Also by JANE HOWARD

A DIFFERENT WOMAN

PLEASE TOUCH: A GUIDED TOUR OF THE HUMAN POTENTIAL MOVEMENT

Jane Howard

FAMILIES

SIMON AND SCHUSTER · NEW YORK

Grateful acknowledgment is made to the following for permission to reprint the materials listed:

Philip Larkin, "This Be the Verse" from *High Windows*, copyright © 1974 by Philip Larkin. Reprinted with permission of Farrar, Straus & Giroux.

Jimmy Long and Gene Autry, "That Silver Haired Daddy of Mine," copyright 1932 and 1959. Used by permission of ABC/Dunhill Music, Inc. All rights reserved.

The New Yorker, excerpt from "Talk of the Town," August 30, 1976.

Owepar Publishing Co., lyrics from "Coat of Many Colors," copyright © 1969 by Owepar Publishing Co. Reprinted by permission. All rights reserved.

To Dr. P. W. Shih

Acknowledgments

This book might have been finished without Alice Mayhew's guidance, or started without Michael Korda's, but it is hard to think how. The memory of Hal Scharlatt, who edited A *Different Woman*, helped too.

So did the family I was born to, and upwards of a hundred hospitable others, of whom only a fraction appear in these pages. For the sake of privacy, a few characters are composites, and many names and places have been changed.

Barbara Grossman and Tony Scherman were inspired researchers. A large and kindly tribe of others kept me supplied, during the three-year task, with perspective, rapport, and suggestions. Some of these are named in the book. Others who were especially generous include Janet Abramowicz, Richard Arnesen, David T. Bazelon, Patricia Bruce, Richard Chapman, Alfred and Roma Connable, Christopher Cory, John Coyne, Andrew Hall Cummins, John and Jane Dabney, Anne Davidson, Susan Edmiston, Joe Eger, Jean Einhorn, Anne Farber, Richard Fithian, Josette Frank, Philip and Kersti French, Alice Gerlach, Celia Gilbert, Robert Glynn, Michael Gross, Hal and Marion Gulliver, Joy and Tom Halsted, Philip Harper, Harriet Harvey, Bill Henderson, Audrey Hubbard, Janice Hutton, Daniel Jacobs, Gladys Jenkins, Stewart Johnson, Sam Kaplan, Billie and Bob Kotlowitz, Irene Kubota, Martine Latour, Theodore and Ruth Lidz, Sterling and Cindy Degener Lord, Katie Letcher Lyle, Rod MacLeish, Bill, Beth and Jane McPherson, Alicia Moore, Susan Nash, Sarah Nathe, Christopher Niebuhr, Bob and Lynn Peterson, Fred and Charlotte Quinn, Paul Ryan, David Scherman, Webster Schott, Bernice Segelstein, Jane Smiley, Nancy Soth, Peter Stone, Kay Vickers, George Vroom, Sally Wells, Carol and Tom Wheeler, Susan Witter, and Fran Zaslow. This list is partial; may those not on it know how grateful I am to them also.

Finally, I am indebted to the Rockefeller Foundation, for an elegant month at the Villa Serbelloni on Lake Como, and to the MacDowell Colony, for six warming weeks by a hearth in the woods of New Hampshire.

Contents

The family, not the individual, is the real molecule of society, the key link in the social chain of being.
　　　　　　　　　　　　　—Robert Nisbet
　　　　　　　　　　　　　Twilight of Authority

Let me start by telling the story of Ethel and the fudge and the sewing machine. Statistics have their place in all this, too, but they will keep for later.

Ethel used to stay with us, now and then, when we lived in Chicago in the early 1940s. Like many young Wisconsin farm women, she came south to earn money doing housework. My sister and I loved her because she was kind and decent and funny and made incomparable fudge.

When Ethel moved back to Wisconsin and married Bill, she remembered how much we liked her fudge. She would send it to us, on our birthdays and at Christmas and sometimes for no reason at all, along with notes urging us to come for a visit. I always meant to pay such a visit but never did until two summers ago.

She and Bill were waiting outside by their mailbox in a yard brightly bordered with flowers when I drove up their gravel road. Ethel gave me a hug. Bill shook my hand. His hand was huge and strong. Ethel had prepared a lavish lunch, a lunch big enough for six more people, but first I had to see her house. Her house had once been a cheese factory; she and Bill had remodeled it themselves. Room by room we toured it. She explained who was who in all the pictures of her children and grandchildren, and where she had got this and that antique. Finally we came to her sewing room.

"This," she told me, "is the room where I mourned your mother's death. I'm not ashamed to say that when I heard the news that she had died I put my head down on the sewing machine and cried like a baby." All that time, without ever seeing us, Ethel had been part of our tribe.

Winnowed Anthems

Tribes and clans and families are what this book is all about. This is a book about connections of chance and connections of choice, both of which lead to families, and the ways these connections can govern and bless and sometimes cripple our lives. This book puzzles over what makes families strong, marvels at their protean endurance, and denies the widespread rumor of their death.

THEY'RE SAYING that families are dying, and soon. They're saying it loud, but we'll see that they're wrong. Families aren't dying. The trouble we take to arrange ourselves in some semblance or other of families is one of the most imperishable habits of the human race. What families are doing, in flamboyant and dumfounding ways, is changing their size and their shape and their purpose. Only 16.3 percent of this country's 56 million families are conventionally "nuclear," with breadwinning fathers, homemaking mothers, and resident children. That leaves 83.7 percent to find other arrangements, which are often so noisy that the clamor resulting is easily mistaken for a death rattle.

Consider these changes:

Parenthood, for the first time in human history, is optional, at least for those who know where and how to obtain contraceptives or abortions. One baby was aborted for every five born in the United States in 1975. Nearly five million American men have volunteered for vasectomies. Ten percent of the world's couples have been sterilized. "PESTICIDE WORK SUGGESTED FOR THOSE SEEKING STERILITY" a headline says. Many people seem to think children are just that: pests. Many educated people of childbearing age are deciding not to raise families at all, or postponing parenthood until it is too late. The more education you have, the smaller the family you are likely to raise. Maybe you won't raise one at all. Maybe you are one of the 15.5 million of us alluded to in the new "Prayer for Those Who Live Alone" in the 1977 revision of the *Book of Common Prayer*.

Maybe you yearn for children but cannot conceive them, news you learn for certain after a series of tests as degrading as the results are depressing. If you then resolve to adopt a child, you may find that adoption is as preoccupying as gestation and can take much more time. Some wait as long as seven years, some forever. Some couples who lack patience pay as much as $40,000 for babies on the black market. Others rent the wombs of women they hope never to see, paying $15,000 for babies who will be at least half theirs by artificial insemination. (For one reason or another, an estimated 20,000 American women are artificially inseminated each year.)

A child who can already walk and talk and remember is not in much demand. Usually, people prefer to adopt healthy babies, the younger the better, of their own race and approximate heritage. But such babies are scarce, partly because many are aborted and partly because the stigma of illegitimacy has greatly diminished. Eighty percent of the nearly 500,000 illegitimate children born each year go home with their mothers, with very little raising of eyebrows.

But a lot of children, shifted from one foster home to another, are literally crying to be adopted. Federal and state governments spend something like $1.2 billion a year to maintain something like 350,000 children in foster homes and institutions. "That figure may be way too low," one adoption official said. "Funny, isn't it—we know exactly how much wheat and how many cows there are in this country, but we don't have a figure on kids. What does *that* say about a nation that professes to care for its children?" At least 100,000 children are available for adoption at any given time, but these children are too old, or too handicapped, or too retarded to be in demand, or they are the wrong color, or available only to those willing to adopt their siblings along with them.

The mothers of many such children are children themselves. The age of puberty has dropped, and so have scruples about early sex. Virginity can go out of fashion as early as the fifth grade. By the age of fifteen, 25 percent of all girls are sexually active. Messages about contraception may reach these girls, but such messages must compete with Top Forty songs like "It's All Right to Make Love on The First Night."

"Radio songs transmit a moral tone and ethical content which encourages their listeners, our children, into premature heat," said the Reverend Jesse Jackson. "It's the fantasy, the dream of motherhood that carries them along," said the director of a program for pregnant addicts. "No matter what realities they've had to face, they continue to imagine themselves in typical TV family situations—mother, father, baby, house." Advertising, one copywriter said, "reflects family life in that it is truly materialistic, exaggerates sex attraction, and suggests that all families can reach the gloriously unreal, totally upbeat, fun-oriented standards we see on the tube."

Parenthood, it would seem, gives very young mothers their first taste—though hardly from the ideal perspective—of what they need themselves: affection, attention, concern. A baby cannot hold its mother, but at least it can be held. A baby can be the object, if not the source, of responsibility.

For a while, after such babies are brought home, their incessant demands are endearingly novel, but the novelty does not last. Not only do babies born of such young mothers tend to be underweight, malnourished, and retarded, and addicted—if their mothers were during pregnancy—to heroin, but they are often abused and abandoned. Their mothers, beaten by their fathers, might in turn beat them. If the parents are married, they probably won't be for long. Four out of ten children born in the 1970s will spend some time in single-parent families, of which 90 percent are headed by women.

Such households can be fragile to the point of pathos, but they still are families. So are those headed by fathers who have custody of their children. So are homosexual couples who have been united in quasi-official church ceremonies called "covenants." So are all manner of other unconventional groupings. "A whale of a lot of people talking about alternative lifestyles are living pretty normal lives," a social worker told me once, and she was right, but a whale of a lot of experimenting is going on too. A headline reads "COURT LETS WOMAN WHO IS NOW A MAN KEEP FOUR CHILDREN"; these adaptable children learned to address this parent of theirs as "Daddy."

A potter in San Diego sulks because the twins of the man she has lived with for two years still don't say hello when she walks into a room. A grocer on an island off the Carolina coast prepares to spend the winter with his "lady," who he knows will never marry him. A dentist in South Dakota hires a "deprogrammer" to wean his daughters back from the International Society of Krishna Consciousness. An accountant in Kansas hires a "snatcher" to get his sons back from their mother. A playwright and his engineer wife, in Vermont, who for years have been unhappily childless, suddenly adopt an unrelated 18-month-old girl and 9-year-old boy.

A Vietnamese refugee mother tries in vain through the courts to get her children back from the Connecticut bachelor who has adopted them. A happily single editor in Galveston adopts her late sister's teen-age daughter and two sons. A newlywed couple in their seventies, in Washington, D.C., insist that they both are happier than they ever have been in their lives. A 747 landing in Los Angeles deposits, among hundreds of others, a man with three children, who are conveyed along a moving floor past elementary school murals to the baggage claim area. There a woman and four other children greet them. The man and the woman embrace. The seven children scowl, balking at the prospect of becoming step-siblings.

Science-fiction fantasies—the colonizing of outer space, the cloning of new organisms from one of 50 trillion cells, the conception of babies in test tubes, extrauterine gestation, being frozen and later thawed—all these phenomena may in time add to the tumult surrounding families. But for now the pictures that linger in the mind are more mundane. On the banks of the Sangamon, a former nun and former priest give their daughter a tricycle. On the banks of the Monongahela, a foster mother weeps saying goodbye to a boy she has come to love in the four years she has kept him. On the banks of the Housatonic, an archaeologist is given the first birthday party of his life by the six people who matter most to him, not a one his relative by blood.

A block from the banks of the Hudson, a car pulls to a double-parked stop in front of an apartment building. The wind blows so savagely off the river that the car doors won't close, once they are open, without fierce effort. Hunched against the wind, a doorman comes out of the building to help carry luggage inside. He has to make several trips; I have been gone for a good two months, and much as I keep meaning to, I never seem to manage to travel light.

"How long you stay here *this* time?" John wants to know as he piles my luggage by the elevator door. If I deny having plans for foreseeable travel he shakes his head: "I know *you*. You go away again soon." As often as not he is right. In recent years I have rarely stayed put for much more than six weeks at a time.

"You don't really *have* a lifestyle, do you?" a shrewd neighbor once observed. Nor can it be said of me, as a women's magazine said once of a publisher's daughter, that I have "found my own idiom."

I'm not sure what a lifestyle or an idiom would do for me. It is bad enough having to choose from the profusion of options for which our forefathers fought at Bunker Hill, Antietam, Iwo Jima and on every battleground since. I am awash in that celebrated and mixed American blessing, mobility. Once, for a birthday, my father gave me a world atlas inscribed, "I hope you get to all these places," and I have got to quite a few of them. By nature and trade I am something of a wanderer. I go off, at intervals, for different reasons: to get, to spend, to talk, to listen, to teach, to learn, to be with the people I love. "Are you still at the 602 number," my answering service once asked, "or shall we refer calls to the 516?"

Not that I don't like where I live. I like it fine. I'd be a fool not to like eleven windows overlooking the river, plenty of jade plants, bright colors, more books than I'll ever find time to read, records that I'll never really listen to, recipes that I'll never cook, and more major appliances than my grandmother or even my mother would have dreamed of. I can go out tonight to hear motets or watch a hockey game; I can walk a block and buy croissants or bagels; I could plan a trip at a travel agency named Shalom Amigo. Several of the people I most like to be with live a short walk or a bus ride away. Others tend to fetch up as houseguests, which is fine as long as they let me carve four solitary hours out of each day.

Have to watch it with that solitude though. Solitude is beautiful and necessary—"it is the lonely buffaloes," as Ford Madox Ford wrote, "ploughing solitary furrows, who have generally produced" the "truths that have eventually swum up to the surface of public consciousness." Jane Austen, on the other hand, achieved her considerable truths in a small rectory room filled with noisy children. It is all very well not to have to wait too long for your turn in the bathroom, but a place too long underpeopled can get to smelling tomblike. "I can't think of anything more depressing," a friend of mine once said, "than going to the store for a single stick of butter."

In excess, and we are nothing if not a culture of excess, our fondness for solitude and privacy and that other American grail, individualism, can get us into trouble. Too much privacy and we won't have anyone with whom to remember, let alone with whom to make plans. Too much individualism and we forget not only our ancestors and our possible descendants but even each other. A "Talk of the Town" piece in *The New Yorker* remarked, a while back, on a fraying of connections that causes us to look upon life as a lone adventure, a great personal odyssey, and there is much in this view which is exhilarating and strengthening, but we seem to be carrying it to such an extreme that if each of us is an Odysseus, he is an Odysseus with no Telemachus to pursue him, with no Ithaca to long for, with no Penelope to return to—an Odysseus on a journey that has been rendered pointless by becoming limitless.

One of the brightest and most sympathetic men I know ended up eating Christmas dinner alone one year, having made such a fetish of not "imposing" on others that others got out of the habit of asking him to. An 89-year-old woman with no kinfolk within a thousand miles fell down one noon on her kitchen floor, broke her hipbone, and lay there on the linoleum for two days before neighbors, hearing her feeble cries, discovered her. She had set great store by not "needing" anyone. Several of my friends pay at least $15,000 a year to the "health-related facilities" that sustain their shriveled, staring parents, each generation wanting "independence" from the other. A crowded hovel might be preferable to such seclusion. Those tyrants have never been fools who punished citizens by restricting them to the "privacy" of their households.

Americans, as Will Rogers said, will join anything but their families. Rather than join them, we try to escape them. Escaping, of course, doesn't work. The harder we try to get away from our families, the likelier we are to repeat their same mistakes. But the illusion of escape is so powerful it probably accounts for many of the migrations to and beyond our shores. Don't tyrannize us, bad King George or Czar Nicholas or you, either, Mom. If you do, we'll be gone, to Plymouth Rock or Ellis Island or to the moon. In motion there is meaning. *Vamos*. Going will save us from having to think. Don't fence us in. Give me a mirror and a subscription to *Self* magazine and let me out of here. There's a catch, though. If I go too far or stay too long I might not be remembered. *Lontan dagli occhi, lontan dal cuore*, it said on an ashtray in a room where I once spent a month in Italy. Out of sight, out of mind. I spent a fair part of my time in that room writing postcards.

It is Thanksgiving, "that day of guilt and grace," as Francine du Plessix Gray has her narrator muse in *Lovers and Tyrants*, "when the family hangs over you like an ox over the sacrificial victim. What a perfect day to go loony." So it is; I have seen plenty of loons lurching through New York subways on Thanksgivings past, brandishing their pint bottles and slurring weepily of old memories. It's a good day to fly, though; not many people do. I had a whole row of seats to my-self on the flight east from Portland to Denver. Everyone else had al-ready gone, over the proverbial river to grandmother's house. I haven't had a grandmother myself for some years now, but I am on my way to join a hospitable clan in Iowa after an hour's layover here. My old friend Emily, who lives an hour away, has come to the air-port. We toast the harvest with a Bloody Mary. The airport is fes-tive; a friendly rancher in a Stetson hat offers us strips of elk jerky from meat he has smoked himself. Emily and I talk fast, as we must, of—among other things—the families neither of us has got around to founding. She, twelve years my junior, is at her peak age for child-bearing. I am edging warily close to the end of mine. For me to have a baby now might be medically dangerous. Still, the day doesn't go by I don't think of the possibility. Not Emily. No babies for her, she has decided, not ever. She will find herself some other kind of family.

"But who will look after you," I ask, not altogether rhetorically, "in your declining years?"

"I'm not going to *have* declining years. A random accident will snuff me out when I'm forty-seven."

Who is to say it won't? Randomness lurks. We gather together, this day and all days, in retreat from catastrophes and mishaps for which there can be no preparing. A rock dropped by a boy from a footbridge falls through a car's roof and onto the lap of a young so-cial worker, killing her at once. A helicopter blade goes awry atop a skyscraper, tumbling to the street below, killing five. A taxi driver loses control of his cab, impaling a young mother against a mailbox; her child watches her die. The few survivors of the collision of two giant planes off the coast of Africa are flown to the special burn unit of a hospital in Texas.

"A lot of people are just plain scared, anymore," someone said to me during my flight from Portland. Scared or at least confused. A snake is imported from Hong Kong, in the sleeve of a jacket, to a K-Mart in Iowa. The sign outside a Georgia motel one week reads, "WELCOME, BASKIN ROBBINS, CYSTIC FIBROSIS AND DELTA PHI EPSILON," and the next week, "WELCOME, AVON AND ACUPUNCTURE." A woman returned to the States after three years abroad marvels that "after just one day here I've already kissed three people I don't even like." A man in the building across the street from a friend of mine plays tennis, alone, in what seems to be his dining room. A woman in my neighborhood walks her St. Bernard, during cloudbursts, in a rain-coat. The dog wears the raincoat, not the woman.

Alopecia nervosa makes men hairless. *Anorexia nervosa* makes women gaunt as skeletons. No rare word these days, *nervosa*. Plenty to be nervous about. We are wary; our connections become hectic and parenthetical. An Episcopalian widow outside Pittsburgh hires a caterer for after her husband's funeral; people in her neighborhood seem to have lost the habit of responding to death with food. A professor is dying, with cruel slowness; his colleagues gradually stop going to see him because, as one explains, "We've worked out our feelings about his disease." Every year we scratch out a fifth of the entries in our address books and write in new streets, new zip codes. One out of five: that's a lot of goodbyes, a lot of transitions, a lot of shelf paper in strange kitchen cabinets.

The globe shrinks. Our options multiply. For the choices that face us, as a friend of mine once said, we need a nervous system entirely different from the one history gives us. A century ago Hegel said that the hard thing was not choosing between right and wrong but between two rights. Now the choice often seems to be between two wrongs. We need limits. We need structure. Some claim that what we need are two-day, $45 seminars in old-fashioned family life, with father as captain and mother as lieutenant and so on down the line. Such seminars draw large crowds. Phyllis Schlafly and other champions of right-wing politics "wrap themselves in the cloth of the family," as Andrew Kopkind has written, the family being "the best available rock in a storm-tossed sea of contradictions." A woman Kopkind interviews tells him that "Lucifer is trying to make it hard for people to have children, to have a family."

American politicians rarely let up on the subject, during and even after their campaigns. "CARTER TO SHACKERS: SHAPE UP!" reads a headline. Everybody hurry up and get married and be like Jimmy and Rosalynn and Amy and Chip and Caron and all the rest of them there in the White House. (What a relief: a pantheon to match and in some ways even to surpass the days of Camelot. The Carters' folksy clannishness is probably as good a reason as any why we chose them, slim though the margin was, over the also wholesome but less numerous Fords.) If dynasties cannot inspire, then they must reassure. That is why we crown them, so they will make us think everything is going to be all right.

"FAMILY HOME EVENING IS HAPPINESS." I keep seeing this legend on bumper stickers, especially in the west. The stickers turn out to be printed by the Mormons, the Church of Jesus Christ of Latter-Day Saints. The Latter-Day Saints are probably the fastest-growing religious organization on earth and quite likely the most familial. Their missionary zeal extends to their own ancestors. Under 700 feet of solid granite in the Wasatch Mountains, not far from Salt Lake City, the Mormons have troubled to quarry giant caverns for the safekeeping of 1.5 billion pages of microfilm records not only of their own forebears but of everybody else's. From all over the world come microfilms of land grants, deeds, parish registers, and probate, marriage, and cemetery records. These records are collected so that all living and future Mormons can trace their families back as far as possible, in order to baptize their ancestors vicariously, "sealing" the pedigrees into families. (The Mormons are happy to talk about this multimillion-dollar project, and just as happy to point out that they no longer countenance polygamy: since 1890, the practice of polygamy has been grounds for excommunication from the church. Some of the 30,000 Americans said to practice polygamy in the American west may once have been Latter-Day Saints, but they aren't now.)

Family Home Evenings, I learned, have been so successful as to inspire similar programs sponsored by the Jaycees, the Insurance Round Table, the Roman Catholic diocese of Arizona, and certain Baptist groups. I thought I'd better see for myself what a Family Home Evening was like, and so during a visit to a midwestern city I looked up the Latter-Day Saints in the classified telephone directory, declared my interest, and was directed at once to go, the next Monday evening, to the home of an eye surgeon and his wife and their three children.

The surgeon's family welcomed me first to the "lesson" which they and all other Mormon families were following that week, in a booklet sent out in 17 languages from Salt Lake City. Since Christmas was approaching, the lesson had to do with giving and receiving. Then, over meringue pie and tap water, we talked. The wife talked more than her husband did, as American wives generally do. "Moral decay is a very great problem," she told me. She and her husband were both worried about threats to the importance of marriage, of parenthood, of women's role in the home. "Educated people are making it seem that it's not intellectual to have children. A lot of people seeing my three children tell me I have more than anyone they know.

"My husband does corneal transplants, and that's fine, but building an eternal family is just as important. It's not easy, but it's very challenging and very fulfilling. I'm building quality children who will become quality adults, not just people who will slouch through life." The quality children were dispatched in their pajamas to bed, while

their parents explained to me their theology and more of their misgivings about American life.

"You know what's the cause of this moral decay?" the Mormon
woman asked. "Immorality is the cause. People don't have perspective on what life is about. There's too much emphasis on momentary
pleasures."

"Basically, people don't believe in God any more," the eye surgeon
said. "They have no more faith. It really does a lot for you as a person to have this faith, and it would even if it was a bunch of hog-
wash, which it isn't."

"Mormons are very happy people, on the whole," said his wife,
"because they know what they're doing and where they're going."

There are times when I wish I could say the same. I'm not so sure
where I'm going myself, or even whether I want to stay where I am.
My apartment hasn't a fireplace, and on plenty of mornings the air
outside is officially declared Unacceptable. For these and other reasons I am subject to periodic cravings for a setting more rural. When
they strike, I circle a few ads in the Sunday *Times* with a felt-tip
pen, head north, and take my chances with real estate agents. I try to
avoid the sort who tell of "lovely homes" and who say things like "if
you so desire, you could put a very unique breezeway in right here."
(More to my taste by far was the Dutchess County woman who told
me, as we drove around to look at her "listings," of the pet she and
her children had just bought for their father's birthday—"He wanted
something big, so we got him a steer.")

What I have in mind, I tell these realtors, is a sprawling log cabin,
near if not on a body of water, within sight, if possible, of some
mountains. It should have an enormous fireplace and a kitchen
roomy enough for a big round table. Taxes should be reasonable,
hardware and stationery stores not too far away, the price modest,
and it would be nice if the house had a couple of porches and maybe
some outbuildings, so that everybody could go off to be alone now
and then, or to get some work done.

The catch, apart from the fact that such finds are so seldom
found, is that I have yet to figure out who "everybody" is. So far
there is no one at whose side I have promised to stay until death or
divorce us do part.

The middle 1930s, when I was born, were lean years for babies—
the leanest then ever recorded. We were few, and much was made of
us. Our newborn footprints were pasted into albums, next to tiny rib-
boned locks of hair. Medical care was far more reliable than it had

been. Most of us grew tall and strong and fertile, marrying early and founding families of our own. A few by now are even grandparents, and all but a small percentage of us have become parents ourselves.

I am a part of that small percentage. What I know about families, apart from the one I was born to, I have learned from the edges of others rather than from the center of my own. My nature, it would seem, is to be peripheral. So far, anyway, my habit is to act as a satellite, orbiting around fixed families by instinct, with gratitude, and for the most part with cheer. For a while, as befit my age and station, I was a bridesmaid, sometimes a maid of honor. In due course I became a godmother, twice in fact and many times in effect. Now I am part of a new corps of inept and unaccredited lay therapists, whose task it is to hear and to try to soothe the woes of the divorced, who are everywhere. Once it was death, as Sean O'Casey wrote, which "dunted into the family life and . . . stunned its functions . . . Nothing would be exactly the same again. There would have to be a new grouping and a new laying out of all things." Now the deaths that dunt us are not so much of people as of promises.

"MAN LITERALLY SAWS HOUSE IN TWO!" reads a headline in a tabloid. That man was upset, plain to see, about his divorce. "HER AUTO RAMS HOUSE OF ESTRANGED HUSBAND" reads another. She, that auto's owner, was upset, too. My butcher tells me he has been to a "divorce party," a celebration, but most people didn't seem to feel like celebrating.

Divorce throws people off balance for a good two years. They shouldn't make any important promises for at least that long. Their friends should be grateful if they can manage to be civil. No use consoling them with the reminder that the Spocks, the McCarthys and even Ann Landers herself are their fellow victims in this nationwide epidemic. Trendiness is small comfort, if any. Each victim's wounds are his own, and they throb as if pain had just been invented. The wounds are a long time healing, and the infection can be contagious.

"Want some free advice? Tell her to *make haste slowly,*" said a real therapist to whom, at a party, I happened to mention a friend's separation. "Half this national plague makes no sense whatsoever. I only wish I knew what makes so many couples rush so mindlessly into divorce." Maybe Edward Hoagland knows, who writes, in an essay called "Other Lives," that

The great leveler nowadays is divorce; almost everybody thinks about it, whether because we expect to be happy all the time—daily, weekly—or because we want the smell of brimstone in lives made too affluent and easy . . . it's as if marriage had become a chancy, grim, modern experiment instead of an ancient institution. We have other lives to lead, we say to ourselves . . . [we may crave] the risk of disaster . . . to touch bottom, see where bottom is, and, coming up, to breathe the air with relief and relish again.

Hoagland is right. The smell of brimstone exhilarates. It also leads to tales of rancor. "Did you win or did Dad?" a boy asks his mother when she returns from divorce court. "We both won," she tells him, but she is lying and her son knows it. Before them stretch new and unforeseeable moments of pain, mostly involving rituals: the stuffing alone of Christmas stockings, the paying alone of taxes, the refloating alone of the raft in the lake on Memorial Day, the carving alone of pumpkins, the observing alone of birthdays, the reworking of alliances with former in-laws. The worst thing about divorce may be the way it unravels the rituals that enact the myths a family has woven about itself, even if the family is only a couple.

Most divorced people will find new mates, their disenchantment being not with marriage but with a particular partner. The urge to establish a new family to replace the old one usually develops soon and strong. Families, for all their vaunted shortcomings, in all their protean manifestations, never fail for long to engulf us, or at least to lure us. Nothing is or ever was more wonderful, more dreadful or more inescapable than families, nor are there many words more perplexing to define.

"We know a hell of a lot more about spacecraft than we do about families," I once heard a man say whose job it had been at different times to study both. "By comparison with a family, a spacecraft is a starkly simple instrument." The etymology of the word "family" is a maze that twists back to Roman times, when *familia*—property, household—derived from *famulus*—servant. The Greek equivalent of *familia* had been *oikos*, which also referred to property. The word that suggested kinship was the Latin *gens*, synonymous with *genus*, whose Greek equivalent meant "nourished by the same milk." A *gens*, according to the *Oxford English Dictionary*, was a "clan or sept, a number of families united by ties of a supposed common origin—common name, common religious rites—or aggregation of families."

Phratries, developing later, were politico-religious divisions of people which arose from but were not limited to ties of blood. *Kin, kindred, house, lineage, sib, clan* and *tribe* all came to mean, more or less, "a group of persons forming a community and claiming a common ancestor." By whatever name, what we now call families have been a fixed institution since our very early ancestors dispersed from Central Asia, heading south to India or west to Greece. Ritual offerings to ancestors are the oldest and most persistent of any human phenomena, common to all cultures. Thomas Hobbes wrote in the seventeenth century that "the beginning of all dominion amongst men was in families, by which was meant a man and his children, or a man and his servants, or a man and his children and his servants." (Hobbes appears not to have been a feminist.)

Historians and anthropologists have gone on at no small length about all this. Libraries bulge with their scholarship. They distinguish between *descent* and *consanguinity*, *marriage* and *affinity*. They explain how rights can be passed to new generations *agnatically*, through the father, or *uterinely*, through the mother, or *bilaterally*, through either. They tell, rather enticingly, of *zadrugas*, which as I had not known are inherited collective ties which unite different extended families in southeastern Yugoslavia. They make quite clear how contemporary is our use of the word "family." Only for some three centuries has the word been applied to what sociologists call "nuclear" families.

It will be a good while before anyone has perspective enough to define today's tribes. Not that the classic tribal spirit has vanished entirely: consider, after all, the tribal nature of wars lately fought in Southeast Asia, in Africa, in the Middle East, in Northern Ireland, at Wounded Knee. But fewer and fewer of us are as tribally defined as our ancestors were. A tribe in the old sense, I gather, was a band of some five hundred people (a likely number to know and be known by sight, and to reach with the unaided voice in open air), who shared a common history, acknowledged a common authority, faced a common danger, and expected a common future. They agreed, more or less, on what was sacred, what was funny, what work had to be done, and who or what was the enemy.

Our ancestors were tribal because they had no choice. They depended on their kinsmen for economic survival because they couldn't trust anybody else. Maybe they didn't even know anybody else. But times changed. Allegiances shifted. People moved and regrouped. Lifespans lengthened; the prospect of a lifetime with one other person lost its inevitability. Once most children lost their first parent at fourteen; now the average age is forty. Geographically and emotionally, it is becoming all but quaint to live in the same climate or time zone with one's relatives.

Nobody, however, has lost the need for what a friend of mine calls "implicitness"—literally and figuratively, a place where, as the poet has it, when you go there they have to let you in, and where at the very least you can waken without surprise. Implicitness is to the spirit what Vitamin C is to the body. Traditionally its source has been tribes and families. Now it is more readily found in looser alliances based less on common ancestry than on common enthusiasm. The hoary and cherished notion that blood is thicker than water is subject to new scrutiny.

"Of *course* water is thicker than blood," two anthropologist friends of mine said one evening, when the subject came up after supper. They said it at once and almost in unison.

"And we speak from two different ends of the spectrum," the man of this couple continued. "She has no parents, and I have eleven."

"Eleven! What remarriers your parents must be!"

"Oh, they are," said the woman. "He can't begin to keep his step-parents and step-siblings straight."

"But you know what it's like, having that many so-called relatives?" asked the man. "It's like having no family at all."

"Does it matter?" I asked. "Do you need one?"

"You might not think so," he said, "but I do."

Everybody does. It is paradoxical. Free—or forced—to define ourselves in a way our ancestors could not have imagined, we long at once for many families and for one, for the adventure of branches and the solace of roots. We long for a balance between the cool of water and the hot pulse of blood.

Money and love have less to do with all this than might be thought. Money, even the absence of it, is not what keeps families going. Economically, families have been obsolete for generations. Children, as someone said, are an economic disaster: to bring one up to the age of eighteen, in New York City at least, costs $85,000. Fathers no longer have children in order to pass their skills along; by the time most children grow up their fathers' skills are obsolete. Once it was families' chief purpose to produce goods together. Now, for most, it is rare even to make ceremonial cookies together once a year. Property, land, work, and rank once defined families far more than they do now. As taxes siphon off more and more of what we earn, the word "heir" loses its old power. Karl Marx was already out of date when he wrote that the bourgeoisie had "torn away from the family its sacramental veil and reduced it to a mere money relation." The reverse, in fact, has come to pass. What holds a family together is not money but emotion. The emotion, however, is not the one that might come first to mind. It is not love.

Love, which Santayana called that "deep, dumb, instinctive affinity," is this world's greatest blessing, all right. No question of that. But love has no structural or inherent connection with family. Families are conventionally supposed to be loving but many are not. Of late, in fact, love among families has become nearly unfashionable. A student of mine once confessed furtively, as if he were owning up to a perversion, that he actually sort of liked his mother and father. The trust that springs from love is no inevitable thing among families. Affection may prompt you to tell your parents or your siblings what is truly on your mind, but just as likely it doesn't. Just as likely you drastically edit the version they get of your life, and receive similar editing from them. Unedited truths, if indeed we can puzzle them out at all, are more the coin of relationships based on water than on blood. "Have families ever loved each other," Walker Percy has his hero ask in *Lancelot*, "except when some dread thing happens to somebody?"

Dread. Now that's more like it. Dread comes closer to what makes a family a family. Dread, and Hoagland's smell of brimstone, and responsibility. "Families are at their best," a friend of mine once put it, "when swords are flashing, trumpets blowing, when the devil is near." Swords and trumpets and the devil, however inconvenient and awful, thrill us with their urgency. They restore to us our mislaid sense of imperatives. Of course I cancel my most cherished plans if the ambulance wails for someone to whom I am responsible. The dread is worse yet, of course, when it is chronic instead of acute, when someone lingers long enough in a state dubious enough to turn my thoughts to euthanasia and test my responsibility to its limits. Generally, people who can affect us this much are our blood kin. They don't have to be, though. Anyone whose death or suffering would undo me as much as a relative's becomes, perforce, a relative. For that reason alone he gets to be part of my family.

Direness, adversity and guilt are not a pretty package, but there is none more compelling. Direness and families have been interwoven since Seth slew Osiris and Abraham offered up Isaac. Familicide, the threat of which prompts half the calls to police stations, is the one crime no culture has ever forgiven. The only crime more heinous, perhaps, is indifference to direness. Recall the shock of the community when Meursault, in Camus's *The Stranger*, went to a movie, and a funny one at that, the day after his mother was buried. Similarly, Arnold Schwarzenegger appalled audiences at the documentary movie about weightlifting *Pumping Iron* when he said no, he had not gone back to Austria for his father's funeral; the man was dead, so what was the point? The point has been on record since Antigone risked everything to bury Polynices. The point is that there must be others for whose sakes we would swim rivers and go sleepless for weeks. There must be families.

"Am I friends with my *cousins?*" asks a man in Kentucky. "Are you kidding me? Those shorthaired assholes? I haven't even *seen* my cousins since I was a kid, and I don't care if I never do. All we ever did when we went to see them was argue over whose turn it was to tend the graves that year. The only thing I liked about those reunions, man, was the way the beads formed on top of the lemon meringue pies. Getting away from my family was the best thing that ever happened to me." But observe what this man does as he rails against the family he was born to: he helps his second wife to frost the cake for her daughter's thirteenth birthday. If our first and second families don't suit us, we go find ourselves a third.

Family imagery pervades religious orders, labor unions, political movements. Nobody's mother tongue, in any fatherland, offers more vivid metaphors for allegiance. Sisterhood is powerful. The *Bhagavad-Gita* outlines the "sacred laws of brotherhood." Teamsters, nuns, and apprentice murderers all band themselves into families. Institutionalized drug addicts and mental patients arrange themselves, even if no one does it for them, into families. The Mafia openly calls itself a family. So did the followers of Charles Manson, so do employees of Henry Luce. The Hanafi Muslims terrorized Washington, D.C., in the spring of 1977 for the same reason the Hatfields and McCoys feuded a century earlier, and Troy was besieged in 1184 B.C.: to settle a family quarrel.

Despots have ever found families a vexation, if not an outright threat. The states of the world, after all, attempt or pretend to be "rational," which families by their very nature can never be. The more "rational" and bureaucratic the world becomes, in fact, the more families matter, greater the need for the passionate and irrational connections which families exist to supply. The most clever politicians in history, and many bumbling ones, have tried and failed to undermine families. Cleisthenes, in 509 B.C., cut away families' power by reorganizing the Greek political system according to regions instead of clans. Plantation owners in the American south forbade their slaves marriage and legitimacy, which was to say families. Hitler, Stalin and Mao Tse-tung all did what they could, which was plenty, to enfeeble the families in their societies.

Israeli *kibbutzniks* rebelled against the Eastern European patriarchal tradition they had inherited. Families have bounced back from all these assaults. Sumerians, Merovingians, and Manitobans all have always sorted themselves into families. Heldentenors and furriers and manicurists all have families. So have actuaries, stewardesses, and tree surgeons. So have you and so have I, although on the surface I might not seem to. With the exception of a few odd tribes here and there, and the extremely occasional "wild child" of the sort about whom Truffaut made his movie, every human being who has ever drawn breath has been part of at least one family. Families breed us, name us, succor us, embarrass us, annoy us, drive us off toward adventures as foreign to them as we can imagine, and then they lure us back. Families collapse, but families expand. They shatter, but they heal. No society in history has ever taken to heart the advice with which the British poet Philip Larkin concludes "This Be the Verse":

> They fuck you up, your mum and dad,
> They may not mean to, but they do.
> They fill you with the faults they had
> And add some extra, just for you.
>
> But they were fucked up in their turn
> By fools in old-style hats and coats
> Who half the time were soppy-stern
> And half at one another's throats.
>
> Man hands on misery to man,
> It deepens like the coastal shelf.
> Get out as quickly as you can
> And don't have any kids yourself.

Nobody ever really follows such counsel for long, because families are a given. Nothing is more futile than to wish they would go away. They won't. Individual ones will of course disappear; to do just that is their biological destiny. Umbilical cords must be broken. But families as an institution, in one guise or another, will survive, because our need for them is so intense it approaches the genetic. "During entire aeons," Jacques Monod writes in *Chance and Necessity*,

> a man's lot was identical with that of the group, of the tribe he belonged to and outside of which he could not survive. The tribe, for its part, was able to survive and defend itself only through its cohesion . . . Given the immense selective importance such social structures assumed over such vast stretches of time, it is difficult not

to believe that they must have made themselves felt upon the genetic evolution of the innate categories of the human brain.

Our capacity and need to be part of one family or another—perhaps
of several—is one of the things that makes us human, like walking
upright and killing for sport and bearing tools. We mix fricatives
and phonemes into speech, we envision our own deaths, we take part
at once in finitude and infinity. We can pick a stranger out of a
crowd and in a short time empower him to hurt or to delight us. We
can confirm and be confirmed by one another, not just as what we
are but as what we might hope, at our best, to become. We can
choose between semblance and being. We know we are naked. We
can laugh. We can blush from guilt.

"The child comes home," Robert Penn Warren writes in *All the
King's Men,*

> and the parent puts the hooks in him. The old man, or woman, as
> the case may be, hasn't got anything to say to the child. All he
> wants is to have that child sit in a chair for a couple of hours and
> then go off to bed under the same roof. It's not love; I am not say-
> ing that there is no such thing as love . . . It is just something in
> the blood. It is a kind of blood greed, and it is the fate of man. It is
> the thing which distinguishes us from the happy brute creation.

The study of what distinguishes us from the "happy brute creation"
is called philosophical anthropology. Immanuel Kant immersed himself in this study in the eighteenth century. He sought the answers to
four questions: what we can know, what we should do, what we may
hope, and what we are. In our own century, Martin Buber pursued
this study further. Buber did not relish being called a theologian or
an existentialist, though he was surely both. He preferred to be called
a philosophical anthropologist, one who "seeks to fix the human," as
he put it, "in the constant flux of individuals and cultures.

"In the most rigid epochs of ancient kingdoms," Buber wrote,
"the family preserved its separate structure in which . . . despite its
authoritative quality, individuals affirmed one another in their mani-
fold nature. And everywhere the position of society is strengthened
by this balance of firmness and looseness." Buber died before he got
around to adding the need for family to his list of answers to the
questions he inherited from Kant—what, that is, makes us human—
but in time he would have done so. That, at least, is the conviction
of Leslie H. Farber, who had many talks with Buber in the 1950s

and who himself defines the family as "that irreducible unit of willed and unwilled . . . connections whose reality lies entirely outside our inclination and whose inescapability is absolute."

In his controversial *Sociobiology*, which suggests a strong link between genetics and the behavior of animals, including humans, Edward O. Wilson chooses for his epigraph these lines from the *Bhagavad-Gita:* ". . . see not the guilt of destroying a family, see not the treason to friends? yet how, O Troubler of the Folk, shall we with clear sight not see the sin of destroying a family?"

An incapacity for family, to quote Farber further, is one of the marks of madness. The family, he has written, "is inescapable. You may revile it, renounce it, reject it . . . but you cannot resign from it. You are born into it, and it lives with you and through you to the end of your days." Not only that, but its memory will prompt you to fashion new families, of blood or water, either in its image or—just as tellingly—quite unlike it. Nobody goes for long without some semblance of a family. If we lack a conventional one, we are certain to grope, ingeniously or awkwardly, for a replacement. We confer the status and importance of relatives on the people at the office, at school, down the block, in the platoon, or wherever else we may find them.

And so, given families' persistence, we might as well think about making them useful and decent. We might try to make them a place where, to quote Buber again, "the heavenly bread of self-being can pass from one person to another," and where "the help that men give each other in becoming a self leads the life between men to its height." Most families, of course, fall dismally short of this exalted aim, and do little or nothing to oppose the effort Buber also saw being made "radically to destroy the mystery between man and man. The personal life, the ever-near mystery, once the source of stillest enthusiasm, is leveled down." Families might as well come right out and celebrate mystery and uncertainty. Whether they mean to or not, they embody mystery; they are a monument to it. Within families we are constantly reminded of what the world's bureaucracies may try to deny: that there exist the unexpected and incredible, the unknown and unknowable. Families provide surcease of a sort from randomness, diverting us from the chaos outside with a tamed, more predictable interior chaos. And always mystery remains. We never entirely figure out what goes on within each other, or within our family as a whole.

Maybe we never will.

Maybe it doesn't matter.

Maybe we aren't supposed to.

My own esteem for mystery is one of the reasons I am so consistently put off by the efforts of well-meaning "experts" from such of the "helping professions" as concern themselves with families. These experts abound. They write books. They hold seminars and workshops and forums. They quantify data. They deplore and exhort and reexamine. They wear celluloid badges at three-day seminars in highrise motels that could just as easily be in Zagreb or Auckland as Milwaukee. They walk down halls that smell of carpet-cleaning fluid to plenary sessions of conferences organized around themes like "The Crisis at the Crossroads of the Family." They hear, or are themselves, Discussants and Resource Persons, who urge audiences to "join *with* me in expressing our appreciation *to* her; she's a very very *devoted* and a very very *human* person."

Their language is a caution. They talk of Affines—that means people for whom you have an affinity—and Surrogates and Male Role Models and Major Intimates and Significant Others (Valentine, will you be my Significant Other?). Multilateral Facilitational Relationships, they say, can "deepen and extend the affectional flow." They talk of Normative Data and Coping Mechanisms and Socializatory Functions and the Lower-Class Value Stretch. Their favorite words are probably Effectuate, Crisis, Volatile and Viable. They recommend Shared Meals As a Core Experience, and Family Strength Acknowledgment Experiences. Hard data have taught them that it is less convenient to be poor and black than merely poor or merely black. They regard families as "a variable of rich variety," best looked at "not cross-sectionally but processually."

"I come out very nonoptimistic about alternative lifestyles," I heard one Discussant say during a panel titled "Androgyny and the Family." As he spoke, his 5-year-old daughter and her Bugs Bunny toy played on his lap. I heard someone else say, "There's a lot of affectional activity in a game of Parcheesi," and that every child really ought to have twelve stress-free minutes of attention from each parent each day, as opposed to the 37.24 seconds the average father gives his offspring.

They warn, these experts do, of technism and presentism, as well as the more publicized menaces of racism and ageism and sexism, and of the possible return of that 1950s specter, the Apathy Boom. They caution against "stressing the rational and individual at the expense of the emotional and corporate." They tell of the "recency effect," which means you remember more of what happened today than yesterday, as opposed to the "primary effect," which means first impressions are strong, and of the "exchange theory," which means that if you take care of my dog when I'm away, then I'll owe you a favor.

One panel, on the subject "Progressive Nucleation," was full of such dense polysyllables that I felt moved to break my usual silence and ask, "Look, can't someone here just please tell me what it *is* that makes a good family?"

The panelists were silent. They were startled. I guess they'd never thought of it that way. Not for a full thirty seconds did anyone speak, and then most of what got said was gibberish, with one exception. The one exception was a woman who said, "Well, I've known a lot of couples where the rocks in her head seemed to fit the holes in his."

Conferences are not the place to learn what I want to know about families. I do better in kitchens and on porches and front stoops. Once, on the sundeck of a beach house where several of us had been invited for a weekend, I asked a boy and girl who seemed to be my fellow guests whose children they were.

"They're their *own* children," said a woman unpacking nearby, who later declared herself to be "a trained psychologist." Well, yes, and the collie is his own collie, too, but that isn't what interests me. What interests me are the myriad ways in which we chance to be or choose to be connected with one another.

A couple of years ago, some friends of mine went off to a three-day family reunion in Rockford, Illinois. So extravagant was this clan's gathering that as a thank-you gift my friends thought of sending a silver tray engraved:

> FOR THREE WHOLE DAYS WE ATE AND DRANK,
> WE OWE IT ALL TO RUTH AND FRANK.

Ruth and Frank, sight unseen, are people after my own heart. I wish I had gone to their party myself. I always crave to meet my friends' relatives, and for that matter, my relatives' friends. I seldom care deeply for anyone who is not, so to speak, a family person, around whom there is not some aura of the clan that bred him. It doesn't matter in the least whether he likes them, or even whether they still are alive. If you and I are to become friends, then each of us will need some sense of this aura, this context, about the other. Sooner or later we will have to know what prisms we got from our families (or are giving to our children) to look at the world through, and whether we (or our children) are turning out to be more or less than what was expected.

The trouble with families as a subject, of course, is that everyone alive is an authority. No conversation with anyone anywhere, however fleeting, is exempt from becoming part of the "research." Every family has at least one Scheherazade, and I doubt that any topic, even the weather, gets talked about oftener or with more passion. The only time people don't talk about families, in my experience, is when they are faced with a list of "interview" questions from a clipboard. That approach may work for experts, or prophets, or social scientists, but it doesn't work for me. My way is to use my intuition as a compass, go where I feel welcome, stay as long as I can manage to, meet whoever is around, help them do what they are doing if they will let me, and try to remember that she who asks least learns most. Then I go home to read, and mix what I have read with what I have heard, waiting and hoping for connections to sprout from the mulch.

This book, an idiosyncratic report on many such visits, is anything but "definitive." It is emphatically not a "study" of the ten most touching or twelve most typical families in America, or anything of the sort. For every family mentioned here I must have met and talked to a dozen others. There were several dozen more, each strongly recommended by a trusted friend for a good reason, which I meant to see but never found time for. To see them all would have taken me well into the 1980s, and I keep hearing about new ones all the time.

Rather later in life than most Americans, I suddenly found myself with a new set of step-siblings: six of them. One has become a friend. Not long ago, in an antique shop, she found an 1891 hymnal called *Winnowed Anthems*. Thinking I might like it, she sent it to me. Little could she know how much it would please me. That title, in a way, could serve for this book, too. This book is meant as a collection of songs of praise, along with a dirge here and there, for some of the families whose stories, for reasons as diverse as the families themselves, have seemed to me worth passing on.

I shall start, as I must, with the first family I ever knew.

The Veterinarian's Cousin

I fear nomads. I am afraid of them and afraid for them, too. I don't know what I would do if any of my dear ones were seized with the wanderlust . . . You don't grow rich in spirit by widening your circle, but by tending your own.
—Jane Bowles,
"Camp Cataract"

WE WEREN'T CATHOLIC, so my parents asked the nuns at Our Lady of Mount Carmel parochial school to leave me out of religious training sessions. Maybe the nuns tried to, but there is such a thing as osmosis. Once when the phone rang in our Chicago apartment, I answered it by saying "Hail Mary" instead of hello. By the time I got to second grade, in 1942, I had brought home sheaf after sheaf of crayoned portraits of Jesus, Mary and Joseph.

"What's all this talk about the Holy Family?" my Congregationalist mother asked her husband, a descendant of birthright Quakers. "What about the *Howard* family?"

What about it indeed?

When my younger sister Ann was five or so and someone asked her what she wanted to be when she grew up, she said, "Oh, just a plain, regular lady like Mommy." I don't suppose our mother saw herself that way at all. She chose to see herself, if I read her right, as: the wife of Chicago's most brilliant and glamorous and dedicated young journalist; intensive care nurse to the two most adorably promising if often germ-ridden little girls in all the Great Lakes region; great-niece of Uncle Demp, William Dempster Hoard, who, as she often told us, had been governor of Wisconsin; cousin to hundreds and niece to seven women, of whom the most revered was the elegant and irreverent Auntie Grace, who blew flawless smoke rings and whose visits never lasted long enough. It was Auntie Grace who first taught me a lesson whose truth I have often encountered since: you don't have to have children to be a matriarch, or for that matter, a patriarch. Two of my most fatherly friends are childless bachelors.*

My mother also saw herself, I think, as a kind of Madame de Staël of the farther reaches of the Near North Side. Wherever she lived became her clan's salon and headquarters. When Uncle Harold, her brother, passed briefly through town to change trains on a business trip, she automatically had us play hookey to join him for lunch. Her tribal instincts were lavished on, but by no means restricted to, blood kin. She sensed that families, like the Holy Roman Empire, are meant to be elastic. However foreign a body may be introduced, it is better to adapt to it than to turn it away.

"It's all a matter of hydrology," as my Uncle Henry once put it. "The easiest thing to do is just let the brooks and streams merge into the rivers." A lot of merging took place in and around us. Ann and I, as a result, were early presented with an impressive frieze of different kinds of kinfolk, a sort of Greek chorus of faces we saw so often that they all seemed like family, whether or not they were.

My father had joked about naming me Omaha, for the horse who won the Kentucky Derby the day I was born, as jokes had been made three decades before about naming him Isaiah, for his maternal grandfather. Nothing could ever come of such whims; automatically we were given the names of English queens and kings, or at least of dukes. Years later, when my sister pretended in some supermarket aisle that her daughter Sarah's name was Cheryl Renée, our Anglophile mother visibly cringed. We were, of course, Republicans. On

* "In primitive antiquity . . . the very name by which [the father] is called —pater— . . . is the same in Greek, in Latin, and in Sanskrit; from which we may conclude that this word dates from a time when the Hellenes, the Italians, and the Hindus still lived together in Central Asia. . . . In judicial language, moreover, the title of pater, or pater familias, might be given to a man who had no children, who was not married, and who was not even of age to contract marriage. The idea of paternity, therefore, was not attached to this word. The old language had another word which properly designated the father, and which, as ancient as pater, is likewise found in the language of the Greeks, of the Romans, and of the Hindus [the Latin word genitor] . . . The word pater had another sense. In religious language, they applied it to the gods; in legal language to every man who had a worship and a domain. The poets show us that they applied it to every one whom they wished to honor . . . It contained in itself not the idea of paternity, but that of power, authority, majestic dignity." Fustel de Coulanges, The Ancient City.

both sides we came from patriarchies, which are well known to spawn conservatives. Our political taste was for reassurance, not surprise. Franklin Delano Roosevelt was no folk hero of ours, and although Hitler and Tojo caused our cousins to be drafted, those despots were too remote to threaten us much. Our battles were mostly fought in sickrooms, and our theater was the family itself. Once when my mother went down to the Loop to shop, she came upon a booth where for twenty-five cents you could record your own voice. Inserting a couple of quarters, and pressing a button, she recorded two songs: "Baby's Boat's a Silvery Moon" for Ann and me, and "Happy Anniversary to You" for Robert Pickrell Howard, then of the Associated Press, later to be hired by the *Chicago Tribune*.

In the Bicentennial Summer of 1976, after eighteen years of marriage, my sister was divorced. That next winter, the coldest and cruelest of the century in central Illinois, she and her children moved from the large "Italian-style Country Villa," as real estate advertisements called their house, to half of a much smaller place across town. In many ways the move was welcome. The mock-Italian house had always been too big, and of late it had developed some quirks: on most winter days they could see their breath indoors, and they were forced to learn odd lessons—for example, to flush a toilet when the pipes are frozen, you need five buckets of melted snow. The small new house would function better.

But there wouldn't be nearly enough room in the small new house for all the things that had filled the big old one, so my sister decided on a drastic pruning. She resolved to get rid of at least half of everything she had accumulated in those eighteen years, from wedding presents onward. Less, after all, is more. She decided, or rather Gloria Liberman and her other friends decided for her, that she ought to have a rummage sale.

What they didn't know, until after they planned that rummage sale, was that they had devised a modern secular ritual. Rituals, according to anthropologists, exist to mark events which are either socially approved, like weddings, or unavoidable, like death and illness. Rituals restore equilibrium; they ease us through times of transition. Few things are as transitional, or as unavoidable, as the consequences of divorce. "Nobody would expect it to be easy, getting rid of all that accumulation," Ann told me, "but I couldn't have imagined what an enormous emotional trauma it would be until the time came. I could no more have had that rummage sale alone than I could have run all the way to Peoria.

"What saved me—what made it not only bearable but actually festive—was my family of friends. You should have seen how they rallied. I didn't have to advertise, I didn't have to make one single decision about what to keep and what to sell or how much to charge. They did it all. Every single decision was made communally, by what we came to think of as The Committee.

"Did I tell you about Debbie Melnik's best friend Anita Lutrin, whom I had never even met before that day?" asked Ann. "She was wonderful. She turned out to be the finest saleswoman in Decatur. Dozens of total strangers came, rummaging through the stuff we'd decided to sell, and when one would pick up something to ask 'What's this?' Anita acted as if she were the one who had been living with the item all her life. She'd pick it up and put it in their arms and say, 'This is a gorgeous piece; it'll be perfect for you. I can let you have it for only so-and-so.'

"You wouldn't believe all the stuff we sold or how much fun the day turned out to be. David Snoeyenbos handled the tools. His wife Jacquie offered people coffee and wine. Claudia Taylor kept Greek records on the phonograph. Joanne Carey sold my queen-sized bed. Marian Ankenbrandt made change. The customers had been to yard sales and garage sales and tag sales, but they never had seen anything like this. When they left, they actually thanked us. John's best friend, Ty's father, Ronald Besalke, who Ty says is the strongest man in Macon County, came to organize the teen-age volunteer help for the move. So did E. Raymond Stanhope and his whole family, including their Australian foreign student. Nancy Roucher, who never has had to lift a finger in her whole life, was down on her knees in our new kitchen, scrubbing out the refrigerator. What would I have done without that Committee?"

"You'd have found another one," I told her.

"So would you," she said, and she was right. Committees of this sort, in ever-changing guises, are one of the recurrent themes of both our lives. It is in us to inspire and to direct such Committees, whose purposes can be as solemn as a post-funeral collation or as silly as seeing someone off for a two-day trip. An uncelebrated birthday offends us as disorder offends a martinet. We can no more let such occasions go unmarked than our ancestors could avoid helping their neighbors raise barns or bury their children. The organizing of such Committees—which of course are really sudden, expandable, and sometimes quite durable substitute families—is as much a part of our heritage as Hoard hands or Howard skin. You might say it is part of our myth.

"We probe our family pasts," as Vladimir Nabokov once wrote, "in search of affinities with oneself, previews of oneself, faint allusions to one's vivid and vigorous Now. This, of course, is a game for old people. Tracing an ancestor to his lair hardly differs from a boy's search for a bird's nest or a ball lost in the grass." But time has proven Nabokov wrong. Genealogy, after stamps and coins this nation's third most popular pastime, now engrosses boys as much as it does their elders. The average genealogist's age has dropped from sixty to twenty. Tape recorders whirr everywhere. What, our astonished forebears ask, you want to know about *my* childhood? Never knew you cared. But now, in the suddenly voguish name of oral history, everyone cares. Much of the craze for genealogy probably stems from, or at least is connected with, the epidemic of divorce. If we can't figure out who our living relatives are, then maybe we'll have more luck with the dead ones. Each of us, in any case, can be his own *griot*—can track down his own family history after the manner of tribesmen in Alex Haley's *Roots*.

Adorned, perhaps, with a $69.95 Golden Divorce Medallion, to "discreetly and tastefully let . . . those around you know you are unattached," we can also buy bumper stickers that say "I COLLECT ANCESTORS," and T-shirts captioned "UPROOT YOURSELF." For $350 we can buy a "rich red oak carving, based upon authentic 15th-century designs," showing our coats of arms, with a "rather unique guarantee of satisfaction." Debrett Ancestry Research, in England, will be only too happy, on receipt of "a cheque for $200," to trace our forebears for us. If we can't find our own ancestors, we can buy tintypes for $3.50 each of other people's—who, after all, will know the difference? Short of the silly extremes to which it can easily lead, this genealogical fervor is a useful thing. Only by knowing your family as the Washington, D.C., psychoanalyst Murray Bowen puts it, can you know yourself. If you have lost and wish to resume contact with your children, Bowen thinks, you shouldn't chase them; you should chase your ancestors. Tune out the noisy foreground and hear the distant drumbeat. But, as Bowen warns, to make real emotional contact with the past is monumental upstream work.

Such work may signal the healthy start of a pendulum's swing from our celebrated and preening narcissism, when the only time that matters is the sacred here-and-now and no face counts but the one in the mirror. For those of us who grew up confident that all within earshot would want to know, at any given time, how each of us was feeling, and why, genealogy is, perhaps, narcissism of a higher order. It gives narcissism some dimension, stretching it to encompass not only our begetters but those who begot them as well. Many is the evening I have sat around, in different rooms with different friends, discussing such matters. Once some of us took turns telling the names of our grandfathers:

"Moishe and Sam."

"Walter and Edwin."

"Llewellyn and Felix."

"Oscar and Mr. Rasmussen."

"*Mr.* Rasmussen! But what did they *call* him?"

"How should I know? He died long before I was born."

"And he was never referred to by his given name?"

"Not that I can remember."

The rest of us, bred with a nearly Confucian awareness of our forebears, were astonished. I knew who my grandfathers were as soon as I knew anything. Harry and J.R., that's who they were. My mother's father Harry, Patrick Henry Nee, was the grandson of a hungry emigrant who left County Clare to work on the railroad in Canada. Harry, brought up in Minnesota, worked on the railroad too. He got to be General Superintendent of the Eastern Division of the Milwaukee Railroad and, as my mother liked to recall, he had the use of a private car. Genevieve Ella Hoard Nee, his wife, was a buxom, kindly amateur pianist who is said to have studied Chinese, and who died when my mother was twelve, leaving seven younger sisters. Their only brother had died during, but not in, World War I. Their paternal grandmother Sarah Katherine White, according to a family genealogy I have just now inherited, lived 75 years and "possessed in a large degree the old Puritan admiration for rectitude, high courage and a contempt for small human meannesses."

Anna Pickrell Howard, my other grandmother, was a schoolteacher before her marriage. Humor could flicker behind her large and often sad-looking bespectacled brown eyes. She crossed her legs a microsecond before sitting down in a chair, the way my Aunt Janet and I sometimes do. She liked to go to the opera when she and James Raley Howard II lived in Chicago. They lived there in the early 1920s, during J.R.'s term as first president of the American Farm Bureau Federation, a post he won in a close race because he "looked and talked more like a farmer than the man from Ohio." J.R. had every reason to look and talk like a farmer: his own grandfather, the first James R. Howard, had bought the first acres of what was to be Homelands Farm for $1.25 each in 1854. He and his wife

Talitha Ann Covington Howard had come west by river steamer and prairie schooner from Ohio, whose saloons Talitha thought were more dangerous than Iowa Indians could possibly be. This first J.R. was descended from North Carolina planters whose Quaker consciences had prodded them to free their slaves and lose their land. They, in turn, were descendants of Englishmen who landed in Virginia sometime in the 1600s, quite likely as indentured servants.

My grandfather's platform, for the Farm Bureau election and always, had among its planks this promise: "I stand like a rock against radicalism." He and Anna were birthright Quakers, descendants of people who called each other "thee." The world whose center was Liberty Township, Marshall County, Iowa, had no clan more staunch than theirs, nor more devoted to education. It was probably the Quaker "inner spirit," as much as anything else, that prompted them to think of all the ways they could, through the Farm Bureau and otherwise, to educate farmers and their families.

I often have wondered why it is, apart from the accident of my surname, but I think of myself as a Howard. What about the other 63 lineages, each one of which, to go back six generations, had an equal genetic say in who I am? "Only by clinging resolutely to one branch, and occasionally swinging to another," as J. H. Plumb has written, "can a family tree be made to look like one: otherwise it vanishes quickly in a complex spider's web." I am not entirely ignorant of those 63 other lines. I even know some of their names. What I do not know are their myths. By chance the Howard myth was the one I heard earliest and loudest, and hear still today.

Families need myths. I heard the Yale University psychiatrist and historian David F. Musto give a provocative talk on this subject. All families, in Musto's view, devise myths about themselves. Myths, Musto thinks, exist to show families where they belong on the map, and not just geographically. Myths serve to unite family members against the confusions of an often hostile world. Myths filter and sort out the world's innumerable stimuli. Such myths—ways of interpreting and meshing with the world—may follow some psychological equivalent of Newton's First Law of Motion: once established, they tend to continue through succeeding generations. Musto was talking in particular about the legendary Adams dynasty, whose papers stretch for five miles and whose myths gave them "a certainty and a sense of purpose that would have sustained one of Darwin's primal hordes through an Ice Age." But he made it clear that you don't have to be an Adams to have a myth.

One of the things to be said about my branch of the Howards is that it doesn't take a funeral to get us together. Three times a decade or so, my father and his sister and their brothers and a varying dozen or so of the rest of us tend to assemble for birthdays, anniversaries, retirements, and other less drastic rituals. The talk at these gatherings, as at most family reunions, is of everyday things: diets, gardens, cousins, politics, the heights and quips and achievements of children. Once—I think it was after my father's seventieth birthday dinner—I heard his brothers' wives Martha and Millie talking as they dried the dishes, looking like a detail from a painting by Breughel.

"What's all this talk about everybody *finding* themselves?" I heard Martha ask Millie. "I don't get it, do you? Haven't you always known who you were? Isn't it nuts not to?" Millie, a retired designer of kitchens for the Department of Agriculture, could only agree. Her parents had immigrated from Scandinavia, as Martha's had from Scotland. I doubt very much that their girlhood concerns included such vaporish crises of identity as preoccupied my generation.

"Don't you envy them their certainty?" I asked my sister, as we finished clearing the table. She nodded.

That certainty, as much as anything, was what lured us both to the flagpole dedication. A flagpole and plaque were dedicated to the memory of our grandfather Howard one Sunday in October of 1977, at the headquarters of the Marshall County Farm Bureau. When my father phoned to tell me about this event, I said it sounded nice but that I couldn't make it. I had urgent work to finish in New York, and flying halfway across the country just for overnight seemed too extravagant and distracting. Ann wasn't going to go, either. Two six-hour drives in the space of two days, at a time when John was having trouble with geometry, would take too much time.

"But you *can't* pass up a chance to have your children feel connected with something beyond themselves," a friend of hers said, and that friend, of course, was right. Inconvenience and geometry be damned; we went. We went to find 22 blood relatives and dozens of descendants of our grandfather's neighbors and friends: a roomful of farmers in their Sunday suits, looking as weathered and reassuring as lobstermen in Maine. Some of their faces we had known all our lives. A man with a magnificent American Gothic look about him stood before a flag and sang a rather long arrangement of the "Pledge of Allegiance," as we all sat with our right hands on our hearts. Ann and I dared not meet each other's eyes.

Before the coffee and brownies we were served reminiscences. J. R. Howard, we were told, had written once that "there is no enduring excellence in this world that does not have its beginning and end in the sweat of brow and brains. When men seek to avoid work, they set aside life's greatest blessing." J. R. Howard could design frame barns in his head, and the barns that were built from these designs were square; they did not sag.

J. R. Howard, his son Henry said, "was a poetic man—not a poet, but poetic in his ability to condense an idea in harmony with cosmic rhythms. As parts appear, they indicate the shape of the whole; he could analyze a problem three-dimensionally, as it was today and as it would appear in the future." J. R. Howard wore barn clothes over his fancy suit to drive cattle to their train ride to the stockyards in Chicago. At a ciphering-down—an evening entertainment by the light of kerosene lamps—J. R. Howard could do long division in his head, as fast as a calculator.

Once in Europe I met a homesick expatriate Ohioan, busy embroidering an eyeglass case for a young woman she wished would become her daughter-in-law. The first thing she wanted to do when she got back to the States, this woman told me, was to embark on what she called a "cousin tour"—a methodical visit to each of the offspring of all her numerous and fertile aunts and uncles. I know many people who would recoil at such a prospect. A lot of people would rather tour sewers than visit their cousins. A lot of people find such reunions so uncongenial that they cannot spend more than a day with their relatives without regressing to a sullen, outdated version of themselves.

"But they miss the point," a friend of mine once said. "It doesn't matter if you don't get on with your relatives. Relatives aren't supposed to be soulmates; for soulmates we have each other." Just so. My cousins and I will never be soulmates, but we fascinate each other all the same. I wouldn't have missed my weekend with James Raley Howard III, D.V.M., and his family. They live in Brawley, California, where Jim is such an expert on arcane cattle diseases that he gets called as far away as Japan for consultations. That whole weekend I was introduced to all Brawley as "the veterinarian's cousin." No description could please me more. Another time, in Minnesota, I rode a bicycle-built-for-two with Jim's sister Judy, outside the house where she lives with her husband and their six children. Someday I would like to see their fertilizer salesman brother John and his family, on their home ground in Texas.

I don't suppose there are many living American females with whom on the surface I have less in common, except for genes, than my other first cousin, Genevieve Florence Nee Glenn. Jenny and her husband Milton live not far from New Orleans in Pass Christian,

Mississippi. I went there to visit in the spring of 1975. It was our first reunion in nearly two decades. Jenny had not been my attentive mother's idea of an attentive only niece; a certain coolness had arisen and lingered. Still, I wanted to see what she was like.

Milton was away on business in Alabama that week; I wouldn't get to see him. "His work habits are so regular," Jenny told me, "that if he's even fifteen minutes late getting home, I'm ready to call the police." But their children Patrick and Bridget, both well into their teens, were home, and so were the dogs Ivor, Wilhelmina, Sven and Michel. Patrick told me it was a tossup whether he would make karate his career or go into "the pipefitting program in Pascagoula." Bridget, who Jenny told me had been "raised on diet cola and only had two pinpoint cavities in her whole life," was thinking of majoring in French at she was not yet sure which college.

"She's not science-orientated," Jenny said of her daughter, "but she's good with plants. Maybe she ought to go into environment, if there weren't going to be such an awful lot of environmentalists looking for jobs as GS-12s. I wonder why it *is* that I've always felt so drawn to government clerks?"

I couldn't help her there. Much about Jenny seemed foreign to me. Her cooking, however, was quite another matter. If her record as a niece had been besmirched, then her cousinly hospitality more than made up for it. It was as if she and I were acting out some script from a yellowing etiquette book, telling precisely how to have a gracious luncheon for hungry ladies. Gumbos, remoulades and creole sauces bubbled on her stove. Hush puppies lurked in the oven, set to Warm. On a bone china platter, under a monogrammed linen napkin, was the classic pecan pie. But first there had to be juleps, in silver cups and crushed ice, with candy canes to stir the sprigs of fresh mint.

"I'll gain ten pounds from this one lunch," I told Jenny.

"Weight *is* a problem," she agreed. "I don't think we *combust* food like other people do. But you're lucky," she told me appraisingly, "not to have inherited the Irish hands and feet—just *look* at mine." I looked, but who could pity anyone with such long-lashed green eyes and such a valentine of a mouth? Elizabeth Taylor's countenance came to mind, as did the early Vivien Leigh's. I saw no need for Jenny to vanish, as she did each morning, for long spells with the unguents and mascaras in her bathroom, from which she would call "I'm just doin' my urban renewal!

"Nobody's going to call *me* Big Mamma when I get to be a grandmother," which in fact she did become not two years later. In her fewer than forty years, my cousin told me, she had not only raised her children but taught sewing to retarded women, imported South African wines, exported lawnmowers, run a combined beauty shop and bar with her husband, and helped with an emergency drive to assist homeless hurricane victims. She and Bridget were both alumnae of the Silva Mind Control Institute—"Down here it's either Mind Control, John Birch, or TM"—and her knowledge of our common ancestors far surpassed my own. The first Hoards, she told me, had come here four or five generations before the American Revolution, and one branch could be traced back to the Crusades. Our more recent ancestors included an ensign under Captain Miles Standish and a drummer boy in the War of 1812.

Sitting there with her sewing kit in her air-conditioned den, a block from the Gulf of Mexico, Jenny talked of these forebears as if they were our contemporaries. I asked what she was working on.

"Oh, a piece of needlepoint for Milton," she told me, "with both our coats of arms."

My generation, the fifth to know Homelands, was the first not to produce a full-time farmer. My Howard cousins lived on the farm for most of their childhoods, calling Ann and me "city slickers" during our frequent visits, pretending we seemed as urbane to them as the Bouvier sisters would have to us. All of us liked the place, where the earth is as black as a fresh cotton typewriter ribbon. On tours of the rooms of its two sturdy main farmhouses, we were periodically reminded that one day *"this . . . will be yours,"* as if we were Plantagenets and real treasures were at stake. But we grew up with tastes and ties that pulled us elsewhere, and farm taxes became more prohibitive every year. Like many family enterprises, this one ran out of steam after four generations. In 1974, after several years' deliberation, the 760 acres were sold. We quit Homelands as our Quaker ancestors had quit the slave-owning South, as theirs had England, as my mother's people had quit County Clare. I guess there simply comes a time to leave, a time to set forth and transplant the old myths in some new soil. I don't suppose it's ever easy.

Three years before the sale of Homelands, we had buried my mother's ashes not on but near the farm, outside the village of Bangor, in a cemetery where generations of Howards lie. It is as peaceful a graveyard in as soothing a setting as any I know of, and I had kept meaning to go back to see it before the bitter January day in 1975 when I went there with Dad and Ann. Aunt Janet took us there this time, after she showed us her new apartment, the one she had bought with her share of the farm sale earnings, in a fancy high-rise building on the western edge of Marshalltown. Nothing could have resembled less the spare white farmhouses of our shared past. This new place was full of .chandeliers and upholstered French provincial furniture whose dominant color, if I remember right, was a sort of vivid aquamarine. In the basement were a Social Room and a futuristic Laundry Room and garage doors that opened automatically.

After this tour we had lemon meringue pie at Stone's Restaurant, Marshalltown's landmark, and drove over the whitened cornfields to Homelands. None of us much felt like lingering there, even though the farmhouse still was vacant. When we got to the graveyard Janet waited in the car, to keep the motor running. The temperature wasn't much above zero, and our breath made little cumulus clouds. Only an occasional jet contrail marred the brilliant sky, and the winds had drifted the snow so that you hardly could tell whose gravestone was whose. The only sounds were the wind and the squeak of our boots as we made three diverging sets of footprints through the powdery snow. Did death embarrass us? Was that why we didn't walk together?

I headed off by myself first, to look for a certain small stone I remembered, a baby's grave it must have marked. A tree trunk had almost surrounded it the last time I had come here. Now only the slightest tip of the stone could be seen, and I bent down to brush the snow off it with my wool mitten. Then I walked back to my mother's and the other Howard gravestones.

Back in the car, returning to Marshalltown, none of us said anything for a number of miles. It was Janet who finally broke the silence. Cardinals, she told us, are the only birds whose feathers are entirely red.

It is December 28. Our mother's Aunt Frances, in California, has sent her usual card hoping we "have a grand time through the holidays, and that the echo of faraway sleighbells will waken you on Christmas morning." Ann and John have gone to the Modern Art Museum. Ann, ever bent on teaching her children to make distinctions, is doubtless asking John as they leave each roomful of paintings which one he would choose, if he could, to take home. Sarah has recovered from an ill-timed case of chickenpox, but we have decided she had better not go outside, not just yet. She is in the living room, playing the hard version of "Chopsticks." Try though she may, she can't seem to get the beginning right. At last, attacking from a higher octave, she succeeds. Sometimes what we Howard-Hoards lack in talent we make up for in persistence.

She and I have just made a double recipe of chocolate chip cookies, adding the optional peanut butter, raisins, and chopped pecans. Sarah has rolled the dough into inch-and-a-half circles and spread them, in rows of four by seven, onto greased cookie sheets. In ten minutes' time the first batch will be done. Already the kitchen is fragrant.

I won't call her in until the timer rings, nor will I go to tell her, in the darkening living room, that she'd better turn a lamp on or else she'll ruin her eyes. Nor will I suggest that this would be a good time to start in on her thank-you notes. I have been saying quite enough of my mother's lines these last few days. In fact, in some odd way, I have become her.

Bean Soup

*There comes a time when you ought to have children,
and I feel sorry for you if you don't.*
                                        —Mamie Doud Eisenhower

I CAN'T REMEMBER quite how old I was when I first lay awake in the middle of the night wondering where that odd steady rhythmic sound was coming from. A train approaching? The bathroom faucet? Raindrops? No, the percussion was closer. It was right on my pillow. It came from me. I heard it from inside my own frail skull, the thumping sound of my own heart. Suddenly, for the first time and for all time, I knew three things: *No one else would ever hear this sound this way, everyone else hears a sound almost like it,* and *someday this sound would stop.*

Until it stops, I look to connect myself with others. I seem to have more luck with small connections than the riskier big ones. I keep hoping the sum of the small ones might have as much substance. Maybe it has and maybe it hasn't. Many of my friendships, in any case, can be traced to parties, which is why I figure that I owe the world a party myself every couple of years. A party, as the heroine of *Mrs. Dalloway* reflects, is an offering. To say no to a party, as John Updike once put it, is to say no to life. So now and then I give a party, to mix things up, see which ions might cling together.

Shopping for a party, I pull to a stop in front of a fruit stand in the country where a sign says "APPLES! $1 A BUSHEL!" Too good a price to pass up. The proprietor, in a worn tan cardigan, shows me an article in the newspaper he has been reading.

"D'you see this?" he wants to know. "See where seventy percent of the people in this Ann Landers poll wrote in that they would *not* want to have their kids all over again, if they had the chance to choose?" I nod. I have seen the statistic, and it shocks me, too.

"Kids," the apple man continues, "are what life's all about, don't you think? What else is the point? You'd have *yours* all over again, wouldn't you?"

"Sure I would," I tell the man. No sense explaining that my children are imaginary. That's what a bachelor friend of mine must have reasoned, too, the day he crossed Wyoming on a Greyhound bus. Next to him on that bus sat a German woman who was delighted to find someone who understood her. She asked how many children my friend had.

"*Fünf,*" he lied. "*Fünf kinder.*" Five children. The German woman beamed.

Why care what apple salesmen and German women think? Because they may be right. Certainly the weight of history and tradition and literature is on their side. What are Shakespeare's first seventeen sonnets other than admonitions to their mysterious addressee to get busy and start a family? "Die single," a representative sonnet concludes, "and thine image dies with thee." Be fruitful. Multiply. Make an honest woman of her, or man of him, and keep the race going. In his autobiography Ford Madox Ford quoted a medieval saying that every man should do four things in his time: build a house, write a book, plant a tree, and have a child. The most important things in life, according to the Koran are money and sons. The chants of Tibet and Polynesia, the sagas and eddas of Iceland, the folklore of Sicilians and Venezuelans and everyone else, everywhere and ever, are family tales. No first sentence of any novel is probably more debated than Tolstoy's, in *Anna Karenina:* "Happy families are all alike, but each unhappy family is unhappy in its own way."

Fictions set in Dublin and Brooklyn tenements, Eastern European *shtetls*, Colombian jungles, Georgia plantations, and Nordic wastes all concern what Joseph Campbell calls the "family romance," that "heavily-loaded, biologically based triangle" of children and parents, "a cooky mold of love and aggression, desire and fear, dependency, command, and the urge for release . . . competent to shape the most recalcitrant dough." Some of the dough is recalcitrant indeed; few of the stories are pretty. The archetypal blood feud of all time is the seamless web of Greek tragedies that stretches from Homer to Euripides, Clytemnestra to Antigone, concerning the grudges and violence engulfing the House of Atreus. One evening I went to see a preview performance of Aeschylus's *Agamemnon*, earliest and most horrible of family dramas. I went with my friend Grace. This production had not been reviewed and had no intermission, so we had no chance to compare our impressions until it was over. I was so beguiled by the music and the staging that it never crossed my mind to think that anyone, least of all Grace, could feel otherwise. But she did.

"I thought that was one of the *worst* productions of anything I've ever seen in my life," said Grace, in her emphatic Indiana accent. "For one thing, the Greek chorus device has always seemed fake. For another, I couldn't understand that singing, or chanting, or whatever it was. Worse yet, I don't see the *sense* of all that stuff about inherited revenge."

"You mean that's not how things were with your clan in Indianapolis?"

"It most *certainly* was *not*."

"But Grace," I said. "Why do you think *Agamemnon* has stood the test of twenty-five hundred years? If it's such a fraud, how come everybody keeps putting it on, paying to see it?"

"Oh," said Grace, "it's sort of like an old Christmas tree ornament. Nobody ever did really like it, but they got used to having it around and couldn't bring themselves to throw it out."

So: the Christmas Tree Ornament Theory of the universality of the family as a theme. Maybe it makes some sense. In any case, the essential charm and the essential horror of all history are familial. The thralldom in which the family holds us obliges us not only to act out involuntary and often dreadful rituals but to keep seeking evidence of what Lionel Trilling called the "mysterious, precarious little flame that lies at the heart of the commonplace." A classicist friend once wrote to me that

right at the beginning of European literature you find two magnificent, warm, loving, unself-conscious families, two "good marriages": one in a tragic context (Hector and Andromache) and one in a comic (Odysseus and Penelope) . . . it is hard to point to any other "relationships" as simply and nobly satisfactory . . . All of Roman literature can be seen as a search (unsuccessful) for some satisfactory human relationship. Hence, in part, all the assorted *machismo*, the hysterical and inhumanely "patriotic" side of the Roman character, so much loved by the writers and artists of the French Revolution. Virgil was a very great poet, but a human relationship between two adults of opposite sexes was something of which he was profoundly afraid; Venus is irresponsible and destructive. The ideal male-female relationship is that between mother and son. Horace is, along with the Mozart of some of the Countess Almaviva's and Pamina's arias, the great poet of love lost somewhere in the past . . . [such poetry] can be excruciatingly beautiful, but where is the background of normality and (God help me!) "fulfillment" against which it might be seen? The sex-obsessed bohemianism of Catullus and the elegiac poets is an aspect of experience that can make good poetry, but it is hardly to be recommended as a basis for society.

However rare "fulfilled" families may be, the search for them has continued from Sophocles down to Sartre, Brecht, O'Neill, Wilder, Williams, and Miller. Television, which the average 18-year-old has spent more time watching than he has in school, abounds with the dramas of families. The Waltons and Bunkers and Sanfords and Hartmans—not to mention the Bellamys of *Upstairs, Downstairs* and the Kintes of *Roots*—have become, for many of us, our own relatives, perhaps because we aren't breeding so many real ones. Voluntary childlessness, social scientists like to say, is "an area in imperative need of study."

If I were a social scientist I might study it myself. As it is, my thoughts turn often to elderly primigravidas, women who bear their first children after the age of 35. Something strikes me as gallant about the gamble these women take. Eggs so long unfertilized can grow stale. One out of every 39 babies they bear is likely to be a Mongoloid or to suffer some other birth defect. These defects can be predicted by a test called an amniocentesis, in which fluid drawn from the mother's belly is examined, but that isn't reassuring enough for most doctors. Most doctors counsel against such pregnancies. "You don't want to be sixty," they ask, "when your son is eighteen— do you?"

"Why ever not?" some women reply. It's a mercy that they do. Several of my friends were born to such mothers. So, I have heard, were more members than not of the French Academy. So, to be metaphorical, was the biblical Isaac, whose birth occurred when his mother Sarah—patron saint of the elderly primigravida—was ninety and his father Abraham ten years her senior. "God hath made me to laugh," Sarah exults in Genesis 21:6, "so that all who hear will laugh with me."

It would be heartening to hear more such laughter. It would be heartening if our reproductive systems could manage an evolutionary change, geared to our greatly expanded lifespans and the urge many women now feel to spend their twenties and thirties elsewhere than in nurseries. It would be heartening if we could postpone parenthood, as men can, until we were good and ready for it.

"I'm forever taking babies on planes," one elderly primigravida told me, "so that the mother can pretend for an hour that she isn't as burdened as she is. Poor nineteen-year-old mothers! They haven't even developed their *own* lives, when along comes this precocious twerp, this *rival*. How can someone that young graduate to the level of returning to the world the kind of love—quite a sophisticated love —that a baby needs?"

"Older mothers, having sown their wild oats, can be better mothers," another woman told me. She is a lawyer who started bearing her four healthy babies at the age of 39. "I wanted those kids so much I went around for weeks with a thermometer in my mouth. I took them to work with me and nursed them in my office. I wouldn't have dreamed of missing the whole experience."

Not everybody feels this way. Many women in their forties and fifties only groan and roll their eyes at the very mention of breeding and chasing small children. But my own sympathies are with the elderly primigravidas. May their ranks increase; may their offspring be whole and bright. Meanwhile I talk in daydreams to children I don't have. The ice is thin and dangerous, I tell one in such a daydream, and I hold you in my arms now as we skate, so you won't drop. There's a lot I've got to teach you. You have to learn to look up at the tops of buildings, not just at what is at eye level. You have to learn to notice the fragrance of clothes dried outdoors, the look of leaves against wet November pavements. You must learn to make angel wingprints in the new-fallen snow, and to bring people flowers, and to decorate walls with topographic maps, and to look up *evensong* and *crankshaft* and *aubergine* and *hogshead* in the dictionary. You must learn where to look—to your father, perhaps—for the things I cannot teach you, which are endless.

We'll make bean soup together, and find people to feed it to. When we go to foreign cities (if there's fuel enough to go there when you're older), we will look for marketplaces, zoos, weddings, and funerals. We'll go when we can to houses near water, and while our clothes are flapping dry on the line in the wind we'll walk over rocks with our sneakers laced together and slung over our shoulders, in case we come to a place too sharp for bare feet. I'll show you how to cut a slice of bread, and when to pull back in your own lane after you have passed another car (if cars still exist when you're older). I shall try to make you understand that certain mysteries are meant to remain mysterious, that hellos imply farewells, that much of what you'll ever learn, from me or from anyone else, is subject to change, and that it is well to speak plainly, and on occasion to lift your voice in song.

The talk turns to children and parents and families wherever I go. On a balcony overlooking Lake Como, one moonlit evening in the middle of an international conference, a man from Massachusetts tells me how it was to be a boy in Minnesota four decades ago. He tells how his father, a teacher by trade and musician by bent, would get up way before dawn to build a fire and put the oatmeal on and then go to the upright piano. One by one he would wake his five children by playing for each the special private melody he had composed. At night he played the same melodies to lull them to sleep. Now this man on this Italian balcony during this conference has children of his own, one of whom plays the piano more brilliantly than his father ever dreamed of doing. Once his son played for this man the same song the man's father had composed. Nothing this accomplished man had ever done, he said, meant more to him than transmitting the gift for music.

My gynecologist is a busy woman. She is booked so far in advance that if you phone her office in October for a routine checkup, you can't get an appointment until January. Even then your waiting isn't over. Some of us outside her office this afternoon have been sitting here for two hours. One of the others who is waiting wears rimless granny glasses and coveralls that look like size 22½. She is probably ten years younger than I am, and looks ten years tireder. In her arms is a fretful infant a few months old, and over her sandals clambers a child who looks about three. To the older child, in a pronounced New York accent, the mother chants a rhyme:

> See saw, open the door,
> Whaddya want, a glass of beer?
> Leave me alone, get outa here.

The older child gets the joke; he knows his mother doesn't want him to get out. He loves the chant, and her, and he begs for more. His mother obliges, repeatedly, patient as a Buddha. When I am beckoned in for my appointment and ask the doctor about this woman, she tells me. The mother gained way too much weight during both her pregnancies, she is in poor health, she is on food stamps. I guess I ought to feel sorry for her, and in a way of course I do. But sorry isn't all.

"I don't like to be around kids," my friend Joan says. "They make me wish I had one myself." Joan, who is 35, has just won another award for one of her articles.

"I know," I tell her, "but I can't stand being away from them."

"You're both out of your minds," says Ginny, a painter whose two children are halfway through their teens. "Do you know what you'd be asking for if you had children?"

"Twenty years," says Joan. "Eighty-five thousand dollars."

"A lot of work," I add, "and a lot of time."

"You can't *imagine* how much work and how much time," says Ginny.

Probably I can't. I try, though.

Passing through San Francisco, I phone an old friend to invite him and his wife to join me in Chinatown for supper. They can't make it, he explains, because of the baby. It's not that they can't find a sitter, it's just that they don't like to leave her. He is in his forties, this first-time father, just as his parents were when he, their only child, was born. (It is striking, the way such patterns repeat themselves.) But he and his wife would love to see me. Won't I come to their house for supper? Of course I will. And before I hang up, wouldn't I like to hear the baby gurgling on the phone, as she has done all morning in her father's arms? Certainly. So the man holds the phone to his infant daughter's mouth. The gurgling stops.

"Well then, just listen to her breathing," he tells me. "It's marvelous, the way she breathes." I listen.

"Very nice," I tell him. "Very rhythmical."

In *Little Women,* Louisa May Alcott wrote:

"I do think that families are the most beautiful things in all the world!" burst out Jo, who was in an unusually uplifted frame of mind just then. "When I have one of my own, I hope it will be just as happy as the three that I know and love the best."

But the real family rhythms of the living models for Marmee March and her husband and their brood of daughters were another matter. Real families inspire as much venom, on paper, as they do treacle.

Green and Black Rocks

We have a country governed by blockheads and knaves; the ties of marriage with all its felicity are severed and destroyed; our wives and daughters are thrown to the stews; our children are cast into the world from the breast and forgotten; filial piety is extinguished; and our surnames, the only mark of distinction among families, are abolished. Can the imagination paint anything more dreadful on this side hell?

> —Timothy Dwight, 1801
> quoted in Henry Adams,
> History of the United States, Volume 1

And may the gods accomplish your desire: a home, a husband, and harmonious converse with him—the best thing in the world being a strong house held in serenity where man and wife agree. Woe to their enemies, joy to their friends! But all this they know best.

> —Homer
> Odyssey, VI, 179

If you are granted wishes for the world,
Enlarge its scope; make work as one with play
In houses built for everlasting fire
Where man and woman burn like seraphim.
> —Peter Davison
> A Voice in the Mountain

FROM THE LORE that has lately engulfed me, paeans to the power of families are harder to extract than attacks against families in particular and the family as an abstraction. "Families," André Gide once wrote, "I hate you!" Nine out of ten of the children he knew, he said elsewhere, would be better off away from their parents. H. L. Mencken alluded to the "mucilaginous togetherness" and Evelyn Waugh to the "hideous lights" of home. Ezra Pound's grandmother, declaring her family a "sty," ran away from it in her eighties. Jean-Paul Sartre's mother told him and Simone de Beauvoir that "it is only now that I am 84 that I have really broken free from my mother."

Even Jesus Christ, in the tenth chapter of the Book of Matthew, makes clear that no earthly power exceeds that of the family: "For I am come to set a man at variance against his father, and the daughter against her mother, and the daughter-in-law against her mother-in-law. And a man's foes shall be they of his own household." He could have chosen no image more forceful.

Dr. Ashley Montagu regards families as "an institution for the systematic production of physical and mental illness in the members." The modern nuclear family, to Susan Sontag, is "a phychological and moral disaster . . . a prison of sexual repression, a playing-field of inconsistent moral laxity, a museum of possessiveness, a guilt-producing factory, a school of selfishness." In his film *Last Tango in Paris*, Bernardo Bertolucci has his hero decry "the holy family that tames the savage, the church of good citizens, where children are taught to tell their first lie, where the will is broken by repression, where freedom is crushed by selfishness, the fucking family, oh God, oh Jesus."

I could add to this assault myself, as who could not? Who doesn't know people whose lives have been stunted and warped by their families? What family is wholly innocent of such warping? But let us bear in mind that families still exist, here and there, whose people abide one another's shortcomings, breed decent children, and sometimes go for days or even weeks without wreaking overt pathological harm. I am connected myself, by water and blood, with at least two such families.

Summer makes me meddlesome. Summer is the season for the merging of the clans. Something about summer prods me to choreograph a big minuet, or maybe it is a square dance, to mingle clans of blood with clans of water. Part of this feeling, I guess, is a notion that one way or another I ought to provide my niece and nephew with cousins.

First I lure them and their mother to a house I have rented near the ocean. We all like the ocean. Nine or so years ago, the first time we all swam in it together, Sarah asked, "Those guys sure put a lot of salt in the water, didn't they?" Those guys sure did. On good days those guys make the surf nice and rough, too, the way we like it. We call the big waves Maytags, because they make us feel like clothing being whirled in a washing machine. Maytags plummet us backwards in shrieking, abandoned somersaults. They make us forget ourselves entirely. We laugh, emerge, hop to shake water from our ears, and flop down on our towels to risk sunburn before the next plunge.

One afternoon Sarah wanders off alone, heading east. A good while later the rest of us notice that she hasn't come back. Ann is afraid she may have drowned. Don't worry, says John. Don't worry, say the other friends who are with us. Don't worry, I say myself, but when the memorial service is over can I ever bear to swim anywhere again? In teams we fan out to look for the missing girl. One friend alerts a lifeguard. Just then Sarah wanders back, puzzled at the fuss her absence has caused.

"I wasn't lost," she says, "I knew where I was all the time."

"I *told* you," says her brother.

At home we hose the sand off our feet and go to welcome more friends arriving on the train, first putting coins on the tracks to be flattened. Many trains bringing many friends flatten many coins; summer is social. Many flies come, too. *Musca domestica* seem to be having a national convention at this very house, with panel discussions and plenary sessions every five or six square feet, round the clock. They keep us awake and reduce us to sending the kids to the hardware store for long sticky gold spirals of flypaper, to uncoil from the ceiling.

"Talk about *tacky*," says Ann. "Talk about Booth cartoons." We had in fact been admiring George Booth's *New Yorker* cartoons of cranky musicians grumping around amid exposed light bulbs, yowling cats, and yards of twisted extension cords. But this house's trouble is not its flypaper or its extension cords. This house's trouble, as far as we are concerned this summer of our lives, is that it doesn't have a history we can absorb. The short history of our own we impose on it is somehow not enough. We need more. As much as we need the ocean, just now, we need photograph albums, ghosts, legends, and a sense of the past. For that reason we head north.

We head north to another house near a lake in the Adirondack mountains. John and Sarah have been hearing about this house for four years now, since I first went there myself. It is a big green lodge of a place under soaring fragrant conifers, set a mile back from the road. For three generations it has belonged to a family I know. The globe is the globe, I tell John and Sarah, which means it is round and any given point on it could claim to be its top, including a street corner in Calcutta or a phone booth in Secaucus. But some places on its surface feel more like the top of the world than other places do, and one of the places that feels most that way to me is this house. See how the lawn curves between the main house and the shed?

They see. They may think me maudlin, with reason, but they get my point. They already know the other children here; we have seen to that in summers past. Together we have gone to Coney Island, to the Bronx Zoo, and once canoeing in Canada. Once we all spent New Year's Eve together in Times Square. High time John and Sarah came here to this place. Four years now I have come here with these three families myself, sampling and adding to this house's fund of myth. Only one of the families with whom I have come here has true claim to this house's history, but the rest of us have seen the pictures in the albums and heard the stories often enough to be unofficial relatives. All of us feel, a little at least, that we too are descended from the grandfather who could skate backwards faster than a horse could run, and from the cartographer great-aunt who wore her hair short like a man's, smoked a pipe, and cut with her jigsaw the animals that hang outlined on the wall of the screened back porch, overlooking the garden. The jigsaw animals hang among badminton rackets and the battered straw hats, between the Ping-Pong table and the table where when it isn't too cold we eat our meals. The table is seldom set for fewer than eleven.

"Granny!" Speaking of meals, what is that woman doing in the kitchen? This is not her day to cook. An elaborate chart taped to the icebox door tells who does what when, to save us from arguing over chores. "Stop it!" we call to her. "You've done enough! You'll make us feel guilty! Don't be a martyr!"

"I can't help it," calls our hostess's mother. "I bake, therefore I am." Incorrigible. Oh well, her brownies will mean we needn't buy dessert when we go to town. What else shall we have tonight? Ham, did we decide? These whole two weeks we haven't had a ham. I could do a glaze with mustard and horseradish and some of those blueberry preserves. You could see whether that vegetable stand up the road is still giving away free cucumbers. You shop. I'll do cleanup. The boys can bring up some of the wood they have just chainsawed for tonight's fire. What, it takes two years for green wood to cure? All right, then, dry logs from the shed.

My first year here nobody would have let those boys anywhere near a power tool. But look now at their penciled heights on the kitchen doorjamb. Tall as we are, they have Adam's apples and learners' permits and embouchures. The girls, with their pierced ears, are musical too, eclectically so. We hear partitas and mazurkas and inventions and rags. We hear spirited debates on the merits of modern performers.

"When she told me she liked Barry Manilow," one girl says of a classmate, "I was physically ill."

"But I think Barry Manilow's sort of cute. It's that other guy who ought to be shot for trying to sing."

"Mom, how come you always wear such shiny plastic slacks? Why don't you get some jeans? You'd look nice in jeans, Mom, really."

"You mean there's hope? You mean I don't have to be as frowzy as I am all the time? Should I get some manacles too, while I'm at it?"

"Will you come and watch us water-ski?"

"And put down *Buddenbrooks?* Do you know how long it's been since I've read *Buddenbrooks?*"

"But Mom, I just learned to go in and out of the wake." They water-ski. They play soccer and softball and badminton and horseshoes and tennis. They play chess and Jotto and Scrabble. (*Ut* is too a legitimate word, it's a synonym for *do*, the first note of the scale. *Ut* a deer, a female deer.) They play hearts and bridge and five-card stud and, when the mood is on them to regress a bit, a card game called Spoon, whose loser must swallow a spoonful of whatever mixture the others can devise. Marshmallow Fluff, with some of the chutney and just a little of the garlic salt, makes an arresting mixture.

The boys nick their cheeks with razors. The girls make melodramatic runs to the drugstore. Self-consciousness is rampant. One dinnertime, even before dessert is served, one girl leaps from the table to shampoo her hair, which she had washed not twenty-four hours before. They tell of their schools, of an Ecology Camp where they are sent to have Learning Experiences. They tell of special seminars called Preparing for the Year 2000. One girl tells of an eighth-grade class called Self-Defense, in which "my Science teacher and my Wilderness teacher were both supposed to throw us to the ground so we'd know what to do if we get raped." They think we don't know that they have smoked, on the sly, and been drunk. No doubt they have done things we can't or don't want to imagine. They don't plan to drink again, though, ever. They don't want to be like us. God forbid. Until four in the morning they stay up talking about us, among any number of other things, and then they sleep till noon. They roll their eyes at us, as we did at our parents, as all children must at all elders. And they're terrible about cleaning up, as we once were too.

But at times we all forget that our generations are meant to be at odds. Two of us and two of them did the job on the male mannequin at Newberry's, so insufferable in his back-to-school polyester that we had to unzip his fly and roll up one of his pant legs. Generational ignorance is no excuse in Charades. A judge who is close to his sixties must act out *Ricochet Rabbit and Droopalong*, a Saturday morning television cartoon program, whether he has ever heard of it or not. My niece, who at eleven does not yet know of Karl Marx, must by the same token do her best with "from each according to his ability, to each according to his need." Her team guesses in 87 seconds. Other times we play Adverbs. You go out of the room until we think of an adverb to act out, and when you come back you will find us all in a pageant, exaggerating as best we can by all we do and say the word we have chosen. Awkwardly. Firmly. Heartily. Surreptitiously. Normally? No, dummy, condescendingly. Grossly. Clannishly.

Storms brew some days, outside the house and in it. Several years ago, soon after I met these people, I asked one set of parents how come their family worked so well. They laughed, and it was not a laugh of joy. I should see it, they told me, on a day when it didn't work. By now I have seen it on many such days. We have all seen one another at something like our worst. At our worst we confirm the accusations of such relentless family critics as David Cooper and R. D. Laing. But we are numerous enough and connected enough not to let anyone's worst prevail for long. For any given poison, our pooled resources can come up with an antidote.

One morning's paper tells of someone in Panama who for a political principle has immolated himself. ("That means burn yourself alive, stupid"; these kids are very conscious of their vocabularies.) But how could anyone choose so hideous a death as that? Could any of us even imagine feeling so strongly about anything?

"Not any*thing*," I speculate. "Maybe any*one*. If it were a question of your dying or mine," I say to one of the boys, "since you've got a lot more years ahead of you, I might risk my life to save yours."

"You *would?*"

"I said I might."

"But I'm not your kid."

Let me come right out and say that the Jacobses aren't perfect, either. I don't suppose any household of five intelligent and complicated beings is. Kathy, my second cousin, who was asked at age 42 to show her identification in a bar, can seem overpowering. Steve, who often vanishes to bed without saying goodnight to a soul, can seem churlish. Tom and Henry, only a year apart, can drive all Pima County to distraction with their endless rounds of unbrotherly rivalry. Even small Jane, to whom I am partial since she is my namesake, is said to be capable of Wagnerian fits of temper. Nevertheless, it occurs to me whenever I contemplate crossing the Mississippi River that I might just make a little side trip down to Tucson, where these people live. Friends from as far away as Prague, Czechoslovakia, have been known to plan their western tours so as to squeeze in a restorative stopover with the Jacobses in Tucson.

The last time I went there I only spent one night in their house. We all left town the next afternoon, as soon as the children were out of school and Steve had finished teaching optical physics at the state university. The six of us, plus seven human neighbors and two dogs, piled into three vehicles and headed south. For eight rattling hours we bounced over rutted roads to camp for four days on a certain secret beach in the Mexican state of Sonora, on the Gulf of California.

"How you doing back there, Juana Grande?" Kathy asks after a particularly vicious bump in the road. She calls me that to distinguish me from her daughter.

"It's like a ride at some amusement park." I recline in the back of the Land Rover atop a pile of duffel—sleeping bags, blankets, rolled-up tents, pillows. These, in turn, lie atop several cases of fruit juice and groceries and beer.

"Be of good cheer," says Steve, who never shifts above third gear the whole ride down. "It'll be worth it. Just wait till you see the green and black rocks in their own habitat."

Already I have seen plenty of these rocks in and outside the house in Tucson. Steve has made four or five previous raids on the secret beach for the special rocks. Specimens are piled all over the house and grounds, waiting to be shined in the tumbler and fashioned into bookends, doorstops, paperweights, tie clasps, steppingstones, earrings, necklaces. Not that the rocks have any intrinsic value. They may not be found in any museum's Hall of Gems. "Unquestionably igneous," a geologist called them when I showed him some of mine, not sounding very excited about it, "with black basalt and green peridotite phenocysts altering to serpentine." Smooth rocks, cool to the touch, nice enough to look at, but only Steve would drive eight hours to load them in every cranny of his car.

Steve is an eccentric. Steve, with his graying corona of frizzy tan hair, is the archetypal absent-minded professor. If Steve is bored or preoccupied he will say nothing, or yawn. But I have never known a more devoted father. Until his children grew too big he bathed each one of them each night. Even now, of a morning, all three of them sometimes snuggle in bed with him and Kathy. He sings to them, too, with his banjo. He plays them songs he composes himself. The songs concern the garbage man, the dog, the kids, the sky, the world. One thing his songs never are is hymns to New York, where Steve grew up. Steve can't stand New York. His 84-year-old mother still goes to work there every day, wearing a bracelet from which hang five silver circles and four silver hearts, each engraved with a grandchild's name and birthday. Steve would rather be his mother's host than her guest.

How was it, his children sometimes ask him, being a boy in New York? He tells how he used to attach a rubber band to a threadless spool so as to propel a match across the street with such force that the match, striking the wall of the building opposite, would ignite. The doormen below were amazed. Then the kids want to know how he felt about the bombing of Japan, the testing of the A-bomb at White Sands, the sonic boom. He tells them. They ask me my views too, and about people I know in the city.

"What do kids *do* there?"

"I know one kid," I tell them, "who broke an elevator."

"He *broke* it? How could he do that? Did he get outside and climb on top and snap the cable?" I don't think so, I tell them, I just know he broke it. Do I have a car? Is it a four-door? Is it a hog on gas? Does it really cost ninety dollars to get it back when the police tow it away? The city, they say, must be awful. I tell them some people think it might be awful in Arizona, with all those drugs, with reporters getting blown to bits for knowing too much. Politics in Arizona are corrupt. The less her children need her, the more time Kathy spends as Precinct Committeeperson for the Pima County Reform Democrats. When Republicans resort to red-baiting smear tactics in local campaigns, she leads the counterattack. When Mexican aliens have trouble with immigration papers, she tries to help them. When liquor stores sell wine from grapes not picked by Cesar Chavez's workers, she pickets. When a Cub Scout leader proposes to take his pack to the Army post, soon after a thorough tour of the Air Force base, she protests that one military facility a semester seems quite enough.

When her friends are having surgery, Kathy's is often the last nonmedical face they see before anesthesia, and the first when they wake up. When Angelita, the Jacobses' cleaning woman, was married in Sinoloa, in a dress Kathy and her neighbor Trish Towle made, the whole Jacobs family went. When word came that Steve's proposal for a sabbatical in Florence had been accepted, Kathy rushed to engage a Milanese tutor. That tutor was a busy woman; if she hadn't been, she might have become an unofficial member of the family, along with neighbors and physicists and Kathy's political "cronies," as she likes to call them, of whom one asked her to be the Best Person at his wedding.

"When are we getting into our high-pitched peak frenzy packing gear?" I ask Kathy an hour before we are to leave for Sonora.

"We're in it now," she says, as she calmly fills Styrofoam cases with coleslaw, bagels, the ingredients for *spaghetti alla carbonara,* and a four-day supply of other groceries. Most people I know, myself most emphatically included, tend to get wrought up about packing for trips. Not Kathy. If the dog throws up on her Levi's, she washes them and finds another pair. If, as once happened, a hurricane forces us all to evacuate a Fire Island house only hours after she and Steve and the kids have arrived, then so be it: she shakes the jigsaw puzzle pieces back into the box and packs, battening down the hatches and heading for land.

With luck, Jane Howard Jacobs will be like that, too. "Aren't you lonesome in there by yourself?" she asks early our second morning on the beach in Sonora, giving me a kiss through the netting of my tent.

"I'm still recovering from that cozy, bumpy ride down here," I tell her. "But I'm glad to see you anyway. Come on in. Hey, where'd you get those big new teeth? Were they expensive?"

"Teeth," Jane informs me, "are free." She unzips the netting to climb into the tent. "You've got a lot of colors in here, haven't you?" So I have. My nightgown seems to be a bright red windbreaker, the sleeping bag a bright blue, and the tent itself the color of an orange.

"But I missed the green flash just before the sun went down."

"Too bad," says Jane. "It was pretty. But we'll find some green rocks. Some green and black rocks. A whole *lot* of green and black rocks."

"Are the others awake?"

"Just you and me. All the rest of the town is asleep, and nobody new has come, either." A sign could go up: GREEN AND BLACK ROCK BEACH, POP. 15, ELEV. 1. The thirteen of us, plus two dogs, could get the world started all over again if we had to. Vegetables might be something of a problem, but we could eat fish and birds, and breed new babies, and use the rocks as currency.

"Let's make breakfast," Jane suggests. We find a can of *jugo de naranja* and light the gas stove to toast our bagels. Keota, the neighbors' Samoyed, joins us. Keota's ancestral destiny is to guard Eskimos in their igloos, but she has adapted admirably to this country of *cholla* and *saguaro*. She leads us on a long hike down the beach. When we return, Tom and Henry and their friends are awake.

"Hey, Big Jane!" Henry, who is eleven, means me. "Look! There's an osprey!" So there is: a beauty. Tom, who is ten, pursues a seagull with his slingshot, in a posture caricaturing stealth. From her tent his mother calls for him to cut it out.

"I hope we don't see any sharks today," says Henry, "because sharks and me don't mix."

"We'll keep that in mind," says his father. The children dig a four-foot pit in the sand. We all play Red Rover, Red Rover except for Steve, who keeps making forays for rocks, stretching the bottom of his faded gray sweatshirt out before him to carry them back. The children scream as one of the neighbors, a man in his early twenties named Keith, hurls them in the air and catches them. Keith's friend, named Linda, tells a story of which I overhear just one line: "Rats are a drag to take for a walk on a leash." Yes, I imagine they are. Keith's and Linda's friend B.J., who looks like a king in his striped orange robe, sings all the verses of "Mr. Bojangles" and tells how the only place he wants to go is Ireland: "My mother, my father, my brother, two sisters and me, not any two of us live in the same state. We're Army brats. I'd like to see County Down where my grandparents lived, but until I save the money to go there, I don't want to leave Tucson. Except to come places like this with you guys, of course."

"Oh, B.J.," says Kathy, "I've started to love you, and that's going to complicate my life, but it can't be helped." A V-shaped flock of pelicans flies overhead. Steve dumps a load of rocks in the Land Rover.

"Daddy! Daddy!" cries my namesake from a cove around the corner.

"I hear you."

"I've found a perfect rock!"

"Better have a look at it." Daddy pops the soap-shaped specimen into his mouth, and then considers it. His saliva deepens the colors, revealing an imperfection which not a whole week in the tumbler at home could erase. "Back that rock goes," he tells his daughter as he tosses it in the water. "We'll let the waves work on it some more. Maybe we'll find it another time. Today we'll look for better ones,

Monkey Cow." That, just now, is Jane's other name. Everybody always has some other name. Steve, himself known at times as Walrus and Hootie for reasons I don't try to understand, is a compulsive rechristener.

In earlier lives he might have been one of the Blackfoot Indians, who changed their names every season, or a worshipper of the Babylonian god Marduk, who had fifty names denoting his various attributes. No telling, ever, what new names he will find for those around him, or why. Maybe that is one of the reasons his family feels spacious: everyone can always try a new identity with the new names. Experimenting with new versions of ourselves, we can say things to each other we would not dare say elsewhere, among people we have to be nice to. That's one thing a family is, Steve once said: a collection of people you needn't be nice to—a guaranteed following.

"What," I once asked Jane, "do you like about your brothers?"

"Nothing!" she answered.

"Oh come on, there must be *something*."

"Well," she said after some thought, "Henry doesn't call me Pig, so I guess I like *that* about him."

Steve and Keith and B.J. go off in the Land Rover, looking for dead cactus to use as firewood. Bill, the next-door neighbor, doesn't join them: "I might just stay here and party." Bill's wife Trish hikes down the beach in search of rocks.

"I myself am going to recline, at this time," says Kathy, "and read Rex Stout in my tent."

"I'll be in mine sorting my rocks," I say. "I can't wait till the next time someone picks up my suitcase and says, 'What have you got in there, lady? Rocks?'"

"Hey, Big Jane," says Tom, "let's play Adverbs."

"I've got a better idea," says Henry. "Let's play *verbs*."

"Let's just play," says Jane Howard Jacobs.

Time for a pause here.

Up to this point I have been talking mostly about my own families —the one I was born to and two of the several I feel part of unofficially—all of which I have known for many years. Now it is time to move on to some of the families I met expressly for the sake of this book.

Each of the families in the chapters that follow shows something about the imperishability of tribes and clans. The cumulative point of their stories is the same one Lucretius made 2,000 years ago: that in the struggle between continuity and change, it is usually continuity that wins.

In these chapters we shall pay visits to what on the surface may appear to be jarringly disparate households. From a lustily noisy black ghetto family we shall move to an oddly still farmhouse where an old-fashioned patriarch rules over six of his eighteen children. We shall visit the church and the business and the living rooms of a big, close tribe of Greek immigrants, then go from there to a number of scattered and different Jewish and southern households. Finally we shall arrive at the headquarters of one of the most privileged clans in America, whose history goes back three centuries.

The lessons I learned in these visits were seldom the ones I expected. Every one of these families surprised me. Most of them amused me. My favorite overheard fragment, at a party in a Jewish household, stays with me still. "Remember that State Senator with the rotten teeth that I didn't introduce you to in the bagel store last Sunday?" a lawyer asked her fiancé. He nodded; he remembered.

"Well," the lawyer went on, "he was the one who hasn't been to Katmandu." I refrained from asking the context of this remark. I prefer to keep wondering.

The eldest daughter of the privileged and wealthy family wanted more than anything else to be "streetwise." The eldest daughter of the black ghetto clan, who is probably as streetwise as anyone I know, wanted—well, we shall see what she wanted. In my visit to one of the southern households, I encountered a man in his seventies with as admirably weathered a face as I have ever seen, and a nature to match. Everyone in the room was drawn to that man. Someone made bold to approach him and ask what we all wanted to know: "You seem to be such a nice person. I'm so accustomed to dealing with people who are essentially rotten that I have to ask: What makes you so decent?"

"Sense of place," the man replied at once. "I had the luck to be brought up by loving and generous parents in a community where everyone genuinely cared about everyone else, before people had to compete so much for land and goods and everything else." Most of the families in the chapters of this section have something of that intense, if slightly anachronistic, feeling for place. That may be one reason why they deal so unflinchingly with direness.

These families are as cohesive as they are for what might seem radically different reasons. The Jews and the Greeks are close because their history has kept them moving. Forced to escape from the Pharaoh or the Führer or their poverty, they scattered explosively, but then found each other and clung together more tightly than ever, wherever they happened to land. The southerners and the blacks are no less close, but for an opposite reason: history obliged them to stay put. Defeat and isolation, in other words, have the same effect on families as a diaspora. Explosion and implosion both keep strong the need for clan.

I had heard rumors about the politics of different kinds of families, and in these visits, at least, those rumors proved true. Patriarchies, like the evangelist's household and, in a gentler way, those of the Greeks, breed conservative, closed families, where a kind of general purdah is imposed: stay home, do as father says. Households ruled by mothers—the black one, for example, and most of those of the Jews—are politically and otherwise more liberal, more open. (By tradition and law, of course, Jewishness may only be transmitted matrilineally. If your mother is not Jewish, then neither are you, even if your father is a rabbi.)

Esteem for religion, ritual and tradition is the commonest and strongest thread that links these families. Tradition, G. K. Chesterton wrote, "refuses to surrender to the arrogant oligarchy of those who merely happen to be walking around." Not all these families have portraits of ancestors over their mantels, but they all are as at-

tached to their elders, living and dead, as they are to their descendants. The sense of inherent structure and continuity they exude, whether they address their mothers as Mum or Mommy or Big Mamma, whether they sup on fried swine or broiled lamb chops with the fat trimmed, is accordingly immense. It is also something of a comfort. Their children grow up with at least a dim notion of what is expected of them, of what roles they might assume.

In 1810, a young Englishwoman who was to become Sarah, Lady Lyttelton, wrote to one of her older brothers about the two youngest boys in their large family, who that happy day had "been told what their professions are to be, and thank God for it, they seem really cordially delighted, both of them . . . Fritz already fancies himself an epauletted, red-coated, well-mounted cavalry officer . . . As to George, he could scarcely keep grave the whole day, after he heard he was to be a clergyman."

Lucky Fritz. Lucky George. Lucky anybody, up to a point at least, on whom the family confers a congenial destiny. One rather envies even those apparently martyred women of the past who were consigned at first to be "the niece" and later "the aunt," devoting their prime years to the care of the old and the dying. Whatever their troubles, such women had a vivid idea of their roles, and knew they could depend on the approval of the only people whose regard made any difference to them: their families.

As a society we cannot go back now to the days of rigid primogeniture, to such a degree of structure and certainty, nor would we wish to. Structure, in excess, can stultify, and frequently does. But so can its absence. The families in these chapters, I think, all somehow keep alive a healthy trace of that structure. That may be one reason why some of their people, most notably the black matriarch, seem to me to belong to what E. M. Forster called "an aristocracy of the sensitive, the considerate, and the plucky," whose members "are to be found in all nations and classes, and all through the ages, and there is a secret understanding between them when they meet. They represent the true human tradition, the one permanent victory of our queer race over cruelty and chaos."

It is time to visit some of these aristocrats.

"He's Been Eating Pork Since He Was *Qualified* to Eat"

IT IS A SULTRY AUGUST EVENING at the Climax Club in Gary, Indiana. I am here at a wedding reception, watching a fat woman in a red dress with a wide smile dancing with somebody's baby. The baby's hair has been plaited into cornrows. The fat woman and the baby don't seem to mind that the air-conditioning doesn't work. Neither do most of the 200 or so other people who have come here to "fellowship." That's what the minister bade us do, earlier today, after he pronounced that a couple named Bobby and Bobbie were man and wife. And so we do: we fellowship.

I don't know either one of the Bobbys. I am here because I know the groom's widowed cousin Cora Manley Taylor. She also, it happens, is a cousin of the fat woman in the red dress. There aren't very many of us here at the Climax Club who can't reach out to touch a cousin.

"That's what I thought *you* were going to look like, before I met you," I tell Cora as we watch the fat woman dance with the baby. Cora and I first met several months before, at her office in a Gary day care center. I went there because I had been wondering what was special about strong black families and somebody had told me that a good way to find out would be to meet Cora Taylor.

"That chick," I had been told, "is something else. You think families are coming apart? Go see the way she's raising those eight kids. Even after they come up, they don't want to leave home. She's probably the best mother in Gary. She's fantastic."

All the superlatives somehow made me picture someone with a lot of laps, like the woman out there on the dance floor. I was wrong. If the fat woman in the red dress was a cake, then Cora Taylor is a piece of toast with the crusts trimmed. She is tall and slim, with straightened hair and gold-rimmed harlequin glasses. Her voice is quiet, probably because it is more her nature to listen than to talk.

"People need somebody to tell things to," she said to me the day we met. "A lot of people, for some reason, like to talk to me. I carry a lot of secrets."

It was an unhappy morning there at the day care center; a vandal had just broken into the Free Clinic downstairs, looking for drugs. "But he didn't find nothin' harsh," someone told Cora.

Children clustered around her when she took me on a tour of the building. A framed birthday poem near her desk was addressed to "The *real* African Queen—the mother who is fly, the grandmother who is baaaad, an elder when experience counts, a counselor in confusion, a peer when one needs the strength of many . . . the flower in the path of the fiery dragon . . ." A hundred or so children came every day to that center for lessons, games, lunches and medical care. Cora's job was to work with their parents, most of whom are employed, if at all, in Gary steel mills or kitchens in Munster or Glen Park. Cora's third daughter Tuffy commutes to her job as a secretary at the University of Chicago. She and her husband and children have an apartment near Tenth and Noble in Gary. Nearly every night they have supper with the rest of the family, at Cora's.

Only one of Cora's other children, her oldest daughter Aretha, lives away from home. Aretha, a veteran of the WAVES, has lived in Philadelphia ever since the Navy transferred her there from Orlando, "but there are so many phone calls back and forth that our bills are all out of sight." Sometimes the calls are routinely chatty— Aretha and her mother both tell of their homework from the community colleges they are enrolled in, Aretha on the GI Bill, Cora because she might want to be a social worker someday—but sometimes they are dramatic. Once, when Aretha felt despondent, she phoned home to say something ominous about her life insurance policy and her children—hinting at suicide. "You just depressed," her sister Roshelle told her. "I'm going to have Mommy call you as soon as she comes in." Mommy did, and told Aretha that "*My* children don't go through changes like that. Besides, the kids wouldn't get the money, anyway. Don't you talk that way, girl."

The other Taylor children all live near the corner of 23rd and Harrison in Gary, around the block from a soft drink plant and down the street from a brightly painted tavern called Thelma's Flamingo Lounge. Their narrow three-story house looks no different on the outside from the others in the neighborhood. "I could sell it for about fifteen thousand the way it is now," Cora told me, "and maybe when I get it fixed up the way I want it, it'll be worth twenty-two or twenty-five." The house has an asbestos siding facade. Three steps lead up to a tiny stoop and an aluminum storm door.

In the long, narrow back yard Cora plants roses and gladioli, avoiding the lunging German shepherd in the yard next door: "I wouldn't advise you to pat him," she says. I'd no more pat that dog than I'd wash my hands in a piranha tank.

Most people, given a choice, would elect to live elsewhere than near that corner in Gary, but if Cora had money, she would buy the house next door so that all her family could live in comfortable proximity. As it is, she is gradually remodeling the place, hiring ex-convicts and friends to do paneling and rewiring. The two things that make this house special are its history and its traffic. The house has been in her family since her widowed mother bought it in 1933, when Cora was five. "My mother worked at the railroad; she unloaded freight cars. When she left that job she went to a factory where they made prophylactics. When she came home from working there she'd go to Turkey Creek, to fish till one in the morning sometimes.

"*Me* fish? I'm deathly afraid of worms and snakes—they're the only thing in the animal world that scare me. When I was carrying Aretha, my sister's boyfriend chased me around this whole block with a garden snake no longer than my finger. What I like to do is work in the dirt: when I get uptight, or the kids make me angry, I'll prune and pull weeds, and it's like therapy."

On Cora's mother's side she is part Indian. Her father, who was killed in a fire when she was one year old, had emigrated to Georgia from Trinidad, where she still has relatives and where she would like to go, if she ever had two weeks to herself—maybe when all the children have completed high school. Her maternal great-grandfather was a white man, "and to hear the way some of them talk about it," her daughter Aretha later told me, "you'd think he was the only ancestor we had. Even though all the others were slaves, the great thing that happened was that white ancestor. I don't see what's so great about white guys—I met a white dude at boot camp. He was homely but sweet, and he had money. Not that money solves everything. It's always the major crisis in family life, but as Mommy said, 'Do you think I could have survived all those years with eight kids and your crazy daddy if I'd let money bother me?' She'd never go on welfare unless she was completely desperate. As kids we sometimes had to put cardboard in the soles of our shoes, but we were *proud*."

Cora's next sister was eight years older, and she grew up feeling lonely. "That's probably why I had so many children myself. Oh, I knew about contraceptives, and tried them all, but either they didn't work or I was too fertile. I'd never have so many children if I had it to do over. I'm sure none of my girls will have such a big family, either. It was hard enough to raise them, and even harder now."

Just after she finished tenth grade, Cora married Augustus Clinton Taylor, a steel mill worker, in the living room of the house she still lives in. When her mother died, the house became hers. All her eight children and two of her six grandchildren were raised there, and the day rarely passes when a couple of dozen visitors don't stop by. Everyone seems to take literally the sign in her living room that reads:

> COME IN, SIT DOWN, RELAX, CONVERSE—
> OUR HOUSE DOESN'T ALWAYS LOOK LIKE THIS,
> SOMETIMES IT'S EVEN WORSE.

Considering how much it is used, the place is remarkably tidy. Volumes of the *Encyclopaedia Britannica* get replaced on their shelves. Issues of *McCall's* and *Reader's Digest* and *Better Homes and Gardens* are stacked neatly. "I read everything that comes my way," she says, "from the Bible to pornography." She gave her daughter Tuffy a whole set of novels about a plantation called Falconhurst—"all about slaves sleeping with masters," Tuffy said, "and having half-breed kids."

On Cora's bedside table, the first time I saw it, were *Robert's Rules of Order* and *The Crisis of Psychoanalysis*. On the dresser were hats, pomades, a dozen or so family snapshots, and cartoons taped to the mirror. "This room is my refuge; it's the only place in the house where I can escape, and even when I do, the children won't let me alone. I never used to let them sleep in my bed when they were little, but now they try to—it's as if they were trying to make up for Gus being gone." Her husband had died of a massive cerebral hemorrhage just a month earlier.

As we talked the mounting cadences of organ music from a church program in "*Dee*-troit, Michigan, area code 313" came up from the radio downstairs. When the choir began to sing "How Great Thou Art," Cora hummed along. On a chair across the room was a tambourine; she was getting ready to go to church, just down the street. She goes there at least three evenings a week, for prayer meetings, as well as on Sunday mornings. She is president of the Ushers' Board, secretary of the Young Women's Christian Council, and head of the nurses' unit. "It's a Pentecostal church; I changed over from the Baptists when I was carrying April, but I've been attending services there for twenty-eight years. The girls used to go too, but they're all backsliders, like their daddy was. They all believe, but they won't sing in the choir or go with me to the services like they used to."

I went to that church once, and I didn't care much for it, either. One of the girls brought along a cynical boyfriend who liked it even less. "You know where these kids' heads was?" he said of the children in the choir. "They was in *Japan!* All that boogie-woogie makes about as much sense as a Munich beer hall. But you have to ask: What would they be doing if they weren't doing this? For a black person to really look at life and see it as it is is to go insane."

"We were all really pissed at Daddy's funeral," Aretha told me later, "because they made so much fuss about his mother. 'If you have to pattern your life after someone,' the pastor said, 'it might as well be Mother Taylor.' Who ever said *she* was the Matriarch Supreme? If there's a saint in our family, it's Mommy. But I've been disillusioned with that church since the first time I came home on furlough from the WAVES. I wore my dress whites there, and when the pastor saw me he said, 'Well! We have a visitor!' Visitor? All I could think was I'd been going to that church all my life. That was the day they started to lose me."

Once, when Cora came home after a church supper, her fifth daughter Roshelle asked what there had been to eat. Shepherd's pie, Cora said. What's in that? Roshelle asked. She was told. "You'll never catch *me* eating mashed potatoes," she said.

"Oh yeah?" said Cora. "That's what your daddy said about beans, but the day came when that's all there was to eat, so he ate them." Another evening, when Tuffy was frying a frankfurter for her son, a cousin professed surprise. "What is this, the Last Supper? Don't you believe in Islam? Don't you know your daddy don't want you to eat no swine, boy?"

"His daddy's not the one hungry now," Tuffy said. "The one hungry now is Danny, and he's been eating pork since he was *qualified* to eat." She thinks of Islam, to which her husband has converted, pretty much what Islam thinks of pork.

That mealtime, like most at Cora's house, was far from tranquil. "My aunt hit me!" sobbed Danny's sister Celestine, pronouncing the word "ahnt."

"*She* started it," said Cora's youngest child Annette, who at eight was just a year older than her niece Celestine, and whose Citizenship

Certificates and Meritorious Achievement Awards were framed all over the house.

"*What* did I tell you about playing with the electric fan?" Cora asked Danny. "You know how lucky you are that that fan isn't plugged in?" She hit the boy with a fly swatter. He fell limp to the floor, looked up, faked a sob, and when nobody paid much attention, snuggled onto his mother's lap.

"Such a charmer," Tuffy said. "When Danny don't come to nursery school, girls there be walking around like the world's coming to an end."

"When Danny *doesn't* come," a sister corrected.

"I can talk right when I need to, at the office," said Tuffy, "but here I like to talk family talk." So does everyone else. I don't think I've ever known a less taciturn household. Nor is there much silence outdoors. It was only by chance, I gathered, that I never happened to hear gunshot sounds when I visited Gary. A woman down the street shot a man dead once, when the older Taylor girls were little, for refusing her a bite of his sandwich. Peaceful interludes never last.

"The rats go next door for a while, when Mommy calls the exterminator, but they always come back," one daughter said. "The boy next door just got sodomized on his way home from the grocery. And once there was a man who looked like a mad dog, who climbed over the back fence and started walking toward the house. Mommy couldn't find the ammunition for Daddy's rifle, so she scared him off with a chisel. She could have done a real job on that dude with that chisel if she'd had to."

The more I talked to her daughters, the more deceptive Cora's placid surface seemed. At first I had thought her almost prissy, the way she had said "purchase" for "buy," and "at the present time" instead of "now," but we all relaxed as we got better acquainted. I also wished more and more that I could have met Cora's husband.

"For a while after Gus passed, *nothing* went right," she told me. "The furnace split down the back, the sink needed a new faucet, the television went bad, the refrigerator went on the blink, and even the plants died. We all had our different crying jags, remembering things about him we would miss. Brian sat alone with his drums in his room all day." Brian was the Taylor who marched with his mother down the church aisle at his father's funeral. Never mind his older sisters; his was the name listed first in the program. Men are made much of in Gary because for one cruel reason or another they don't always stay around for long. Augustina's boyfriend went to California; Roshelle's can't seem to find a job; "Dan doesn't earn much singing baritone," Tuffy told me. "If I ever marry again I'll find me a rich man, because I *know* what a poor man is like.

"That's why I thought you might want to come to our cousin's wedding," she told me. "I thought you might not *live* long enough to see any of *us* get married." She and her mother were the only legal wives in the whole clan. "It's kind of a family tradition," she told me, "for us to get pregnant in our senior year of high school." But no babies could be more welcome than those raised here.

"A house *needs* a baby," Cora once said as she held her newest granddaughter, Jamila Zainab Karima Taylor, whom Roshelle had asked her to name. Nobody will hold it against Jamila if her father doesn't find work, but everybody realizes how rare her grandfather Gus was. "He'd kiss each one of us goodbye when he went to the mill," April said, "but he was strict, too. He didn't like it when we went around barefoot, and he couldn't stand for us to wear Afros or wigs. He'd say, 'What you want to go around for with your hair lookin' like a rabbit's butt? Women ought to look like *women!*'"

"Even in the later years when he drank," Cora said, "Gus would come up here and we'd still have such good discussions. We've always been a great family for talking. Sometimes the girls and I sit here talking till three in the morning. There's no subject we can't bring up with each other—drugs, sex, crime, the danger of unknown strangers. However bad it is, it's better if we talk it out. Gus liked those talks as much as any of us did.

"His doctor warned him not to drink, because his pressure was skyrocketing—just the opposite of mine, mine's too low—but he couldn't seem to stop. Why? Maybe he was tired. Maybe vodka and beer made him forget that he wanted to do more than he felt he could accomplish. He was so spiritually knowledgeable, so politically wise, such a good speaker—but when he was drinking I'd be tense all day, wondering how I would find him.

"When he started drinking heavy, I'd feel like I was in a void all by myself. I'd stay up here in my room and not go out, and I knew *that* wasn't *me*. For a while I went to a counselor. It was good to have someone outside the family to talk to. He wanted Gus to come too, but Gus wouldn't."

Taylor women don't tend to pick men who are easy to manage. "When their husbands and fellows don't come up to their father's standard, it disappoints them," Cora said, "because that standard is embedded in them more deeply than they think. Their father, even when he was drinking, made sure he took care of his family. Not all girls are so lucky."

"Dan's been having a hard time looking for a job," Tuffy said of her husband as she hid the hot dog buns. "He was a big shot at Gary West, breaking track records, but since the Army gave him a medical discharge, nothing's really gone right for him." I found Dan Williams hard to talk to. Mostly when we were there together I would sit and admire the way he looked, the stylish trick he had of rolling a basketball up one side of his arm and then down the other.

"Aretha has the best man of any of my girls," Cora said. "Oh, she and he have their troubles, but he's special—he's a career Navy officer—and so was she. She's not only an artist and a writer and in college, but she was one of the first women and first blacks to work on the newspaper on her base. She's bright, Aretha. She's got quite a future. When you get to Philadelphia, you ought to drop by to see her and her children."

A couple of months later, I did.

Aretha Taylor White and her children live in a third-floor walkup apartment in a dismal reconverted row house in south central Philadelphia. She wouldn't let me into the kitchen. "I've got so many dirty dishes piled up in there, I wouldn't let *anyone* see," she told me. "I can't *wait* till Traci learns to wash dishes." Traci, her six-year-old, and Augie, who was four, stared at me for a few minutes while Aretha made instant coffee. I looked around at her artwork. A number of her paintings and carvings were on display, but what struck me most were the pictures, every four feet or so, of Mel, the children's father.

There was Mel in enlarged black-and-white snapshots, Mel in tinted formal portraits, Mel in his full-dress Navy uniform, Mel in a bathing suit, Mel with and without his mustache and glasses. The man in a painting of Aretha's called "Pregnant Woman and How She Got That Way" looked pretty much like Mel, too.

"Good-looking man," I told her when she returned with my coffee and an ale she had poured for herself.

"I almost forget how he looks," she said. "Here it is Thursday morning, and he said he'd be home Monday night. He's been in Florida for three weeks taking a special race-relations training course the Navy sent him to. 'Take the bus home,' I told him when he called last week. 'The bus'll get you from Pensacola to Philly in thirty-four hours.' I know; I checked. But no.

"No, Mel said he could save money by getting a ride back here with a buddy from the course. Driving would be cheaper—it wasn't as if we had cash to spare. But cheap or no cheap, next time he goes somewhere I'm going along, and so are the kids. Never mind missing school: I'm smart, and so are they; I can teach them myself. Their daddy's smart too, which is why you might think it would occur to him to call up to tell me just *how* much later he's going to be.

"Of course I did tell him the phone might be disconnected, because we don't always pay the bills when we're supposed to, and some of those bills have been high lately. But even so, wouldn't you think he could pull off the road to find a Western Union, and at least send a wire? Couldn't he at least tell me when to expect him?

"Of course, for all I know he could be dead. Maybe I ought to be afraid. Maybe his family knows and they're not telling me. You never *saw* anything more depressing than the place where they live, near some bakery outside of Denver. Six of his thirteen brothers and sisters live at home there, and you ought to see the way they twist him to get him to do what they want. One of his sisters even conned him into buying her a forty-dollar plastic chinaware set. How do you like *that*, with these kids here needing shoes the way they do?"

Traci asked for a piece of candy. "You eat *all* the candy that was here yesterday?" Aretha asked. "Must have been a hundred pieces. Oh all right, you can split this piece of licorice." For herself she poured another glass of ale, then showed me a poem she had written to Mel called "Silk Sheets and Wine." She liked to write, she told me, especially when it was raining, or when the television was on. She was going to write a novel someday, and its title would be *A Nigger Is a Bitch*.

"That's the title Daddy suggested. We used to talk about things like that a lot. He wanted me to keep on in college till I got my Ph.D. Maybe I will. Maybe I'll go back in the Navy and do more editorial work. Want to see the papers I edited?" Sure I did, so she went to get them. While I read them she kept staring at the wall behind me.

"No," she decided, "Mel's not dead. I'd *feel* it if he were. He's on his way here, and I know where, too. This isn't the first trick he's pulled in the seven years we've been together. Once he left at four in the afternoon, saying he was going to wash his car, and you know when he came home? Seven in the morning, that's when.

" 'I met some of the fellows,' he told me, 'and we decided to wash our cars together.'

" 'Oh?' I said. 'Until *seven?* In the *morning?*'

" 'Well,' he told me, 'we found an after-hours club.'

"Next time that happened, I was waiting for him with a .32. That's when he decided maybe we ought to move someplace where it'd be easier to find babysitters, so we could get out *together*. So we moved here, but it turns out the other people around here aren't what you'd call the babysitting type. So for a while what we'd do is all four of us go places together, even the kids, to places like the zoo."

"That gives me an idea," I told her. "Let's get out of here. It was too bright a day to sit indoors, and I was getting nervous myself, watching that phone not ring.

"Go away, bumblebee, get away from my kid," says Aretha. We came in my rented car to Fairmount Park, a twenty-minute drive from the phone in South Philadelphia. Waiting for our lunch we look out over the Schuylkill at sculls. Traci is afraid of the bee that hovers over our table, but Aretha hugs and comforts her.

"I love my mother," Traci tells me, "and someday I'll find a place where there are no bumblebees, and go pick her some flowers."

"That's sweet, baby," Aretha said. "You know what *I'm* going to do? I think I'll have some flowers sent to Mommy. At Daddy's funeral I kept thinking: All these flowers and he can't smell a damn one. Lord have mercy."

She has big ideas, Aretha. She would like to open a nightclub "with out-of-sight prices" called the Club Gazelle, with an island in the middle of the dance floor where a mother gazelle and her baby could graze, with soft jazz and "music for *couples* to dance to." I'd like to take an ocean voyage sometime, and ride naked on a horse in San Francisco, and go on the Johnny Carson show, and tell Sammy Davis, Junior, what an Oreo I think he is.

"There's not really too much left for me to do. I've already sung before two thousand people at a state church convocation in Gary, and you know what I did then? I fell off the stage. People thought I must have been touched by the Spirit, until they heard me say, 'Oh, shit!' I figured that was as good a time as any to quit the choir.

"If I don't stay on in college I'll go back in the WAVES. I joined in the first place because I was the baddest thing that ever hit Gary, Indiana; I grew up a smartass kid and I knew I needed to learn to do what I was told to without any lip. Mommy didn't think I could accept that kind of regimentation, and for a while she was right; boot camp was the worst ever. It wasn't as bad as the Marines, though. A girlfriend of mine joined the Marines and they'd tell her, 'I don't want to hear a lip smacking or a cunt clacking, all I want to hear is feet cracking!' That girl had sand flea bites all over her legs, because she couldn't scratch or swat while standing at attention.

"In the Navy I worked for a while in the machine shop. It was a terrible job; I'd have to work both shifts with no overtime. That's when I started drinking; I'd bring cough syrup to work and after a while it'd take me more than a fifth to get bombed. If my husband saw me drinking malt ale he'd be pissed off; it has more alcohol in it than beer."

We are back in the apartment now. Still no Mel. The phone hasn't been disconnected; when we pick it up we get a dial tone. Aretha puts a record on the phonograph—it is the "1812 Overture"—and conducts it at the dining room table, with a pair of chopsticks. "Mommy tells me I ought to be flattered to be Number One with Mel," she said, "but I want to be the *only* one. Or else. In fact, I'd be in Mommy's house in Gary right now, only Mommy wouldn't want me. She says I've got too much going for me to leave Mel. Besides, Mel wouldn't even let me go there for a visit while he was in Florida.

"He probably figured that if I got with my sisters, I'd run in the streets and meet men. My sister Augustina ran a little wild, sometimes. Poor Gussie, I worry about her, she can't find her identity. She was Daddy's favorite, and she never even knew it. They were so alike in so many ways, little quirks they had in common. I hate to see her screwed up, because that's an intelligent girl there. Every now and then I get a card from Gussie and that means she wants to talk, so I call her." Augustina, I have noticed, is the only Taylor daughter who doesn't look busy and stylish. Her sisters hurry in and out of the house in fashionable costumes, with much on their minds; she usually sits staring into space, wearing a bathrobe. Once I asked her what was wrong, and she said her navel hurt.

"Maybe if I went home I *would* go a little wild for a while," Aretha is saying. "Mel knows that as long as I stay here in Philly, I'm Miss Goody Two-Shoes. Well, he's going to find out that this is my last pair of that kind of shoes. Anyway, he should talk. He told me he wasn't married, when we met, because he knew I didn't date married men—I'd learned from experience that married men mean trouble.

"I believed him, and forgot all about Thighbone and Reno and all the other men in my life, and wrote home that I'd finally found a dude I wanted to spend the rest of my life with. And not till I ordered the invitations—not till Mommy had bought an airplane ticket from Chicago (Daddy couldn't come because there was only enough money for one of them to make the trip)—not until I'd gone and got a *dress* to get married in did I find out, by checking with Personnel, that Mel never really did get a divorce from the woman he'd been married to before, in Japan.

"And you know what a *thing* I've got against Japanese women? They won't let men wash their own *anything*—they've got to wash it for them." Aretha takes me to her closet to show me the wedding gown she never has worn. It hangs among Mel's suits to remind him. "See how pretty it is, with the jacket and train? This brocade cost five dollars a yard, but brocade's my favorite material, and you just watch and see if I don't wear this dress someday after all. That's what I got it for, and that's what I'm going to do with it.

"I'm going to marry *Mel* in it, too. Nobody else. I'm not fickle. If I were fickle I'd take up with some dudes from my class; I have chances. But I'll wait. Meanwhile, when people ask how long we've been married, I'll just keep on saying, 'Long enough.' It's none of anybody's business.

"Maybe what we ought to do is fight more. Mommy and Daddy really fought, but all we do is argue. Maybe arguing isn't enough. I could fight if I had to. I can shoot an ant pissing on cotton. I'm a good rifle shot; my daddy used to take me hunting. My mother's got a beautiful double-barrel shotgun. My own next gun's going to be either a .357 Magnum or else a nine-millimeter with hollow-point bullets, the kind that sound like a cannon and explode inside like shrapnel.

"Melvin knows all about the hurts I've had in my life, and every now and then I tell him, 'I'll kill you, darling, I'll blow you away,' but I wouldn't really do that. I'd sooner castrate him, call an ambulance, and get him to the hospital. Must be the Scorpio in me coming out. The time to get a man is when he's asleep, and you know what? Sometimes that motherfucker falls asleep while I'm *talking* to him!

"One night when he fell asleep I got really pissed. I walked out carrying the tool I use for my woodcarvings. On the street a strange man said, 'Don't you know what can happen, lady, if you come out here alone at night?' I showed him the carving tool. He just said, 'Look, I'll be honest with you; I'm trying to get me a stable. Any time you want work, give me a call.' But that's not the kind of work I want to do. What I want to do is pour hot grits on Mel's feet, so I could incapacitate his running power and his ass would be *mine*. Or throw hot noodles on him in the shower so he'll look like a puzzle."

Darkness falls. The phone still sits silent. "Let's go get something to eat," I suggest. Aretha leads us to Gino's, a franchised hamburger place. As we wait for our order, a sleek car pulls up outside, and

Aretha surveys its driver. Luckily he can't hear what she says to him: "Oh, blood, you look so *tacky*, running around in that big Cadillac—you probably haven't even paid the rent."

Back home the phone still has a dial tone. Its silence screams. The children yawn, but Aretha doesn't put them to bed. "They're all the company I have," she says, "so I let them stay up longer than they ought to."

"Do birds go to sleep?" asks Augie, as he squirms on her lap.

"Yes, boy, just like people."

"When?"

"When they get hungry." Later she tells me how hungry she has been, on occasion, herself. "When Mel and I first lived together, there was a week when all we had to eat was popcorn, and it made him so sad he'd go into the other room and cry.

"You know what my idea of soul food is? Never mind neck bones and greens; my idea of soul food is lobster thermidor."

The phone rings. At last. She lets it ring four times before she picks it up.

"Oh. Hi, Mommy."

But not all fathers are so shy about phoning, as I learned in a visit to a quite different sort of family.

"He'll Visit Maxine's
Leg Off"

A FEW YEARS AGO, when Otto Muller and his third wife Maxine and six of the youngest of their eighteen children moved to the outskirts of Baltimore, they put a sign outside their house that said "THE CHAPEL ON 97—TEACHING THE NINE STEPS TO THE TOTALITY OF BEING A CHRISTIAN." They hoped that the sign might attract strangers, who would knock on the door to hear Otto's message. Otto, who once was a prosperous hairdresser, gave up his business to become an evangelist. But not many strangers were dropping by. Evangelism wasn't keeping Muller very busy. At least it wasn't in the spring of 1975, when I visited Muller myself. I didn't go there to learn about evangelism or hairdressing, though it turned out I heard plenty about both of these subjects. I went there to try to get some sense of a family with eighteen brothers and sisters and an old-fashioned, strong, and present father. I had been wondering about old-fashioned fathers for years.

I had been wondering, I guess, since an evening several years before, in a restaurant on the Upper East Side of Manhattan, when seven or eight of us sat around after dinner talking about our mothers. We talked about our mothers, one by one and with considerable feeling, for quite a long time. This impromptu seminar about our mothers could have lasted all night. Everyone was garrulous on the subject except for one man, who wore a tie clasp and a pin-striped suit, and didn't seem to get the point.

"Why are all of you going on so about your *mothers?*" this man wanted to know. "Why is it nobody ever talks about fathers?" Obtuse of him, the rest of us later agreed. In this society, the rest of us concurred, it is mothers who spin the webs and build the networks which, like it or not, give us our notion of what families are. In all American social classes, when the subject is families—as the subject so often is—it is the mothers who talk the most. They are also the ones who get talked to: thousands more of us telephone home on Mother's Day than on Father's Day. "Her mother and I do," men say when asked who giveth this woman in marriage.

Strong fathers, in this society, are rare, for good if sad reasons. The traditions of American jurisprudence exclude fathers from definitions of family. Much of the traditional authority of fathers has been taken over by governmental and corporate bureaucracies. Nine out of ten children in American slums are legally fatherless, sometimes because fathers must abandon their families if their dependents are to qualify for public relief. In modern American televised mythology, fathers are belittled, portrayed as ineffectual buffoons, referred to in some circles as "male role models," "live-in sperm donors," or "surrogates." It may well be, as Robertson Davies writes in his novel *The Manticore*, that "the fathers you choose for yourself are the significant ones . . . no man knows his father."

It may also be that all this is changing. Some maternity hospitals invite fathers to take off their shirts to learn how it feels to "nurse" a newborn child—a variation perhaps on the primitive custom of *couvade*, whereby fathers go through the motions and actions of childbirth. In divorce proceedings, more and more fathers are demanding and getting the custody of their children. Nine hundred thousand American children under the age of eighteen, of whom 50,000 are not yet in school, now live with their male parents. Perhaps in time we will take steps to follow the example of Sweden, where fathers, like mothers, can take a seven-month leave at full pay after a baby is born (and 90 more days off, any time, before the child is eight). Maybe by the twenty-first century fatherhood in America will be different.

But for now, with strong fathers as rare as pileated woodpeckers, I had a notion that I ought to go find one, talk to him and see what his life was like, see what he might have to say that could be instructive. Quite by chance, I heard about Otto Muller. Muller, who had fathered sixteen children of his own, was bringing up two adopted ones as well. From what I heard, he was a man of unswerving faith in himself and the path, or rather paths, he had chosen. I also heard that he liked to talk. I was fairly sure that what he might have to say would be new to me: never before had I met a patriarchal evangelist who had forsaken a career in hairdressing. Muller, apparently, had been a masterly hairdresser, too; several women liked his work so much they had it put in their wills that he should give them their final coiffures.

I heard about Otto Muller from Martin, the seventh of his eighteen children. Martin, alone among the eighteen, was following his father's original profession. Martin worked in a beauty salon in Little Rock, Arkansas, where I once paid a visit. Even in his early twenties, Martin had quite a following himself; in the firmament of Little Rock he was a star. I had to wait a week to see him. It turned out that he liked to talk, too.

"If you're a hairdresser," this young man with long-lashed brown eyes told me, "people either think you're queer or that you're balling every chick in town. But you know what they say—small minds talk about people, medium minds talk about things, and great minds talk about ideas. I like to keep myself in the latter two categories. I learned that from my dad. Dad used to be a hairdresser here, too. He had a beauty school and a chain of three shops, and about eighty-five employees. But four or five years ago he gave it all up to become an evangelist. He got the call, and sold his business, and left, and went to Bible School in Idaho, and met Maxine.

"Maxine's his third wife. My mom, who had fourteen of us, died when I was eight. I don't remember her much, but nobody could replace her for me. Dad's second wife expected me to call her Mom, but I couldn't. She wasn't for me and she wasn't for Dad, either. After a couple of years they split up. She took the two kids they had together off to Montana. Maxine, the one he's married to now, she brought two kids of her own with her. Their father was a fireman who died of smoke inhalation. My dad's just like a dad to those two little ones now. He disciplines them just like he disciplined us. That's the way it should be. If we respected authority more, we'd have a better country.

"I wouldn't trade my dad in for no man in the world. He rules all eighteen of us with an iron fist inside a velvet glove. He could have handled a family twice the size of ours. Once he almost did. Once he and my real mom thought about taking in another thirteen kids, when their father was killed in an explosion. That father and his wife were the only people who ever invited our whole family to dinner. Another time, Dad came close to adopting another family of four. If a situation got a hold of his heartstrings, he said, there was no telling what he might do. It probably would have been fine if he'd adopted more. I wouldn't trade coming up with so many brothers and sisters."

("Come up," it crossed my mind, was what they said in the Gary

black ghetto, too. Rural children are "raised." I was "brought up."
What, I wondered and still do wonder, is the difference?)

"You have a lot more going for you in a large family than people
do in smaller ones," said Martin. "When I was a kid we all worked
together a lot. When Dad remodeled the beauty school here, from
the ground up, we all helped. Even my married brothers came back
to help with the job. We made up our own crew. Like Dad used to
say, why hire it when you've got it? He always felt like you've got to
teach your son a trade. I started working for him in the fifth grade,
cleaning his shops and folding towels. I'm the only one who went
into the hairdressing business, but all the others had to learn the
skills, how to use things best and get better attention.

"Popular? Dad sure was. Women would come from as far away as
California to have him do their hair. I've seen men I would consider
top international stars who couldn't dress a head of hair as well as he
could. Possibly I could do as good or better a job myself, but I'm not
out to beat him. I just do my job. I specialize in haircutting. It's my
first and only great love, except for cars." In considerable detail Martin then told of a cross-country trip he and four brothers had made,
in several vehicles, to surprise a sister in Idaho on her graduation
day. But he no longer felt like traveling, at least not when we talked.
He had been as far as Europe, and all he wanted to do now was stay
in the salon and keep working.

"Listening is a lot of what I do," he told me. "Maybe that's why
I'm talking so much to you now—I listen to my clients, patrons, patients, sons-of-bitches, whatever I feel like calling them. Hairdressers
probably listen as much as shrinks do. I'm not always in the mood to
hear what they have to tell me, but the majority of them are good at
figuring out what mood *I'm* in. It doesn't embarrass me a bit to ask
if they're having their period, or if they're on the pill, or if they're
pregnant. All those things affect how your hair looks. Pregnancy
makes hair look even limper than menstruating does. A lot of girls,
after they've had a kid, their hair will change.

"A lot of your curl look is coming back now. Hairstyles change
every seven years. Long hair won't go out, ever, because men like it.
Women's Lib is a big bunch of bullshit. Women were more liber-
ated *before* they started doing all this pushing. If they had more
sense, they would play it more cool. That's what my dad says. He
knows a lot about women, as much as he knows about raising kids.
He thinks lack of discipline is the basic problem in most families
today. Now and then, he thinks, you've got to take kids out in the
toolshed and whip the shit out of them.

"In the long run it makes for closer families. Dad and I are pretty close now. I go home for long weekends sometimes, even though it's a hell of a trip. It's worth it, though, to get to talk to Dad. I consider him to be a fantastic lecturer. Sometimes I'll argue with him even when I don't disagree, to get his point of view better. Like he says, a stagnant mind is a dead mind. There isn't anything stagnant about him. That's why he retired before he was fifty, to go wherever Jesus leads him.

"I'm not so sure about church myself. The church today is getting more turned away from the Bible than it should. You go to church to hear about religion and what you hear about is money. It helps to have fellowship with people, but it's hard to find fellowship anywhere. I guess when I was coming up I found it in my family. I guess that's part of why Dad had so many of us. Maybe you ought to go talk to him yourself."

Maybe I ought to, I figured. I didn't expect that this hairdresser-evangelist and I would have much in common, but that was part of his allure. Maybe what he would have to say about families would be significant; maybe his ideas would speak for thousands of people whom I otherwise would not encounter. So I phoned him, a few months later when I was back in New York, to ask if I could come by for a visit. I had to go to Washington on other business; might I stop by overnight outside Baltimore to see him and his family? I might indeed, he said. He and Maxine would be real glad to meet my train.

Duane and Wayne and Dolores and Jim and Arlene and Bill and Renée were off and married, scattered from Tampa to Juneau. Martin, the hairdresser, was, as I well knew, in Arkansas. Raymond was in the Army, at Fort Knox. Jeanne was in Alaska, too, getting ready for her wedding. Karen and Kevin were with their mother, Muller's second wife, in Montana. Those were the absent Mullers. But Randy and Ronnie and Ricky and Terry and Leslie and Darlene, home on one bus from three different schools, were running toward the house right this minute, at three in the afternoon. Having spent most of the day hearing their father talk about these six young Mullers, I finally would get to meet them for myself.

"Watch out if you get to talking with that Terry," the patriarch warned me. "He'll visit Maxine's leg off, sometimes." But none of the brown-eyed, fair-haired young Mullers felt like visiting with a total stranger, at least not so soon. They all rushed out to the barn behind the house, to see whether the pregnant goat Nana had yet given birth to her three expected kids.

"We probably won't get to see it happen," their father told the children. "Unless they're in trouble, newborn goats are as difficult to catch as newborn horses. When I was a boy we'd never see the farm-house horses up the road drop their foals." There weren't any horses in the barn behind this house: just goats and cats and chickens. When Muller's first wife died, each of her thirteen children got a legacy of $108, and several of them had spent their money on goats. Goats, they told me, are good suppliers of milk.

"We're hoping Nana will have three real healthy does," one child said. "Bucks smell worse than does, and bucks have to be penned in alone. They're more trouble." These children seemed to know plenty about goats and poultry and carpentry. The boys had helped their fa-ther build the triple-decker bunk beds they slept in upstairs. They also had helped build new fences. Their father believed firmly in fences.

I had left New York very early that morning, but I felt as if I had crossed half a continent and at least half a century as well. Here was an archetypal self-contained giant family, all right—such a giant one they didn't need anybody outside it, or did they? Was it my imagina-tion, or did these children seem somehow lonely? There wasn't much time for such ruminations. Since this was Darlene's birthday, tonight would be a party. The dinner menu, like all Muller meals, had been planned for two weeks. Maxine Muller, two decades her evangelist husband's junior, was efficient. She was also unobtrusive, in her bouffant hairdo and long skirt. She looked like a faithful reader of *The Total Woman* and *Fascinating Womanhood*. The topic she most warmed to was fashion.

"Most of the time, anymore, I do wear a long skirt," she volun-teered, "because I like it better than slacks. I only wear slacks to do heavy work in the barn. I wear pantyhose and acetate panties as sel-dom as possible, because polyester material doesn't breathe. It causes yeast problems with women, did you know that? If you're sexually ac-tive, cotton panties are better."

"Her infections get transferred to me," volunteered Otto, "and that kind of itch can make you lose your mind. Long cotton under-wear is better."

"Mmm," I said. That's all I can ever think of to say when people answer questions it would never have crossed my mind to ask.

"Very few women have the legs to wear short skirts," said Maxine.

"Besides," said Otto, "most mature men aren't interested in pieces of property walking around on public display. Why take home merchandise that everyone else may have handled? When customers used to squirm around in the salon, to cover their short skirts, I'd tell them, 'Lady, if I see something I haven't ever seen before, I'll wave. Otherwise, will you *please* set still?' "

In his hairdressing years, Otto told me, he had prospered enough to earn more than the governor of Arkansas: "The *Wall Street Journal* was my Bible. I made good investments. We're still living on the stocks I bought then. Business was good. One of the keys to success is to have friends thirty-forty years older, who help you the way you later help someone else. Through the years I've maintained friends much older than I am, in diverse businesses. It's a simple law of the universe: people only move to gain a benefit or avoid a loss. That's the whole secret. I had the blessing of many friends who were leaders. One of the secrets is not to let 'A' know that you're the reason 'B' hired him. You have to learn to pick people's brains. My twenty-three-year-old son Jim is unique, because he's a brain-picker. You should also ask yourself two questions, every time you meet someone new: Does he like me? Can he help me?

"Things went well for me in business. I had seventeen suits, five or six sport jackets, more shirts than I could count. I had up to eighty-five employees; I'd worked my way up from seventy-five-cent haircuts to nineteen-dollar sets. I'd thought of going to barber school after the war, but moved to cosmetology because it was a better field: I could see that home permanents would make this the biggest thing in the world. Permanent waves are coming back again now; people are regaining their integrity and respect. Abstainers' hair sets last longer. Sex means sweat, plus all that running of hands through the hair.

"Backcombing, when it was done right in the proper proportion, could be beautiful. There's a recipe: you should never see over a third of the head, a third of the right shoulder, a third of the left shoulder. Jackie Kennedy still looks like a horse headed for a county fair. Nature gives you a rule: put your hand down at the highest protruding vertebra; your hair should never be shorter than that. I'd go to conventions, talk about these things. At conventions others always wondered why I'd spend so much time in my room alone: it was because I never otherwise had a whole bathroom to myself.

"But I had to make a choice, between backcombing and another way of life. I thought back to the veterans' hospital I spent some time in after World War II, where a World War I veteran in the bed next to mine would stand up every fifteen minutes, stretch his arms, say 'Oh, shit,' and then set back down. That man was dead already. A lot of people are. It's really pathetic to see people walking around who've been dead for thirty years, looking for a free lunch. Not just veterans, either. Plenty of women walk around that way. That's why this time I didn't marry a woman my own age.

"Most women my own age act dead. All they think about is curtains and ruffles. Maxine was different. She was a widow when we met at a Christian singles group. We've been married two years now. My main idea when we got married was to help her out. We didn't go into this arrangement with a bundle of 'love.' This word 'love' gets people confused. A lot of garbage floats around this country under the name of 'love.' Love, the way I see it, is when in pheasant season I observe the rules and the quota, so the generation following will have *their* pheasants. And love is living within my income, so I won't mortgage my children and *their* children—between my six married children they have three grandchildren so far—to the national debt.

"Anyway, Maxine and I went into it as friends, and maintaining that friendship is the best thing we've done. The first year of marriage, the Scriptures say, a man ought to stay home getting to know his wife, and I was glad I quit my business in time so I could do that."

Muller's new calling came during a meeting of the Full Gospel Businessmen. When he found at that meeting that he could speak in tongues, a minister suggested he go to a seminary. Ultimately he did, in Idaho. "When we moved to Idaho we first bought a farm with about eight thousand Christmas trees. We sold those trees that year, and when I saw the way grown men would almost stomp me to death to get those trees, that ended Christmas for me. That was the year we decided against presents. I asked the kids, 'On your birthday, would you want everyone else to get a gift?' They said no. So I said, 'Well then, why on *Christ's* birthday should everyone get a gift? So now we give presents whenever it seems right. Why set in July, if you know what one of the boys wants, and wait until December to give it to him? One year I got Randy a set of tools in the middle of the summer that's paid for itself a million times over. He repairs lawnmowers, can wire almost anything, and is a first-rate cook.

"We all do a lot of work around the place here while we wait for our ministry to expand. The gift of tongues has put a fire in me; it's given me a commitment. It's a long walk ahead. When you're following a calling, there's a training period, and that's what we're doing here, now. It's a new field for both of us. Just now we're in the

process of walking alone, waiting for the ministry of the lost, the
drunks, the prostitutes. There's no calling for us in intellectual circles; I seem to have the unique knack of being sandpaper to those
people. We just want to tell the news to whoever we meet. Somebody plants the seed and sows the ground. It takes a hundred years
for a fig tree, thirty for an English walnut, and a few months for a
tomato. It doesn't bother me that we don't seem to be in the tomato
business. I thank God that when I was a hairdresser I had my day of
being on top; now I can go for the rest of my life without that
feeling.

"What matters most now is my family. I'd like to raise my own
family as wisely as my father raised his. I look on this house the way
I look on eternity: as a continuous learning session. What we have
here is a training center where each child can learn to be either the
head or the heart of another home. If I expect lovable grandchildren,
I had better raise my children to be lovable men and women. That's
how my own father raised us. My father was a farmer who could
have been a schoolteacher if he had just gone to college one more
month. I would call him to seek his wisdom even when he was in his
eighties. He taught me how to think, and to make mistakes and decisions. Decision-making is the greatest legacy a parent can give a
child.

"My grandmother was a decision-maker, too. She was completely
deaf, a lip-reader, and a beautiful person. Her husband died in a fire
when a kerosene lamp exploded, setting in that rocking chair right
there, when I was nine months old. Grandma was four feet eight, a
mighty little woman who raised twelve tall children. She was a little
spitfire, Grandma was. When she was ninety years old she could still
knock you down if you went wrong. I was fairly handy with a pair of
boxing gloves myself, as a kid. My father had boxed Jack Dempsey.
My father was a powerful man, who could pick up a calf and lay it
on its side. In the service he got a hole behind his ear he could stick
a match in. His other ear was sharp as a radar system: when he took
the cotton out of it, he could hear from here to that fence.

"I grew up on the edge of a Catholic community. I was the out-
sider there. There were only five of us Protestants in the whole high
school. It was kind of tough to be the only one left when the priests
came to take all the others on a picnic. But it showed me how
minorities feel." I wondered: Had it really? How then could Muller
go on to say that "some Jewish individuals are just about as homely
as a person can be. And these little tutti-fruttis coming in openly
flaunting their homosexuality, they make me want to vomit. At a

queer bar in Detroit where I went once, during a convention, I thought it was funny to see two men necking, but now it makes me sick. Reprobate minds, that's what they are, and they're flagrant. There's no *way* a homosexual can be a Christian. Gay churches, the way I look at it, are satanic. As for blacks, you know why they *became* black, don't you? Noah, after the flood, made wine and got inebriated, and Ham gossiped about him, so that's why Ham was cursed to be black. The Hamites settled in Africa. That's why when I gossip about someone, I am in blackness. We become a prisoner to our own gossip, and that's what blacks remind me of."

The afternoon grows late. Sun streams through the windows, thawing the snow outside and turning it to slush. I look at this brown-eyed man with the tan crewcut, the open-throated shirt, the slight paunch, the incessant talk. I look at my watch, and think how far away are tomorrow morning and the station. I think how few of my friends have more than two children, to this man's eighteen. Does that mean this man's philosophy has a better chance of enduring into the twenty-first century? How gloomy, and how elitist of me to think so. I also wonder how a house with six schoolchildren in it can be so oddly silent. Muller suggests I go upstairs to talk to the children. Their views do not greatly differ from his, which I suppose shouldn't surprise me.

"We just had Black Emphasis Week at school," one young Muller tells me, "and the Negroes put on a play. They really feel sorry for themselves. They've already *got* equal rights, but it seems like they want more. They skip classes a lot. You never see any Negroes in Auto Mechanics or Building Trades or Electronics. They're in a lot of shop classes, but they goof around. Some white girls go with black guys, but I think that's sick. I think you ought to date your own color. There's a Korean girl in my math class. Korea is over there in Asia somewhere."

The young Mullers talked of television programs, of the difficulty of finding a place to hide in a big family, of their favorite period at school, which, as I might have guessed, was Lunch. They also talked with spirit, as all American children seem to want to do, in all families of all income brackets, of cars.

"If I had a lot of money," one said, "I'd get a truck and make it look like a real rod, and use it for roddin' around." Roddin' around: has there ever been a pastime more American?

"If he's disgusted," one of the Mullers said of their father, whom even his two stepchildren seemed to resemble, "he'll tell us off individually."

"Yeah, 'individually,'" replied another, in the day's only effort at sarcasm. "'Individually' in front of everybody else. I can't stand it when he does that. It's like he's looking right through you."

"Sometimes he'll literally wash out our mouths with soap," another Muller said. "He likes us to listen to Earl Nightingale on the radio, because Nightingale teaches you to increase your sales, do creative thinking, use your ideas, test them on the job, lead the field."

I have given and been to many a birthday party in my time, but none ever quite like Darlene Muller's, that evening in Maryland. Darlene's birthday party made the Mormon Family Home Night I had been to earlier seem like an evening of esoteric Adirondack charades. Darlene's birthday party turned out to be another of Otto Muller's "learning sessions." After we all had sung "Happy Birthday" to the girl and watched her open some presents, there came a chorus of "This Is the Day the Lord Hath Made," with all Muller hands lifted in Pentecostal surrender. Then all the children took out their spiral notebooks, because it was time for their father's sermon. The topic was telephone manners.

"Smile when you're on the phone," their father told them, and they wrote that down in their notebooks. "Identify yourself, if you are the caller. If you answer, and someone asks for your folks, don't say they're not home, say they can't come to the phone just now. If you're the one making the call, state your business right away. Get to the point. Stand up straight when you're talking. Don't slouch. Remember, we are salesmen every day of our lives. Even if whoever is at the other end of the phone can't see you, you still are selling yourself to him. He needs you. Remember how, when Cain killed his brother, God's punishment was for him to be a vagabond alone? We all need each other. Remember the needs of other people. The average person thinks of himself nineteen out of every twenty minutes he is awake. If you can make him think he is important to *you*, then you are ahead of the game."

Later, after supper, Muller expounded on his philosophy for me. "The whole world is made up of people who don't have enough sense to come in out of the rain," he said. "That's why we have these training sessions here. Every evening we have Bible study and discussion, sometimes for up to an hour and a half. It take three years and four months to read the entire Bible. One of the things we notice in the Bible is one hundred six different references to hair. It's a hard, cold, brutal fact, but if you're going to buy the Bible, you take it all the way. The Bible makes it clear that the only people long hair wasn't an abomination to were the Nazarenes. Christ came from Nazareth, but he wasn't a Nazarene. I was very upset with Martin, when he wore his hair long for a while, to conform with the crowd. But he had left home, and I tell my boys that after they are away from home, they are out on their own.

"A man that wants to be a buddy to his son is a fool. You have to let them develop their own lives, away from your influence. I'm tickled to death to have them come back here to visit, one family at a time. When more than one family comes at a time, it's too chaotic. I'm a firm believer that, once a child is married, the best thing is for them to go off and create their own home. As long as they are here, they help with the carpentry and the animals and everything else there is to do. If there's one thing I can't stand it's a freeloader, or a lollygagger. On school nights, for instance, eight o'clock is an awful good time to head for bed."

It is quite a bit beyond that hour now. Johnny Carson's deadpan face is on the television screen. Maxine, in her long skirt, is pouring crème de menthe into her blender to make us another batch of Grasshoppers. Grasshoppers—crème de menthe mixed with heavy whipping cream and brandy—are one of the day's surprises. I wouldn't have expected to sit around watching Johnny Carson and drinking grasshoppers anywhere, much less in a former hairdresser's house purporting to teach "THE NINE STEPS TO THE TOTALITY OF BEING A CHRISTIAN."

Muller tunes down Carson's monologue so his own can be heard better. This time his tangent is gun control. "Many's the time, traveling alone at night, when I've saved my own life by showing a gun. I don't go with the theory that the criminal has rights. The way I look at it, you lose your rights as soon as you commit the crime. You know what should happen to those mentally deranged wards of the state who commit crimes? They should be shot. I'm prejudiced, I admit it, but is the guy selling pornography the only one with rights? Don't I have the right not to expose my daughter to what he sells?

"What business does the Supreme Court have trying to change all that? The good lord willing and the creeks don't rise, we all ought to take a long look at why people really act, and what causes their problems. One of the things that causes their problems is weak families. Strong families start with good marriages. I wish Maxine and I could make it to a silver anniversary, but I'm not too hopeful.

"I'm fifty already. I've already got a lot of miles on my odometer. But I can't complain. Maxine and I are getting along gloriously, and with Marge, my first wife, I had more in nineteen years than most people have in a hundred. Marge and I were more than friends—even after nineteen years we would still go out in the country to find a spot to drink beer and make love until three or four in the morning.

"Marge died of an embolism, after surgery. The surgeon did his best. His best wasn't good enough. That's all there was to it. I couldn't pump life back into her, much as I wanted to. Terry was only a year old when Marge died, and from there on in, if he had a bath, I was the one gave it to him, until we started our string of housekeepers. Being a widower gave me a closer feeling to how a mother must feel.

"Two years after being a widower I married again, but that time, instead of getting a wife, I got another child. She and the two children we had together are in Montana. I'd give a lot if those children were here. She allows our eleven-year-old daughter to date, which doesn't seem right to me. But then a lot of things don't seem right to me.

"Another woman wanted me to father a child for her, no strings attached, but I somehow didn't feel that the role of a stud was all that appealing. It turns me off, using children as a bargaining commodity. What sort of an example would a child like that face, not even knowing who Daddy was? That same woman was the product of a divorce herself, and very wealthy—if I had needed a meal ticket, she would have provided me with one for the rest of my life."

Johnny Carson's face has long since faded from the screen. I must leave early in the morning. I get up to start for bed. Muller assures me that if I want to shampoo my hair in the morning, I can have the use of "a regular salon-type drier." He and Maxine walk me up the stairs to the room where I am to sleep, past photographs of all eighteen children, his first wife, and Maxine's first husband. "We felt like the children ought to remember their real parents," he tells me. "As I hear Maxine's children tell about their real father—whose parents, by the way, have been very gracious about taking me in—I wish I had known him. He was a very dynamic individual, who was going places. I think he and I would have got on famously."

"I *know* you would have," says Maxine, from the top of the stairs. "But I didn't really start to wake up and come alive until I met you."

We had eaten Darlene's birthday supper at a huge table, 5 by 14 feet, a table capable of seating 24, which the Mullers had bought years before from German craftsmen. An admirable table, almost as nice as a round one, but the Mullers didn't seem to care much for it.

"We're going to cut this table down in the summer," the evangelist told me. "The way it is now, it's a real white elephant. We couldn't get rid of it if we wanted to."

This news did not seem so symbolically grim as it would have the day before I met the Mullers, nor did small families seem so forlorn. Even only children, for whom I had always felt a certain automatic pity, no longer seemed pathetic. My evangelist host had his virtues, of which not the least was his confidence, but I could not envy his children.

The Muller who had impressed me most that whole day was young Terry. After supper Terry had offered to go with me when I said I felt a sudden need for a walk in fresh air. Terry was the one who, his father had told me, sometimes would "visit Maxine's leg off," but he didn't seem to feel loquacious this evening. He didn't say a word until we had walked several blocks past THE CHAPEL ON 97.

"Have you ever felt," he asked me then, "that you were the only one real, and everyone else was a robot?"

I told him I had.

Leaving the Mullers, I wondered if patriarchies had to be so absolute, or whether connectedness had to be quite so self-contained. Why couldn't a father's rule be gentler? A Greek clan—as foreign to Otto Muller as cheese is to chalk—was to teach me that it could indeed.

"I'm Afraid He'll Squeeze His Brains"

*Thou art the master neither of thy property nor of thyself;
thou and thy estate, all these things, belong to family;
that is to say, to thy ancestry and to thy posterity.*

—Plato,
Laws, XI

I COULD START with the young father at the picnic, holding his year-old son as high in the sky as his muscled arms could reach. I could start with my stroll down the hall of the St. Spyridon parish house, past framed picture after framed picture of Sunday school classes. I could start with Lilia's house, or Alexandra's, or either one of Nick's. But I guess it makes more sense to start with the pizza.

They don't call it a pizzeria, the Westboro House of Pizza, because it's no more Italian than they are. They call it a pizza because it is Greek. Put a quarter in its jukebox and you hear *bouzouki* music while you wait for your order. I have put a good many quarters in that jukebox since my friend Nick Gage first took me there, to meet one of his pizza-owning brothers-in-law. With luck I expected to put in a good many more. I would no more drive through east central Massachusetts without a stop at this pizza, in fact, than I would pass up a swim on a hot afternoon.

There's nothing fancy about the place, outside or in. You'd have to call it unprepossessing. It is a small white frame building just across from the Bay State Abrasives factory, on East Main Street in Westboro. On its walls are coy kittens and cute Snoopys, painted on black velveteen in day-glo colors. They are for sale, but they tempt me no more than the electronic tennis game does. What lures me there, instead, are the food and the family that serves it. The food's quality, in an age of franchised swill, is rare. The family's cohesion in an age when so few people care what has become of their kinfolk, is rarer still. The brothers who own the restaurant enlist the help of their wives and children and relatives to keep it open thirteen hours a day except on Thanksgiving and Christmas. Theirs is as close as any clan I know. Their kind of closeness, however, may be as doomed as the cry of the loons on the lakes to the north.

These people belong to a clan of about eighty Greeks. Their clan, in turn, is part of what might be called a tribe of some 4,000, who in the past seventy years have migrated to the environs of Worcester, as their countrymen have done in similar numbers to other New England cities. Most of the Greeks I know in this family, and many outside it, came from the tiny adjoining villages of Lia and Vavouria, in the northwestern province of Epirus, near the Albanian border. Their collective story is at once unique and universal. They came to Worcester for the same reasons my own ancestors came from England in the seventeenth century and from Ireland in the nineteenth; for the same reasons people now swarm in from Haiti and Korea and Mexico. They came because things were tough at home.

Christos Nicholas Ngagoyeanis came in 1910, when he was seventeen. A cousin, already settled in Worcester, had sent him the money for his passage. His mother assumed that she never would see him again, and wailed as his ship disappeared. On the ship he had a dictionary and a lesson book, and taught himself enough English to find menial work right away. Sooner than most immigrants could, he progressed to less lowly jobs. He was also thrifty. When he had saved $300, he bought a shop of his own, called The Spa, where he sold newspapers and candy. Then he went back to Lia to reassure his mother and find a wife, and to sire two children. Before the second child was born he returned to Massachusetts, then to Greece to father two more children, then to Worcester again, and then back to Greece where his fifth and last child was born.

His wife would not join him in Worcester, though he wanted her to. She felt she belonged at home, looking after her grandfather and aunt. Her children, born United States citizens because their father had become one, all eventually joined him in Worcester. She probably would have joined him too, sooner or later, had she not been the victim of a Communist guerrilla massacre in her village in 1948. Her murder is this clan's tragedy. Her husband's prosperity—sufficient to allow dozens of his relatives and *patrioti* to follow him to Worcester —is this clan's pride.

Papou, the patriarch, has long been half-bald, but his brown eyes, behind gold-rimmed glasses, are alert. He makes one think of those Caucasian centenarians whose great age has recently been traced, in part, to the strength of their families. "I have a brother in the old country who's ninety-eight," Papou said. "He goes hunting up in the Alps, follows the wild rabbits way up in the mountains, up in the caves. I don't hunt here; it's dangerous. Here they make mistakes; the hunters here get killed, instead of the deer. But God bless America. I have no wish to go home to Greece except for a visit. I know more people here now than I know in my village. I have my doctors here, my friends here, my grandchildren here, my car here. I've been driving since 1919. If I can't have a steering wheel, sweetheart, I can't live."

Papou is loved and revered wherever he goes in Worcester. Every chair he sits in becomes, for the while, a throne. He is his clan's founder, and his fifth child and only son is its hero. Clans need heroes as much as they need founders; at their best they have someone whose accomplishments the rest of the world can join them in applauding. For the clan he was born to, Nicholas Christos Gage fills this need superbly. His sisters talk of him as if they were reading from scripture. I have friends who have felt special all their lives because they came along after their mothers suffered five or six or seven miscarriages, and others who feel special because they were long-awaited only children, but compared with Nick Gage, these people are like victims of child abuse.

"When my mother had Nick Gage, oh boy, I swear we celebrate for forty days," says Lilia, the third of his four sisters, who was six on the "hot hot day in July" in 1939, when he arrived. "I remember, the midwife had my aunt go get my grandfather and give him a special cap to wear called a *capella*, because after the four girls my mother finally has the son. Everyone is so happy that we hurry to make the special cakes called *tiganites*. For forty days we dance."

Nick Gage—his sisters and kinfolk usually refer to him by his full name—came from Greece at the age of nine with high resolve. Talented in mathematics, he thought he would become an engineer. When he won an essay contest, he changed his mind and decided on a writing career instead. Newspapers hired him early to do stories and articles. He started to earn money. He also helped his immigrating relatives. Streaming across the Atlantic in growing numbers, they needed someone to figure out tax returns, citizenship papers, driver's licenses, and other American obstacles. Someone had to interpret their new country to them. The someone was Nick.

So it still goes. "Nobody would ever think of buying property without consulting Nick first," one cousin said. He arranges immigration papers, advises about all manner of things, and works so hard on his own projects that Papou is "afraid he will squeeze his brains." He has done screenplays, television series, books of nonfiction, a novel, and investigative reporting, most of it for the *New York Times*, whose Athens bureau he was sent to manage in the fall of 1977. His *Times* colleagues and New York friends regard Nick as a dashing and generous fellow, quick to pick up checks, preoccupied with ambition, whose conversation never strays for long from his background. He looks something like certain Praxitelean statues.

His sister Lilia, who helps her husband with the pizza, doesn't look much like Nick except for her eyes and her hair, which, like his, is light brown. Lilia's hair is teased into a beehive, a style popular among women one generation removed from peasantry, and one of the teeth in her dazzling and unfeigned smile is gold. She is as central to her clan as her brother and their father. She provides a service no clan can do without: she is its switchboard. She is the one who knows, at any given time, where her eighty closest relatives are and what, more or less, is on their minds. She knows who is about to have surgery, who might be on the brink of engagement or marriage or divorce, who may be having what she calls "the trouble with the school," and who has reservations to fly to, or return from, Athens. Someone in this clan is always packing or unpacking a suitcaseload of presents: sheets and pillowcases and towels and shawls for the other side of the Atlantic; jars of holy water and charms to pin on children's clothing to ward off the evil eye for this side.

Lilia, born Ylikeria, believes in the power of the evil eye. So do most of her kinfolk. They take their superstitions seriously. When something is lost, they tie a knot in a towel, calling it "Satan's beard," and tell Satan they won't untie it till he helps them find what they're missing. Above Lilia's television set is a shelf which has become a sort of shrine. On the shelf are icons, framed family photographs, palm fronds, a string of red and blue Christmas tree lights, and a jar of holy water imported from Greece in a plastic pop bottle, from which she takes a sip "whenever I don't feel so good. I swear, honest to God, it helps." Ancient Greeks had holy altars with sacred fires where they worshipped their ancestors; on Maxdale Street in Worcester things are not so different.

This clan owes much of its vigor to the concentrated energy it gets from Papou as patriarch, Nick as hero and ambassador, and Lilia as switchboard. It also draws strength from the drama of its history—so

central a figure as a mother, so recently slain by so vivid an enemy as
the Communists—and from the urgency of its task: to wrest a living
from the ambiguities of the new world. Sense of place is a source of
this clan's richness, too. Families tend to fall apart, as my own has
begun to do, when their members aren't sure where on the face of
the earth they belong. The more places a clan can manage somehow
to hallow, the longer the clan will last. In this respect, the Worcester
Greeks are wealthy. They know where their ancestors lie, on both
sides of the ocean. Papou knows in which lot in which Worcester
cemetery he'll be buried. All these Greeks know where their work is,
most of it in pizzas like the one I visit. They know where to go to
worship, too, to Saint Spyridon's Church on Russell Street, where
they all get married and christened. And they know where to find
one another. With the exception of Nick Gage, who has moved to
that most acceptably remote of destinations, Athens, nobody is farther away than Pawtucket, Rhode Island. Lilia's sister Alexandra was
a little nervous when one of her sons first went to college thirty miles
away in Boston. "When somebody leaves the family," she said, "we
worry too much."

Homesickness is the least of this family's worries. Should a pang of
nostalgia for the Old World ever strike a Worcester Greek, he need
only wait until Sunday to turn his radio dial to station WNEB or
WORC, to listen to an hour of records which their listeners may
dedicate, at $12 or $15 each, to honor name days, anniversaries, chris-
tenings or trips to Athens. "When Nick and I were married," Joan
Gage told me, "it took a whole extra hour for them to play all the
records people dedicated to us. And when our children were born,
they dedicated a lot more, mostly songs from Epirus. Eleni dedicated
a song to Elenitsa called 'You Grew Up in My Hands.'" Eleni, one
of Nick's numerous distant cousins, moved in with the Gages to help
care for their children. When she got married, she wore Joan's wedding gown, and Nick gave her away.

Joan Gage, Nick's wife, isn't Greek. By heritage she is a Swedish
Presbyterian, by birth a Minnesotan. She and Nick met at the Co-
lumbia Graduate School of Journalism. When they got their diplo-
mas, in 1964, Nick's father met her and said, "Too bad she's not
Greek, I like that girl." That girl did the best she could to become a
Greek, converting to Nick's religion and learning his language, bearing him three children and keeping on writing herself. We found
plenty to talk about, the three of us, when a friend introduced us in
New York. The more time we spent together, the more I heard
about Massachusetts and the pre-Civil War house the Gages had

just bought. They always seemed to be running up there, so that Nick could give commencement addresses at his nieces' and nephews' schools, or to help dye eggs red for Easter, or to celebrate Christmas or Thanksgiving, or to help some cousin open a new pizza.

"They work hard at those pizzas," Nick said. "The trouble with Greeks is that they aren't good organizers. They're all chiefs and no Indians. You'd think that with two or three hundred Greek pizzas within a seventy-mile radius of Worcester they might form an association, to buy the stuff they need more cheaply from the manufacturer, but no—they each like to control their own shop. Same way with florists and other small businesses. It's mainly a Byzantine culture now, but when I read Homer and Kitto and Edith Hamilton about the ancient Greeks I feel some connection with them, too. They had the same self-reliance and the same inability to organize. But you ought to come to Worcester sometime and see for yourself."

So I did. I got in the habit of stopping at the pizza even when I was not hungry, ordering an Extra Special to heat up later in whatever kitchen I was bound for, because an Extra Special makes a splendid house present. Its base is a crust made from dough baked fresh daily, on which is piled a layer of cheddar cheese. Atop the cheese go more layers: of ground beef, mushrooms, anchovies, sliced meatballs, sausage, baloney, pepperoni, green peppers, onions, and a final layer of cheddar. Nothing comes from a can; all the ingredients are fresh. The name Extra Special is an understatement.

Once I asked Prokopi Economou, Lilia's husband, where the Extra Special recipe came from. Prokopi and his brother Christos manage their pizza restaurant together. Prokopi smiled, the sort of smile politicians wish for and can't often emulate. Then he tapped his remarkably round head. One of his nephews who happened to be around—in this clan several nephews are always around—protested.

"It's not *your* recipe," said the nephew. "It's my father's."

"You're wrong," said Prokopi, whose American customers call him Paul. "I'm the one who taught your father to make the pizza."

"But he had a pizza five years before you did," said the nephew. "You worked for him before you got your own place; that's how you learned the recipe."

This argument never was settled. No matter. Such kidding is a constant ritual among Greeks. They joke with each other, quarrel with each other, hire each other, and when need be, lend each other money, paying it back with no interest, on the honor system. Once, at a picnic in Worcester in honor of the Prophet Elias, patron saint of Nick's native village, Nick told me that if for any reason he needed $300,000 right then, that very summer afternoon, "I could go around to the people at this picnic and collect it, in cash, no questions asked."

Not much cash seemed to be changing hands that afternoon, though, except for the man who went around collecting dues for the Liotes Association, the club for people from Lia. Nick paid his dues three years in advance, and thanked an elderly cousin in a black peasant dress for giving us fresh pastry. She in turn thanked him for arranging for one of her sons to immigrate. A lot of thanking went on. But mostly, it was a day for dancing. The circle of dancers got so big it became a spiral, winding under the grove of oak trees. *Bouzouki* and clarinet players from the orchestra took turns doing solos. When the moment seized them, different Greeks advanced to the head of the spiral to do special acrobatic steps of their own. One picked up a glass of wine with his teeth, draining it dry. Nick, who led a dance or two himself, invited me to join the circle. It didn't matter, he said, that I didn't know the steps. It turned out he was right. People had better things to do, when I took the hands of strangers in that circle, than to look at my feet. People were smiling. They were smiling at the elderly women in black peasant dresses, and at young women in polyester pastel maternity dresses, and young fathers holding their infants high up in the sky to pose for photographers. The sky that afternoon, everyone agreed, gave off a light that seemed remarkably Greek—more Greek, some were saying, than that in Greece itself.

"It *is* more Greek here than it is in Greece," said Nick. "I was invited to Greek Week in Birmingham, Alabama, a while ago, and so was the Greek ambassador to this country, who was born in Athens. Even he didn't know how to do these dances. I kidded him, and said I wouldn't appoint a nondancing ambassador. People who live in the cities, they don't keep up the village dances."

"But we danced plenty when we went to Greece," said Prokopi, who had just returned with his family from their first trip home in eight years. They had been to see his parents, Lilia's mother's grave, and all their surviving relatives in both their native villages. "For two days we danced until three-thirty in the morning, by the church up on the mountain, under the big tree that's thousands of years old.

"We have a fine trip, never mind that it cost eight or nine thousand dollars. We didn't go on a charter. Why should we take a charter? I bought open return tickets, because what if my wife wants to stay longer, or come home sooner? We want to stay there as long as we like. We took taxis back and forth between her village and mine.

The people in mine thought I sounded American, because after twenty-two years in this country I must talk Greek with an accent."

"We visited hundreds of people," said Lilia, "but the first day we got there I didn't see anybody at all. I only went to my mother's grave. I went there every other day, too, to light a candle. One night I went to sleep with an aunt, because she was crying a lot. Every lady I see in both the two villages was crying for my mother. I cry too, when I'm there. It was terrible, when the Communists killed my mother. They captured me and tried to kill me, too, and they tried to make me a soldier, make me learn to shoot with the gun. I was hiding, I had nothing to eat, but some nice soldiers helped me escape to Macedonia, where my grandfather found me, and got word to my father that I was alive. My sisters and brother had already escaped to America, so then I went, too. Sometimes now people make fun of me, they say, 'Why you all the time so happy?' I say, 'I was unhappy as a young girl, I should be happy now.' But I cry, I get mad, when I think of my mother.

"In the old country, the kids they respect the parents more than here," Lilia said. "My husband is fifty years old, and he still is afraid of his father. He should be. Here, if you have to hit your son sometimes, you should be able to. The parents have the right to punish the son. Kids have to respect somebody. They need to be looked after. Even now, my son is nineteen, I wait up till he comes home. We never go to bed till the boys come home."

"On Father's Day and Mother's Day," said Prokopi, "I send my parents ten dollars—why not be a sport?"

"The clan," Joan Gage said later, when we talked in her kitchen, "gives everybody terrific strength. There really *is* safety in numbers. This family, for example, gives you a prescribed behavior for every situation you can think of. No matter what tragedy might come along, they have it codified. They tell you what you're supposed to do. If someone dies, you keen and wail and it makes you feel better. If someone's born, you wait forty days to take him to the church to be blessed and up to a year to have a christening. On your son's name day, you have a big party. On your daughter's, you have a little one, if any. I guess these people are sexist—sure they are—but there'd be no more point in telling them that than there would be to tell you or me that we weren't born with wings.

"Nick is more conservative than any of his sisters. If one of our eighteen-year-old nieces comes for a visit, and goes out on a date, he'll want to know where she is going, with whom, and how late. He's a patriarch already. He really believes all those codes and rules of conduct. I myself grew up to be much more lenient and liberal, and therefore less secure. But I'd be a far less happy person than I am now if I had married some All-American English major, and sat around smoking pot.

"The family, to these Greeks, is everything. The only 'love match' of any of Nick's sisters—the only marriage that wasn't arranged—is the only one that ended in divorce. Girls are very closely chaperoned until they get engaged. Engagement's a very formal thing with a big party, and maybe a new set of rules, maybe not, depending on who the girl is and who her parents are.

"Greeks define their relationships much more intricately than we do, so they'll understand what they owe each other. The closer the bond, the greater the obligation. They have two different words, for example, for sister-in-law. Your brother's wife is your *nyfi*, to whom you are less close than you are to your husband's sister, who is called your *kouniada*."

The two of Joan's *kouniades* whom I met were Lilia and Alexandra. They both live near enough to drop by at least once every day when Joan and Nick and their children are in Massachusetts, bringing food and presents and gossip. Lilia and Alexandra fascinated me, and still do, because they live as close to each other as I at times have wished my own sister and I did. They live right next door. Their identical split-level houses were built the same year, by the same contractor, in a suburban section of Worcester.

Their lives are uncannily symmetrical. Both their husbands own and run pizzas, both have two teen-age sons, both are so preoccupied with their clan that they have little time or energy left for the other neighbors on Maxdale Street, let alone the world beyond. As I talked to them I kept wondering, Could my sister Ann and I get on as well if we lived next door? Would we want to, if by chance I regarded Decatur or she Manhattan as more than a buoying place for an occasional visit? Would we abuse our siblings' right to be less nice to each other than we ever would dare to be to anyone else? Would the laughing rapport which we achieve at our best outbalance regressive snippiness? I rather fear that for us, as for many pairs of siblings, it might not. But Lilia and Alexandra are different. They probably couldn't imagine living any farther apart than they do. "Each of us always knows what the other one is thinking," as Alexandra said. In their early years in this country, after all, even when they were young brides, they and their father and brother and sisters all lived under the same roof. Pizza made them prosperous enough to escape, but they didn't elect to go very far.

The day I chose to visit their house seemed a promising one; it happened to be the same day Lilia and Prokopi were having the priest over from St. Spyridon's to bless their house and banish the evil eye. An exorcism! Would that not be dramatic? How could it fail to be, with a robed, chasubled, bearded Orthodox clergyman moving from room to room, swinging his censer, murmuring incantations, telling the devil to get out of here and leave these good Greeks alone? That was more or less what the priest did, the day I first went to Lilia's, but the whole occasion was somehow strangely prosaic. It was rather as if the exterminator were coming. Papou, who lives with Lilia and her family, wasn't even there, and Prokopi left as soon as the ritual was finished.

The priest sat down for coffee with Lilia and her sons, and they chatted in Greek. Later she told me what he had said. "'You got to believe in God. When you believe in the religion, you get up in the morning, you wash your face, you make the sign of the cross, and you thank God you have a good day today.' The priest tells my sons to listen to their father and mother, they know better than you. Watch it. Don't mix it up with the bad kids. My boys believe him, they *do* respect. I teach my boys religion. It would be nice to have the daughter, because when the daughter gets married she is closer to the mother, but so far I'm happy with my boys." For their part, her boys seemed eager for the priest's visit to end. I was, too; I wanted to see how Alexandra's house differed from Lilia's.

It didn't differ much. Her dominant color was green, to Lilia's yellow, but she had the same furniture of puffed, tufted, plastic velvet. A plastic cover protected a plastic bouquet of flowers from dust. The windowshades were drawn. Maybe at home in Greece this family had seen enough sun, enough dirt. Certainly they hadn't seen enough television; only during the priest's visit was Lilia's set turned off.

"I don't like parties as much as my sister does," said Alexandra, "and I don't like furniture as much as I used to, either. I used to be crazy about the furniture, but I don't think about it now. What I think about now are the soap operas. I watch *Love of Life* and *Search for Tomorrow* and *Guiding Light*. Sometimes I sit all afternoon watching the television. It relaxes me, makes me feel part of more families.

"I used to sleep with a dictionary under my pillow, and think I might want to go on to more school, but I don't think that now. My brain is too old now. What am I going to do, if I go to school now? I'm forty-three; how long am I going to live, another forty or forty-five years? If I don't see the world, at least I see Cape Cod. That's okay. I know enough, I've been enough places. Our other sister, she wanted to be a doctor, but she quit school when she was sixteen to work in a bank, to help my father."

Once Nick speculated that if he had stayed in Greece he might have become a shepherd on a hillside, or a taxi driver in the city. Never, said his father. "My wife and daughters and I would all have worked to send Nick to college, even in the old country," Papou said. "I'm so proud of my son I'd like to walk up on the air. He knows everything he's ever learned. He never forgets. My own education was different. I went to school only in the evenings. I was a money-maker; what I learned was from school in the evenings and what my customers taught me. But money you can lose. If you have millions you can lose it. Education you can't lose. God bless America, my grandchildren are born on good soil. It's a dream come true for my grandchildren to go for vacations to England, to Italy, to France.

"America is different from Greece. The Greeks don't like the girls, because in the old country they have to pay the boy to marry the girl, but in America it's different. In America my four girls all get married right away. Girls like mine are good. If I have six more girls like these, I'd like it fine. God bless America a million times! Bread alone, if you eat it in the States here, it tastes like a steak. I love the history of my old country, the old people, but not the new people. The new ones are pro-Communist. I can't forgive them. My son, he forgives everybody. He's not so mean as me."

Every time I went to Joan's and Nick's, at least a dozen relatives and neighbors were wandering in through the porch from the yard to the kitchen, and back out again. On my last visit, Christy and some neighbor children were outside jumping rope. One of the neighbor boys came in to borrow a piece of paper, on which he later spelled out "I LOVE YOU MISES GAGE." Mises Gage gave him a hug. Elenitsa was on the floor of the porch, transferring animals into and out of her Noah's Ark. Papou sat on the reclining chair, telling more about his early days in this country.

"Nine months after I got here I bought my shop in Worcester, for $300, which in those days was a lot of money. I worked peddling vegetables, selling fruits and vegetables to millionaires' wives, and setting up pins in a bowling alley, and working in a factory that made tea strainers. In other factories I made looms and pistols. I was class A1 in the war, but they didn't make me wear the khaki because what I was doing was more important, I was making the crankshafts. Did

you ever see how they make the crankshafts? It's rough, very rough—
I made thirty-two crankshafts a day.

"My big mistake, my foolish mistake, was not bringing my wife
over right away. She was fourteen years younger than me, I should
have brought her here with me. She told stories of what she heard
about the States, she told of swimming pools big as a room."

"But she love the family too much," said Lilia. "She said 'If they
take my child away, I'm going to stand up and they can shoot me,'
and this is what they did."

Lilia would probably do the same thing now, if life in Worcester
obliged her to, for her own two sons. "That's why we work so hard
in the pizza," she said. "I work sometimes fifteen hours a day, till my
whole body is all swollen. But we have to do it for the kids, so they
won't have to work as hard themselves."

"The kids, they don't always appreciate," said Prokopi, "but you
have to do it for them anyway."

"But maybe we do too much for them," said Joan. "How can we
raise them not to be spoiled? Is it good for them to grow up having
everything they want?"

"Maybe you're right," said Alexandra. "Maybe bad experiences
make them strong, keep them from growing up soft. But still, I don't
want my kids to have the life we had."

This issue, of course, will never be resolved. Marina, youngest of
Papou's thirteen grandchildren, gurgles on behalf of all her generation, and accepts the homage of her aunt Alexandra.

"Hello, *kukla*," says Alexandra. "*Kukla* means dolly. Hello, dolly."
The dolly produces something like a smile. So, at once, do all the
rest of us: Lilia, Eleni, Joan and I. Eleni gives me a quizzical look
and asks the others a question, in Greek. Joan translates. Eleni wonders how I can run all around the countryside alone in my car, free
to come and go as I wish. Papou had seemed to wonder the same
thing, when I came into this house earlier this afternoon: he told me
I "walked like a captain," which Joan said wasn't necessarily a compliment.

All the Greek women confess they find it odd that I should live so
far from my parents and only sister. They care enough about me to
come right out and say they wish I would get married. Alexandra
wonders if I ever have tasted *ouzo*, the anise-flavored Greek liqueur. I
have, often, but am pleased to accept more now. What luck: in the
only bottle of *ouzo* at hand there is only a scant inch of the liquor,
which means that if I drink it, my chances of finding a husband will
increase.

Alexandra mentions that this is her name day. Everyone agrees that if she were a man, they'd be having a big party to honor her. Since they aren't, I lift my glass to toast her, and the others raise their cups of coffee.

"Maybe by my next name day you'll be married," says Alexandra, "if you drink the last of the *ouzo*. You should have a big wedding, like Joan's and Nick's, when we roasted the six lambs. Have a big wedding, and invite a lot of Greeks, because the Greeks know how to do the weddings."

Eleni doesn't speak English, but she follows what is being said. She runs to another room to show me the pictures Joan took of her own wedding, the year before. One picture shows her and her husband at the reception, beneath a tree in the Gages' yard. In the other picture they sit rather shyly on a bed, under a canopy, looking into each other's eyes. She is wearing Joan's bridal gown, which I recall having seen hanging from the second-floor railing, so its train could trail down unwrinkled. The Greeks are indeed fond of weddings, as they are of all ceremonies, even small ones.

Now, for instance, Prokopi and his son Fotios, who have been out in the yard with the children, declare that they and Lilia must leave to go home. Prokopi's brother Chris is in charge of the pizza tonight, so they can go home to watch Home Box Office. "It costs more," says Prokopi, "but you get the better programs, without the commercials for the cat food. It's worth it to spend more, to keep the boys away from the robbers and the bad kids. We need to keep the family together."

So Prokopi and Lilia get ready to leave. So does their son Fotios, who is called Freddy. Freddy is a big tough kid in the middle of his teens, who looks like a football player. Before he leaves, he bends down to squat on the floor of the porch to give his three-year-old cousin Elenitsa, whom he is sure to see tomorrow, a kiss goodbye. Lilia will surely see Christy tomorrow, too, but before she leaves she scoops him up and lifts him high and gives him the kind of hug most people only get at airports, after long absences.

"Gee, Christy," says one of the American neighbors who has come to play. "You're lucky to have so many people who love you."

"Christy is named for your father, right?" I ask Nick later when he comes home.

"Yes, and I'm named for *his* father."

"And he'll name his son for you."

"He'd better," smiles Nick, "or I'll have both his legs broken."

This web of secure connectedness is hard to leave. I almost want it to trap me. I keep postponing my departure, hanging around an extra hour and then another. When I do finally back out of the driveway, I make a side trip to the pizza, for an Extra Special to heat up at home later. Things are frantic at the pizza. Big crowds hold numbers, waiting for their orders. Prokopi's brother and his children rush from oven to sink to cutting board to cash register. The phone rarely stops ringing. This family is in high gear, working together to produce something that it would seem at least half of Westboro is eager to consume. They don't sit around wondering how come they work so hard. They know why. They work hard so that their children will have it better than they did.

And, to be sure, their children will grow up knowing, with a certainty that would have made their ancestors marvel, where their next meal will come from. Hunger won't plague them. But choices probably will. People will enter their lives who know nothing of the rituals of Lia and Worcester, becoming their friends, offering them possibilities. They will be distracted. They will spend less time dyeing eggs red on the Thursday before Easter, and doing the dances at the picnics. The fabric that keeps their clan a clan will unravel.

Cut it out, I tell myself, as I pull onto the interstate. Don't be mawkish. Why feel any misgivings about the future of such ostensibly lucky children as Fotios and Christy and Elenitsa and Marina and all their cousins? Why should I envy their parents, and theirs and theirs, the urgent clarity of the problems it is and was their lot to solve?

At a party in New York I met the Greek-born concert pianist Rita Bouboulidi. We sat with plates of hors d'oeuvres in our laps and talked of Greek families, particularly of her own. Her mother, she told me, had died of cancer in Greece during Rita's scholarship year at the Paris Conservatory.

"The family hid the news from me," said Rita. "I only found out by chance, when someone who didn't know wrote me a condolence letter. I was studying; if I did not pass my exams, I would lose my scholarship. My mother told them, 'First she finishes with exams, then she finds out about me.' When she died, at age fifty-six, my father declared a strike from life, and little by little he disappeared.

"One of the things I don't understand about the U.S. is the detachment from family, which I am far too Greek to approve. If the

U.S. could develop the sort of family attachment Greeks have, it would be miraculous. In a divorce case between a Greek man and a Greek woman, for example, they would *never* end up, as couples do here, as 'good friends.' Friendship isn't possible after Greeks divorce."

Miss Hogan Phoned

And may her bridegroom bring her to a house
Where all's accustomed, ceremonious; . . .
How but in custom and in ceremony
Are innocence and beauty born?
                    —*William Butler Yeats*
                    "Prayer for My Daughter"

FIVE TOP TULSA LAWYERS have advised Sidney to cancel all of Patsy's charge accounts, but that isn't the way he wants to approach their divorce. He would prefer not to approach it at all. If he had his way, they would reconcile. They've had their differences, sure, but after fourteen years don't all couples? He is ready now to listen to Patsy, the way she says he never has, but she is through. She wants Sidney out, so out he is, and he tells his story in a hard, tight voice, not at all the way he usually talks.

One of the things Sidney dreads most is breaking this news to his Polish immigrant parents, back in Minneapolis. They, as he says, don't need this. They have had *tsuris* enough, bringing up him and four other children, of whom one is retarded, in a new country. Sidney, more than any of the others, has kept his parents reliably supplied with fresh *naches*—honors—and reasons to *kvell*: full scholarships, graduation *cum laude*, smart grandsons, Junior Chamber of Commerce awards. They didn't like his marrying a gentile and they didn't like his firm's transferring him to Tulsa, but they liked it fine when he sent them a copy of Who's Who in the South and Southwest with his name listed.

Sidney's father is an exterminator. His company sends him all over the Twin Cities, in an unmarked truck when he visits fancy suburbs, with a pressurized sprayer of Malathion. When Sidney tells of problems at his office, which he does often, his father says: "Look, you don't have to work standing up, do you?" and indeed Sidney doesn't. Sidney has a desk, a door he can lock, and a secretary. He gets paid to go to conferences and seminars. He has earned enough to buy a big old house on a two-acre plot filled with trees. He loves that house and he loves those trees. Before his wife got so engrossed in graduate school, where she is studying to become a marriage counselor, he used to love preparing French toast, on Sunday mornings, with her and the boys. Theirs was a family with all kinds of rituals.

Now the bewildered boys keep their sleeping bags at Sidney's tiny studio apartment downtown. He tries to pretend it is fun, having them there weekends, but they know better and so does he. His parents keep writing to ask after these boys, rarely mentioning their mother. Even though Patsy became their daughter-in-law in a Jewish ceremony, they never really liked her. For a couple of months Sidney's answers to their letters have avoided all mention of the looming divorce, but when his parents write to say they are thinking of spending their vacation in Tulsa, the news can no longer be concealed. When Sidney tells his parents, on the phone, his mother consoles him, advising him to find a Jewish girl next time. His father agrees.

"*Feh!*" says the older man. "*Goyim!* What do they know from families?"

Some of us know plenty. A Jewish friend was amazed when I told him once of my inherited compulsion, on arriving in a strange town, to phone not only my own relatives but other people's as well. "I thought only Jews did that," he said. The once clear line between Jewishness and the American mainstream grows ever more blurred. A North Dakota friend once wrote to me about a schoolmate's wedding she had gone to in Santa Monica:

Judy married a nice Jewish boy who is a paraplegic and has a good job with the state of California, working for the disabled. They had a gorgeous rabbi, *mishpocha* from the entire eastern seaboard, especially Long Island and Miami, a wheelchair contingent, a deaf contingent, with sign language interpreter right beside the *chuppa* [canopy], several common-garden-variety L.A. freaks, Rinpoche devotees complete with third-eye jewel in middle of forehead and yards of flowing muslin, a free spirit who is single and eight months preggers, another free spirit who is very, very gay, Judy's parents from Bismarck, and little me. If only the Founding Fathers could see this, I kept mumbling into my champagne.

I would like to have been at that wedding myself. It sounded far more heartening than most of the recent news about the ancient Jewish tribal passion. That passion, which has sustained and defined most Jews for many centuries, has lately and measurably begun to cool. Councils of rabbis convene to lament the leap of divorce rates among their traditionally monogamous followers, and even among themselves. Alcoholism, once all but unknown among Jews, is so no more—far from it. Elderly Jews can be just as forlorn and neglected as elderly anyone else. Tabloid series bewail the disappearance of that lovable and, it once seemed, imperishable stock figure, the Jewish mother.

Good riddance, some say. Those tribal bonds, like houses with too much custom and ceremony, could suffocate. No doubt at times they could and did and do, but it is disturbing to think that Jews, having survived Pharaoh and the Holocaust, should feel as unhinged by the late twentieth century as the rest of us do. The rest of us in this society have relied greatly on Jews for what many of us lack ourselves: an invisible but quite effective family network, sustained by ritual and elastic enough to encircle whoever needs encircling. Jewish families, better acquainted than most with grief, by hearsay at least, have a tradition of compassion, irony, and humor, not to say resilience, which is contagious.

Arriving in Iowa City to teach for a semester at the state university, I was asked to a brunch one Sunday where I met a painter, also there as a guest teacher, who turned out to come from my same neighborhood in New York. When I asked her what she missed, her answer was immediate: "Yiddish!" I knew what she meant. I too missed, among other things, the shortcuts provided by the Yiddish language. In English we say "my son-in-law's [or daughter-in-law's] mother [or father]; in Yiddish the words are *macheteneste* or *machuten.* Ever so cumbersomely we tell of "my brothers and sisters and their wives and husbands and their children and their spouses' parents and siblings and a few of their oldest friends"; how much simpler to call such a network a *mishpocha.*

I have been relying on *mishpochas* myself, Jewish and otherwise, since long before I ever heard the word. The more *mishpochas* I can belong to, on however temporary a basis, the better off I feel. Once, on a visit to my own family in Illinois, I broke out in a sudden and annoying skin rash. Where did I turn for help? Where but to my niece's friend Rozzy's father's celebrated "Uncle Sonny," Dr. Hyman Burstein, the busiest dermatologist in Macon County. Ordinarily people must wait weeks to see Dr. Burstein, but the *mishpocha* connection entitled me to immediate treatment. The rash, thanks to a salve prescribed by Uncle Sonny, disappeared at once.

So, in other places over the years, have a number of less visible ailments. I felt uneasy about moving into an apartment in Coralville, Iowa, until I found the Welts next door. Theirs was not a large *mishpocha*, consisting as it did only of Peter and Elinor, but it did the job. It made me feel encircled. Of a Sabbath eve I could find Peter and Elinor lighting the candelabra which was the only object Peter had brought with him from Berlin. Whenever I felt the need, and sometimes when I didn't, I could hear tales of Elinor's girlhood in Omaha, where she had taught Hebrew school and where her *bas mitzvah*—thirteenth birthday ceremony—had been the biggest that city had ever seen.

I also felt uneasy a few months later, reporting to Athens, Georgia, for a term of guest teaching. I knew virtually nobody there, and could only hope that the legendary southern hospitality would ward off any seizures of loneliness. It didn't, until I telephoned Elinor Welt's sister Bonnie Pike and her family in Atlanta, and met Burt and Dot Sparer in Athens. The Sparers at once invited me to their daughter Lisa's *bas mitzvah*. More persuasively than I would have thought possible, Lisa told at that ceremony how lucky she felt to be a 13-year-old Jew in Athens. She sang part of the service herself, at the lectern. So did the rabbi. So did her father and her mother and her twin brother and their dentist. Her grandmother *kvelled*. So did her Prussian great-grandmother Omama, on a visit from the "health-related facility" where she lives in New York. So did I.

Once I heard of a father who not only planned but cooked himself a banquet to celebrate his daughter's becoming a woman. That father, of course, was Jewish. His ceremony seems tame compared with the African tribe that once obliged its girls, as a puberty rite, to catch water insects with their mouths and kill a tethered chicken by sitting on its head. Most of us have lost all touch with such open acknowledgment of reality. In 1949, when an Episcopalian friend of mine got all dressed up for the first date of his life, his father looked at him and said, "Well, you're looking pretty spiffy, aren't you?" and that was that. So much for the onset of manhood and whatever it might imply.

Once I saw a litter of Labrador Retrievers born during a dinner

party on Central Park West. The timing was amazing—a puppy arrived at the end of each course. Otherwise, like most middle-class
Americans, I have witnessed births and deaths only on screen. Gen-
teel people, after all, arrange to do such things in hospitals, not in
public. We may send Mother's Day cards and mark other guilt-
inspired "holidays," but as a nation we are not much attuned to the
numinous. It takes a funeral to remind most families of the ultimate,
and some don't get together even then. I find this regrettable. I think
there are plenty of lesser occasions worthy of attention, too. "Every
day," as Joan Didion once wrote, "is all there is." If we would follow
the Jewish example and enliven our days with more ritual, we would
be better off.*

My own clan owes a good part of its strength to the reflexive way
we dye and hide the eggs, wave the sparklers, bake the cakes, carve
the pumpkins, stuff the turkeys, deck the halls, and ring out the old.
Little of this has anything to do with theology; left to our own de-
vices we didn't say grace, and our churchgoing was occasional and
perfunctory. These practices stem, instead, from our need to ac-
knowledge seasons and solstices. Religions have endured, among
other reasons, because of the scaffolding they provide from which to
suspend such traditions. All the Jewish families I care for, and the
gentile ones too, feel strongly about ceremonies that link them to the
earth, to those who have trod it before them, and to one another. I
only wish more of my Jewish friends were in the habit of marking
Passover with dinners called Seders, a 3,200-year-old ritual honoring
the bonds that link individuals to families to Judaism.

In springtime I used to make my wistful way along upper Broadway, past shops barred shut for Passover and beaming neighbors on
their way to and from temples and Seders. No Jew at Christmas
could feel more left out. But at last I learned the power of the carefully placed hint, and one spring got asked to what must have been
the two most heartening Seders on the Atlantic seaboard, one in my
own apartment building and the other at several pushed-together
tables in Philadelphia. Twice I got to sing "Dayenu" and the song
about the one kid goat, eat the food, drink the wine, hear the Four
Questions and the fearsome list of plagues the Hebrews had barely
escaped, help say the prayers, and meet the *mishpocha*.

After the Philadelphia Seder the daughter of the household told
how, when she first went to college, her Presbyterian roommate shyly

* The United Methodist Church booklet *Ritual in a New Day: An Invitation*
has overly earnest prose, but the rites it suggests—for naming, moving, divorcing,
preparing to die, and reviving the old custom of footwashing—make sense.

asked, "Ellen, is kosher a spice?" It isn't. Kosher, Ellen explained, means among other things having two sets of china, one for meat dishes and the other for those containing milk. Kosher households need a lot of cupboards. "One year I said *screw* these dishes, I can't *stand* all these dishes," my New York hostess told me, "but I figured I had to keep the whole thing going for the sake of my mother-in-law. These things die out if somebody doesn't keep them going, and the somebody in our family seems to be me, so I figured it was my *drang*. But you know who raised a fuss, when I threatened to get rid of all the dishes? Not my mother-in-law. My kids."

The next year I was invited to a New Jersey Seder by a young friend whose father and grandmother both had died since the Passover before. I almost didn't go, figuring that these two absences would make the occasion too private and too gloomy. But then I remembered Jerry's telling how he had felt something oddly like joy when he, as eldest son, had been required to throw the first handful of sod onto his father's lowered coffin. "It gave me a feeling of rightness and profound connectedness," he said, "because I remembered seeing my father do the same thing for *his* father." How could Jerry, at 24 or any other age, preside over a depressing Seder? I went, and it wasn't. It healed not only the sting of death but several less specific anxieties.

I know another young couple named Diana and Daniel, who live together. They aren't married. Diana's widowed mother wishes intensely that they were. A member of the Great Books Society of Hartford, Connecticut, she knows better than to sit *shive* for her daughter, as if she were dead, but the hour never passes, when these two women are together, without a recital of the virtues of wedlock.

"She even tries to *bribe* me," Diana says, as she and Daniel and I drink tea and eat banana bread on the floor of their three-room apartment. "She says she'll get me a Cuisinart if we get married. A big part of the problem is that she doesn't know what to *call* us. Daniel she refers to as my 'er—friend.' As for what I am to him, that really stymies her. 'Slut' just doesn't have the right ring to it."

"She thinks I'm ripping Diana off," says Daniel, who is working toward his doctorate in history, "because Diana earns more money than I do." Diana is an advertising copywriter trainee.

"She wouldn't even come to visit us for two months after we moved into this apartment," says Diana. "When she did, we thought maybe we ought to lay a sword down the middle of our bed."

"When we go to *her* place, I sleep alone in the basement," says

Daniel. "Maybe Diana's cousin's wedding next week will mollify her some."

"Maybe, on the other hand, it won't," says Diana. "You want to see a family drama, you ought to come to that wedding with us," she tells me. "My cousin Sherry is marrying a *convert!*"

"But Gil doesn't like to talk about his conversion," says Daniel. "He figures it's private, which makes me like him a lot more than I usually like accountants. When Sherry's father got divorced from his second wife, Gil wrote him a terrific letter, quoting some ancient rabbi who said how a good divorce is better than a bad marriage."

"Sherry's father got divorced *twice?*"

"No, his first wife—Sherry's mother, Esther—died five years ago. After that he was married for just ten months to an Israeli war widow who had come over from Haifa to look for a husband."

"It was the idea of it that got him," says Daniel. "The idea of a *galut* Jew, one of the Diaspora, marrying someone from Israel, appealed to his sense of romance. That and the blending of families— Shulamith had five kids, he has four—he loved the idea of being an Old World patriarch."

"Those five kids came here speaking only Hebrew," says Diana. "You talk about *dynamics*, you should have seen those nine kids together at Uncle Howard's dinner table."

"He misses those kids a lot more than he misses Shulamith," says Daniel.

"Who could miss Shulamith?" asked Diana. "When she went back to Haifa, Uncle Howard practically gave a street dance to celebrate."

"What did she do that was so awful?"

"Oh, gossip about his inadequacies to the neighbors, ask to use the neighbors' phones and make calls—not collect ones—to Haifa. Beneath her cold exterior there turned out to be even more coldness. Now he's on the lookout for somebody new: someone who's interested, he told me, in three things: the English language, sex, and music. He plays the oboe, you see."

"He has found a lady friend," said Daniel, "but she's nineteen years younger, and wants kids, and he's not sure it would be fair for him to be sixty when a child of his was ten."

"I know a man who's *eighty* who has a child aged ten," I told them, "and that family is one of the better ones I know of."

"Anybody who tries to make recipes or draw diagrams for how to construct a family," said Daniel, "is either stupid or arrogant."

"Or both," said Diana. "Come with us to the wedding."

I did go to the wedding. Like the exorcism I went to at the Greeks' house, the event was less interesting than what happened before it and after. Not that the dogwoods weren't in perfect bloom, outside the suburban synagogue's picture window. Not that the rabbi didn't wax metaphoric, evoking as he did "the sculptor Michelangelo, who said, 'It isn't I, it's the form embedded in the rock that's important; I just chip away at the excess to reveal that form.' In that same way, Sherry and Gilbert, you now have the beautiful privilege of chipping away at the excess in each other.

"Your essential natures have been set by your families—however you view one another and act toward one another, your family traditions will stand in the background, waiting to give whatever support you might need. But now it is time for the real you to emerge. May you never grow tired of the labor."

"We should have given them chisels for a wedding present," Diana whispered to me. Her mother, sitting on her other side, gave her a glare. Poor Diana's mother. Gilbert stamped on the glass. Sherry smiled under the canopy. They kissed. Flashbulbs popped. We all headed for the reception in the garden behind Sherry's widowed father's gigantic house. We represented, you might say, many walks of life. Some among us wore suits that must have cost four hundred dollars, while others looked as if they belonged on the park benches of Broadway in the nineties, mumbling and feeding pigeons.

"Why am I so popular all of a sudden with the bugs?" asked Sherry's father's Aunt Ida. "Look, even in my coffee cup there's a little living something just flew in. He should live and be well, of course, but somewhere else."

"I wish Esther could have been here today," said Bubbi, Ida's sister and Howard's mother. "I kept thinking how proud she would be. But there wasn't time to brood on that or anything else. Such a day! From the first thing in the morning it was 'Bubbi this! Bubbi that! The hem's gone out of my dress!' I had to be an actress, pretending to be a lot calmer than I felt."

"It must be nice to be so needed," said Aunt Ida.

"Not needed, *wanted*," said Bubbi. "You're wanted too, Ida, and you know it. Howard wants us all here. But when he thanked me for coming, I said 'What are parents for?'"

"You've worked hard enough now, Mom," said Howard. "No more kitchen duty. Why do you think we hired the cateress? Let her do the work—you take it easy."

The cateress, a graduate of Erhard Seminar Training, was an inspired cook. Spinach snuggled in her cannelloni. Her wedding cake was fruitcake, which she had learned was Gil's favorite. When everyone exclaimed over giant, fish-shaped salmon salad, arched under fins made of cucumbers, she said, "I learned taste from my mother. Both my mother and I have perfect taste."

"But it looks like World Wars Three, Four and Five in that kitchen," said Bubbi. "I was just trying to help. I've been helping all my life. You think it was easy, coming here from the Ukraine when I was eighteen?"

"I'm sure it wasn't," I said.

"You're right, young lady," said Bubbi. "I'd work from seven in the morning to seven in the evening, and once when I didn't have any money I walked all the way from Canal Street to 125th."

"Guess how old I am?" asked Zaide, Bubbi's husband.

"Seventy, maybe?" I said.

"Seventy plus sixteen! But I'm feeling good, and I'm feeling proud."

"You should," I told him. "I liked the prayer you said when you blessed the *challa*."

"How do *you* know the name for our bread?"

"I know lots of Jewish families."

"You see a good Jewish family starting today," said Bubbi. "Isn't that Gilbert a doll?"

"I could go for him myself, if I were a hundred years younger," said Aunt Blanche.

"Can I bring you a drink?" asked Zaide.

"No, Dad, you sit still," said Howard. "Here, let's have a special drink." From a cabinet on the porch adjoining the garden he took a wine bottle whose label read "MAZEL TOV, SHULAMITH AND HOWARD."

"Oh Uncle Howard," said Diana, "you don't still have *that* stuff around? From such a sad mistake of a wedding as that?"

"Just this one bottle is left," said Howard. "Let's finish it off." He poured glasses of what turned out to be exceptionally sweet Michigan burgundy, the last of a case he had been given for his wedding to the Israeli. "What I'm doing now," he told me, "is what I call decathecting—separating myself from the memory of that whole big mistake. It isn't easy, but I'm coming to see Shulamith as the extremely troubled, extremely stubborn lady she was. She never wanted to trust me, so I finally and reluctantly had to realize that I couldn't trust her, either. But who ever thinks about trust? I never thought about trust in my marriage with Esther, any more than I thought about having two lungs. That's Esther there," he said, pointing above the cabinet to a photograph of a woman with large, tender eyes and a nose so magnificent I remarked on it.

"Once someone asked Esther if she had ever thought of having the girls' noses fixed," Howard said. "Can you imagine? Wouldn't it be criminal to tamper with a nose like that?"

"It would," I said.

"Shulamith used to call this house Esther's mausoleum, and maybe she was right. One of our big mistakes was to start a whole new marriage on such old ground. If I get married again, we'll start on neutral territory. I'm thinking of selling this house now—it's much too big for just two children left at home and me—but I don't want to do that until I find a new wife. What I'd like to find meanwhile is a couple to move in with us, so there wouldn't be so much wasted space. If the wife of the couple would do the cooking, I'd let them live here free."

"People are always telling me I should sell *my* big house and move to some singles condominium," said a divorced cousin of Diana's named Yvonne. "I guess it would be sensible, now that the divorce is final, now that my four boys are all grown and gone, but I just can't see living in a tiny place. I *like* big houses and the sounds of people; I like comings and goings and keys in the latch, so I've taken in lodgers. They have kitchen privileges. Sometimes they and I have breakfast together."

"Like an old-fashioned boarding house," said Daniel. "It doesn't sound bad. It sounds sort of nice."

"What happened to Al?" asked Diana, of Yvonne's ex-husband.

"He's moved to California. He has a new wife who makes the sort of fuss over him I never could, after we stopped being infatuated with each other."

"How long did the infatuation last?" asked Daniel.

"Two, three years," said Yvonne. "Until our boys started coming. When all four were born, Al took to calling me 'Mother.'"

"Oh God," said Diana.

"He didn't see why I wanted to get my master's in chemistry when the kids were in school—he'd say, 'You're just a victim of Women's Lib.'"

"You'll find somebody new," said Howard, "if you look."

"I'm not in any big rush," said Yvonne, "but I *am* looking. I keep busy. I've joined a Single Professionals group—we go skiing, we play tennis and bridge, we go to the theater, we have book reviews. Next month we're having a discussion of *The Prophet*."

"Each to his own," mumbled Diana.

"What was that, young lady?" asked her mother.

"What's going *on* in here?" asked Gilbert, the bridegroom, coming out with Sherry to the porch where we sat.

"Just family undercurrents," said Diana.

"Undercurrents?" said Daniel. "Are you kidding? This family doesn't have undercurrents, it has tidal waves! Hey, where are you guys going on your honeymoon?"

"Los Angeles," said Gilbert, "to visit some relatives."

"But we're really not flying there till morning," said Sherry. "I shouldn't tell you this, but tonight we're going to stay in a hotel near the airport! I figure if you don't stay in a hotel the night of your wedding, then when *do* you? I've only stayed in one hotel before this in my life, and that was when I was ten, with five of us in one room."

"Let's have some more wine," said Howard, reaching for the bottle labeled "MAZEL TOV."

"Not *that* stuff," said Gilbert. "Hold on a second." He went to another room and brought back some champagne. "This is more like it," he said as he popped the cork and filled our glasses. "*L'chaim*," he said as he lifted his own in a toast.

"That means 'to life,' " said Zaide, for my benefit.

"She knows," said Diana as we clicked glasses.

Now and then I think about marrying a Jewish man myself. In a life beset with ambiguity and surprise, their power to attract me is one of the few constants. One of these, fifteen years my senior, was a poet named Ben with whom I traveled to England several summers ago. We didn't hit it off. We were both more relieved than sad when, after five quarrelsome weeks, Ben decided to fly off alone to visit friends in Sweden.

There, mercifully, he met Sigrid, a serene and distinguished chemical engineer with three grown children. Soon Ben and Sigrid were rearranging their lives to spend all the time they could together.

"As a couple," I heard from another friend of Ben's who met Sigrid before I did, "they're like some improbable transistor radio made from odd bits of wire found on the streets of Calcutta, all tangled and twisted. To look at such a radio you'd never think it could possibly work, but the amazing thing is that it does—it works wonderfully."

Ben and Sigrid spent most of the year together—her profession brought her often to New York—but remained single. "After five decades of privacy and independence," he told me when enough time had elapsed for us to renew our friendship, "I can't quite give it all up, not even for her. These separations give us breathing space, and make me appreciate all the more what we have when we're together. You know something? I never knew anything could be so good."

"*Mazel tov*," I told him, so truly happy for their good fortune that I wasn't even jealous. If it could happen to them, I figured, then maybe it could to me too someday. And what difference did it make, at their ages, if they didn't commit themselves legally? But a year later came one of the most astonishing letters I have ever received, with a Swedish stamp, addressed in Ben's unmistakable blackslanting hand.

"Guess what Sigrid and I did last week," the letter said, after a paragraph of inquiries about my health and comments on the weather. "We got MARRIED!" A harried chief magistrate in Sigrid's town registry—"she must have been on leave from the dog licensing department," Ben speculated—had pronounced the necessary words. Ben, everyone figured, must have been the oldest first-time groom in all the history of Uppsala. His knees had knocked. His blood had felt like sherbet. But at the age of 56 he had done what all his life he had been avoiding.

A fortnight before Sigrid could leave Sweden, Ben had to return to the States. Soon he made a trip to the Long Island nursing home where for some years his mother had been languishing. When I first knew Ben we would go to that nursing home together to visit the old woman, whose life had not been easy. Widowed before Ben was even born, she had long ago buried her only other child. She had spent her adult life selling sportswear in a department store, and on days when she felt strong she would recall for us the code expressions she and other clerks at that store had used, so that customers wouldn't know what they were saying.

"If a strange or crazy-looking customer should come in," she told us once, "and I'd notice him and want to tell the girl at the next cash register, I couldn't just say, 'Get a load of that one, will you?' so I'd call out 'Miss Cook! Miss Cook!'—which sounds like Yiddish for 'take a look'—as if I wanted the supervisor to come. Or, if I was having trouble closing a sale—if a customer who had been just about to buy a ninety-dollar suit was starting to lose interest—I couldn't call 'Help!' so what I'd say was 'Miss Hogan phoned!' That meant 'Come quick, before this customer gets away!' "

It saddened me to learn that as Ben's mother grew more frail, she no longer told such tales. When I asked Ben how she was, he usually answered, "She's just there—she sits there. Once she told me, 'I get mixed up.'" But the day he visited after his return from Sweden, she wasn't mixed up at all. This time, when her only surviving son broke to her the most momentous news of his life, all vagueness fled the 88-year-old woman's countenance. "She drew herself up in her chair in strictest maternal fashion," Ben wrote to me, "and said, 'I *hope* you married a Jewish girl.'"

Ben doesn't normally tell Jewish mother jokes. He agrees with Irving Howe that "sentimentalism is the besetting sin of the Jewish turn to ethnicity." For Sholom Aleichem as for T. S. Eliot as for James Joyce, as Howe once said in a commencement address, "the province, the ethnic nest, remains the point from which everything begins and without which, probably, it could not begin; but the province, the ethnic nest, is not enough, it must be transcended."

Gradually, with what might be called all deliberate speed, the same lesson is being learned in the south.

Hurry Back

ONCE, ON A STREET CORNER near the Mason-Dixon line, I stood with a man from Louisiana waiting for a light to change. We weren't in any special hurry to get where we were going, but the light stayed red for so long that I lost my patience. Seeing no traffic coming from either side, and being by nature a hurrying, jaywalking Yankee, I dashed across. My friend stayed put until the light turned green, then ambled over to join me.

"There you have it," he said. "The whole difference between a northern and a southern family upbringing."

"What have families got to do with traffic lights?"

"The way I was raised," he explained, "I'd no more think of disobeying a red light than you would, apparently, of holding one sacred. That's one reason I've never had any trouble with any authority—in school, college, the Marines, or any job. To grow up southern is to know instinctively who is boss and what the rules are."

"You almost make me envy you," I said.

"You almost should," he answered. "It's not for nothing that southern families are such a myth unto themselves."

Few myths are better-documented. Hear the lyrics of southern songs:

> I'd give all I own, if I could but atone
> To that silver-haired daddy of mine.

and

> I know we had no money, but I was rich as I could be
> In my coat of many colors that my mama made for me.

Reread Faulkner. Read Tennessee Williams and Flannery O'Connor and Erskine Caldwell and Eudora Welty and Carson McCullers. Reflect on the Compsons, Sartorises, Snopeses, Winfields, Kowalskis, and the O'Haras of Tara, Miss Pittypat Hamilton, and the Tarleton twins vying for Miss Scarlett's company over barbecue. Consider the actual Longs, Thurmonds, Talmadges, Byrds, and Wallaces, not to mention the descendants of Kunta Kinte. Think of all the blacks in all the ghettoes of all the north whose only annual change of scene is to spend two hot August weeks with their ancient southern mothers. As Herbert Gutman has made quite clear in *The Black Family in Slavery and Freedom* (Pantheon, 1977), they are wrong who would claim that black families are, or ever have been, weak ones. Gutman quotes a slave ship captain whose diary in 1682, includes this passage:

> . . . I once happened to have aboard a whole family, man, wife, three young boys, and a girl, brought here one after another at several places; and cannot but observe here what mighty satisfaction these poor creatures expressed to be so come together again, though in bondage. For several days successively they could not forebear shedding tears of joy, and continually embracing and caressing one another, which moving me to compassion I ordered they should be better treated aboard then commonly we can afford to do it . . .

Both races' heritages make for remarkably close southern clans—as tightly rooted, and as determined, as the kudzu vines which spread north and took root outside Washington around the same time the Jimmy Carters began to expand and extend right there in the White House. "The south," as another of its children told me, "is a cauldron, a stew—southern families really *are* more eccentric, and more colorful, than those you'll find anywhere else. They're also harder to figure out. Sometimes they extend in pretty funny ways—just think of all the kings and queens crowned by all the *krewes* at Mardi Gras."

Think and hear and read and watch and marvel, because "whether you like them or not," as my southern friend went on, "families here are different from other families, as Fitzgerald wrote about the rich. We're different because we're a *sight* more familial. In the south, more than anywhere else in this whole country, the bonds of family can tighten into bands." So I was to learn for myself, when I spent ten weeks in the south in the spring of 1975, the year before the Carters relinquished their privacy. The journalism school at the University of Georgia asked me down as a visiting lecturer to teach a one-term course. This, I figured, was my chance to investigate the myths about the clans of the south. I hoped they would be still true. Behind and among the Bonanza Sirloins and mobile home parks and shopping malls I knew I would find as readily in Georgia as in Montana, I hoped there would be families as distinctive as the accents of the south. I figured it shouldn't be hard to get some firsthand sense of what southern clans were all about. Those clans, I further figured, would engulf any well-meaning and curious visitor with their legendary hospitality.

On the last point I was somewhat mistaken. "Ten weeks," someone later told me, "is both way too short and way too long a time to spend in the south."

"Graham Greene," I said, "once wrote that the proper length of any visit is either two weeks or eighteen months."

"That's true," my informant said. "If you'd come here for just a fortnight, that would have been quite different; knowing the end was in sight—if you'll pardon me—we would have feted you with luncheons and parties. Down here, you see, there's a kind of twenty-five-year trial period before we take in a stranger. Southerners don't see the sense of investing all that emotion, all that risk, in people who tend to fly off in who knows what direction every other whipstitch."

"There's a sort of rule down here," another southerner told me once, "that when you give a party you never let people talk together for more than three minutes, to keep things moving. Once a rather iconoclastic friend from New York was here for a party and got into three or four fairly promising conversations, only to have each one interrupted by his hostess, who would say 'David, I *know* you'll want to meet so-and-so.' So David finally got up and put two chairs together in the center of the room and said, 'Goddamnit, we might as well play musical chairs; you screw up every conversation I ever get into,' which was really a *stunning* shock to everybody."

"Why, I have so many roots myself," said an anthropologist in Georgia, "that I'm almost *over*supported. I used to have a beau who'd address me as 'y'all' even when we were alone in a room, so vivid was his sense of my tribe." I heard a great deal about the strength of such tribes. I heard of a small boy in a town nearby who in fifteen minutes could ride his bicycle to the houses of both his two grandmothers and all four of his great-grandmothers, not a one of them a step-parent. I heard of a woman in her sixties, a grandmother herself, who went to see her parents, in their nineties, three times every week. "Their neighbors don't think that's nearly often enough," she said. "They accuse me of shocking daughterly neglect."

Southern families are intense, all right. Four sisters and a brother, all unmarried and in their sixties, have spent their whole lives under the same one roof. A childless married couple in their fifties giggle conspiratorially about how late they like to stay up—sometimes until well past midnight! "Oh, we just have a high old time," the wife said, "laughing and playing our records!" Once she had given some thought to adopting a baby, since they couldn't seem to have one of their own, but never got around to it. They didn't get around to it because her father—not her husband, her father—forbade them to. Just as well: a child in the house might give them less pleasant reasons to stay up so late.

The man from the old New Orleans family never did take me to see the oil well by moonlight, that night fifteen years ago in San Antonio. He had meant to; he had said we would go there when we shared a taxi into town from the airport. But instead we got to talking. This man wore a monogrammed shirt, the reason he had decided on the plane that he wanted to meet me, he said, was what I thought of as my Rachel Carson dress. I told him I had bought that dress to replace another, which I had burned.

"You burned a dress?"

"Someone told me to; someone told me the dress I was wearing was that awful. So I did. I stuffed it down a friend's incinerator, and borrowed some clothes from the friend to wear home." We sat in a hotel lobby that had an alligator tank, drinking bourbon. The man talked of his late father, who had said it was okay to be snobbish if one had a reason to, and of his wife, from whom he had been separated ten months now, and of his children. He would rather lose an eyeball, the man said as he tossed a crumpled wad of paper into the air, than one of his children. He also talked of his mother. His mother was quite a talker. I ought to meet her. In time I did.

Winter mornings can be cold in New Orleans. The oilman's mother sat by the fire. It crackled. Her manservant brought her her usual breakfast: two fried eggs, two thin slices of whole wheat toast, coffee. The steam from her coffee rose in the sun that slanted onto the jewel-toned rug. When I came in to join her, she bade me have some coffee cake. I declined.

"But you *have* to have some," she said. "It's Sara Lee, which the Duchess of Windsor said was the only good thing about America." Oh well then, I said, succumbing to the cake and to her story. At some point every year, she told me, the sun fell all the way over there to that corner of the room onto the pure white porcelain statue, the statue she had in her room in Paris. She remembers the day the statue arrived back here, how starkly white it looked being unwrapped by blacker hands than I am used to seeing in the north.

"Essentially," she told me, "I was brought up by blacks. I have no recollection of my mother until I was six years old, and I don't believe she ever cooked a dinner in her life until I was eleven. We had a housekeeper named Mrs. Green, who when she couldn't think of anything else to clean up, gave us enemas. A psychiatrist once told me I had the worst possible background; it was a wonder, he said, that I wasn't locked up.

"My family regarded themselves as the toniest kind of southern aristocracy. When my grandmother felt the call of nature, speaking of such unseemly matters, slaves would surround her and stretch out their skirts so no one could see what she was doing. That's the kind of background I come from. Once, when a young woman failed to comment on a relative's new dress, in the town where my mother grew up, they led a pony upstairs in her house. Ponies, as you know, will go upstairs but not down. They had to take down the whole side of the house to get that pony down, on a ramp.

"Men in such a culture don't want wives. They want mothers. I married my first husband because I thought he'd be depressed if I didn't. I thought, This is nice for him, he really likes it, it doesn't bother me too much; why not? It wasn't smart, but then I wasn't raised to be smart. My mother could never forgive me for being Phi Beta Kappa. She would have preferred that I have an illegitimate child."

Most of the southern stories I heard concerned women. I heard of one lady who never opened a door in her life but always carried a black silk handkerchief with her, just in case she might have occasion to touch a doorknob. I heard of a widow who refused to move out of her enormous mansion because "I *killed* my husband to get him to earn the money to furnish this house, and I'm not going to leave it." I met many women with men's or family names, a practice someone said arose after the Civil War, stemming from the fear that since so many men had died, the names might die too if they were not passed on to females.

My ten southern weeks began just before what one woman called the "Green Rain—the one rain we have every year that changes the whole look of things." Change the look it did; never again do I expect to see such azaleas, such dogwoods, such tulip trees and hickories. All these were splendid. So were the metaphors: "tight like a mule sphincter in fly season" and "mean as a boiled walrus." So were the grits, the barbecued goat meat, the red clay, and the café where I heard that a widow once went alone to order four meals: one for her late father, one for her late husband, one for her spiritual mentor, a Dr. Holman who had "gone to India to study altruism," and one for herself. "She had kind of flipped," a neighbor of this widow told me, "but of course we didn't admit it, because down here we protect our own, and she was one of our own, all right."

"Hurry back!" the waitress said when I left that café myself. They said that everywhere in the south, the way they say "thank you much"—giving "much" two syllables—at cash registers in the midwest. I seldom felt much yen to hurry back to the south. Most of the people I grew to like there were also outsiders, who'd come from Nebraska or Korea or New York. But there were exceptions. There were, for example, the Philpotts.

You don't use words like "nuclear" or "extended" when you talk of the Philpotts of Henry County, Virginia. The Philpotts, to their credit, don't talk or think that way at all. They talk in plain cadences that sound like questions, in an accent that to my Yankee ear made "aunt" sound like "ornt," and "home" sound like "howm," as in the sentence, "We're having a reunion at Fairy Stone Creek to welcome home one of our aunts."

I went to that reunion. The Philpott who invited me was named Patrice. Patrice was nineteen that spring. I first met her on the campus of the Southern Seminary Junior College, in the foothills of the Blue Ridge Mountains, a two-hour drive northwest of her home town of Bassett. "Sem," as her college is called, had asked me for a two-day visit to talk with classes about writing, so I took a break from my ten-week visit to Georgia. My real reason for going was to listen, not to talk. Most of the students there were majoring in equitation—horseback riding. I knew so little about that subject that I figured we would have refreshingly little in common.

Patrice, a friendly, narrow-eyed blond girl, hung around after one class to talk not of horses but of her family, with such fervor that ten minutes convinced me she might be the most tribal young woman on either side of the Mississippi. "I'd go home every weekend, if I had a car," she said. "Once I went for five whole weeks without seeing my parents, and it nearly killed me." Bassett, she told me, is in the white pine and tobacco country twenty miles north of the Carolina border. Her grandfather and his two brothers all lived within a quarter-mile radius of each other. Her father managed 1,100 of the

2,700 acres that had been in the family for six generations, since the first Philpotts came south from Maryland.

Tradition had kept the Philpott clan strong for that whole time. "On the Fourth of July," Patrice told me, "we always fry millions and millions of fish in the cabin by the lake. It used to be that all my cousins would come, but now some of them are starting not to. We're losing some of our sense of belonging. Now so many Philpotts, and others too, are moving out of Bassett that it's hard to tell *what's* going on. My grandfather's children and his two brothers' children all still live at home, but my cousins are starting to move away, which makes me right sad. It scares me to think that our family might not go on. In this past century we've hardly changed at all, but what's going to happen in the *next* fifty years?"

"In grade school," Patrice told me, "after I didn't make cheerleader, I dated the son of some mill people, who told him, 'Don't you know there's no sense your going out with a rich girl like her?'" But by most standards the Philpotts aren't rich. They make no pretense of belonging to that species called FFVs—first families of Virginia—most of whom have money. From what I could tell, the Philpotts were wealthy chiefly in their sense of tribe. "Once somebody came to one of our reunions and said that if he died and could come back as someone else he'd want to come back as a Philpott, because the Philpotts have more fun," said Patrice, "but he didn't know how much *work* goes into all that fun. We're some hard-working people, we Philpotts." Her father works at a lumber factory in addition to managing the land. Her mother has a job in an insurance office. As for Patrice herself, she had just "nearly *killed* myself over a term paper for Textiles that my roommate had the nerve to say I'd plagiarized from hers."

Hard work: that is one of the Philpotts' myths about themselves. Later I learned the other. Philpotts, I heard, have "never seen a stranger"; they don't sit back and wait for it to come to them, whatever "it" might be, preferring to go get it themselves; they are hospitable, eschewing front doors in favor of the friendlier ones that lead straight into kitchens; they believe that the hardest thing to open is a closed mind, and they help each other. If any bad fate should befall a Philpott, perish forbid, there'd be no need to call for outside help, so quickly would other Philpotts swarm to the rescue.

When Patrice said I ought to visit Bassett myself, as soon as I had a chance to, I felt as if a Rockefeller had told me which mat the key was under at Pocantico Hills. When my Georgia duties were done I made a point of stopping by in Bassett, just in time for the Fairy

Stone Park reunion. But I got there late. Kindly ladies with narrow eyes much like Patrice's were wrapping what was left of their pies in foil, getting ready to carry them home. Granny, Patrice's father's mother, took my hand in hers, which was dry and warm, and led me around to meet such Philpotts and Prillamans and others as remained at the picnic, and to sense the spirit of those who had gone before. Most of those present scolded me gently for my tardy arrival, but assured me there would be other reunions. I believed them. It was quite plain that in a world of uncertainty and dread, one sure thing is that the Philpotts of Henry County can always come up with some reason or other, every few weeks or months, to stage another family reunion.

"Jee-ma-*nee*," the Philpotts said, "gol-*lee*, good*night*. If she's come all this way to find out about us"—they were talking about me—"then we'd better show her who we are. Let's see, why *are* we so special? Has she met A.L.?" A.L., I learned, is Patrice's father Charlie's double-first cousin, and the Philpott clan's hero. Every family, however humble, has its hero—if not its lieutenant-governor then its choirmaster, its all-state diving champion, its postmistress—the one all the others work into their conversations as often and as proudly as they can. A. L. Philpott, Granny told me, "not only is in the General Assembly, he *is* the General Assembly. At the House of Delegates they used to tease him and say he had enough family to put down the opposition right there. He's one of the most forceful, dynamic speakers you ever heard. Twice he was voted the most influential member of the legislature. He's not in favor of the Equal Rights Amendment, because he thinks a lot of things are in there that if women understood better, they'd be against it, too." But Philpott women are not necessarily docile. Joanne, Patrice's mother, would rather work as a licensed agent at an insurance office, "than stay home and make strawberry preserves, like someone said she ought to," her daughter told me. "She says she'd rather earn her own money to go out and *buy* the preserves."

A.L. chose not to talk about the E.R.A. to me. Instead he told me the history of Fairy Stone Park—fairy stones, he said, are little rocks shaped like angels' tears turned to crosses—and Philpott Dam Park, which was once on Philpott property, "then it went to the Feds, and was worked on by the C.C.C. and the W.P.A. The Confederate bills they paid for it never were redeemed." A.L., I heard, was the son of John, one of the three original brothers who settled these acres. "When those brothers dissolved the lumber-mercantile family business partnership," Patrice's Aunt Edna told me, "they didn't keep but one account for all three. Only when they got married did they divide up all the accounts. When John took a contract to do something with the dam, they sent him a check for it and he divided it with the other two. Now *that's* what I call loyalty."

The next afternoon we visited Aunt Edna. "Aunt Edna had a heart attack," Patrice told me, "and since all the fluid's gathered around her heart, she has to lie down for an hour after every meal." Aunt Edna is the widowed mother of Pewee, who lives way over on the hill. She received us regally. On her bedside table were *Times to Remember* and *First Lady*, and a family Bible, with a clip inside of a picture of Pat Nixon, with a penciled note: "Isn't this lovely?" We also visited John's widow, Aunt Gertrude, in whose living room photographs of the women in the family were framed in gold on one wall, facing wood-framed pictures of men across the room.

Birdsong wakened me that morning in Patrice's bedroom, which she had insisted on vacating for me. I woke between striped pink and lavender sheets, and beheld around me the artifacts of her life: a college beer mug, animal figurines with whimsical faces, Anya Seton's *Green Darkness*, Norman Vincent Peale's *You Can If You Think You Can*, a Girl Scout merit badge banner, a Valentine candy box, electric curlers, a picture of a young man, a camp sign with her name burnt on it, stuffed ice cream cones, and posters captioned "LOVE CAN WARM THE LONELIEST PLACES" and "DO YOU LOVE ME OR DO YOU NOT? YOU TOLD ME ONCE, BUT I FORGOT."

Breakfast that morning was creamed dried beef on the screened-in porch on Granny's side of the house she shares with her son and his wife and their daughters. Creamed dried beef on the screened-in porch while the dew was still on the roses. One of the dew-covered roses was our centerpiece. Granny told of her church, the Primitive Baptists. "What we believe," she said, "is that your destiny is determined before the foundation of the world. My father was a religious man who lived his belief by day. What he believed, and I do too, is that God foreknew what you would do and how you would live, and that we were all born to either go to heaven or to hell."

"But if it's all foreordained," asked Patrice's younger sister Jamie, "then what's the point of trying?" This question was not resolved that morning. Granny did agree that there were a lot of good people who hadn't joined the Primitive Baptists, and that you don't have to join a church to get to heaven. But her own baptism had been "the most wonderful thang on earth—I was totally immersed in a creek in the middle of winter, and didn't feel one bit cold."

Strong faith, many think, makes strong families. A corollary exists to link the decline of family with the decline of organized religion. The families I see most of on my own time tend toward the secular, but consider Cora Taylor, Otto Muller, and Papou Ngagoyeanis: can there ever have been families more tightly knit than theirs, or more intensely religious? So too with the Philpotts, and a number of other cohesive southern families. Churches in the south are nearly impossible to escape. An agnostic divorcee I met who had moved to Atlanta from Minneapolis got so tired of having neighbors ask which was the church of her choice that she finally thought of a scheme to silence them. She and her children would get all dressed up of a Sunday morning in their best clothes, pull out of their driveway at half-past ten, return a couple of hours later, and never tell anybody that where they really had been for that whole time was at a Dunkin' Donuts.

Not so the Philpotts, or anyone else to speak of in Bassett, where the Baptists and Methodists compete for newcomers. "The Baptists were declining," Patrice told me, "until Reverend Page, a new Billy Graham-type guy, came in two years ago. He's so emotional I even got drug into it myself—I went to a revival where everyone else was cryin' and I got to cryin', too. I do feel like people have to go to church every *noun* then, even though I can sense God myself when I ride through the woods on a horse."

Patrice's parents, her mother told me, are "both real active in the Methodist church. Charlie was on the board of trustees, president of Methodist Men, and taught Sunday school. I was treasurer of the Women's Society of Christian Service, and on the Methodist Youth Fellowship. I do Scout volunteer work, too. Charlie comes along and helps me with that. He likes it better than getting involved in Kiwanis meetings and such. It doesn't pay for both members of the family to get involved in community work, because if you do that, all you can hope is to meet each other coming and going, if you're lucky. I keep pestering for the public schools—been to every board meeting since January—and I've taught kindergarten and substituted in third grade, worked for the Census bureau measuring for bomb shelters—that was pretty silly, now I look back on it—and worked in an architecture office, too."

"We haven't fully country-ized Mama yet," Patrice said. "When she came here in 1957 she had lived in bigger towns and even in Europe, and she still has some of her city ways. She's still afraid of the animals, sometimes." Joanne was married at age twenty to Charles Philpott, who, as Patrice said, "looks just the way he did in his V.P.I. graduation picture. He used to be in the mortgage business, but now he's at the factory. He's the most unprejudiced man I ever met, and very observant, too. His job is to buy lumber from all over the U.S., and he knows so much about the lumber business he can tell you all about whatever floor you may be standing on. He plays golf some, but he doesn't go in for country clubs and that sort of thing. He'd rather hunt or fish or talk to cows."

"You done shot your schedule up," Charlie said to me, as my visit to Bassett kept lengthening. "You shot it up plumb."

"But she's got to find out more about us," said his daughter Laura. I wished I had at least a month to learn more about the Philpotts. Later that day they took me on a tour through the green-and-yellow landscape and wild daisies and ragged robins, back to Fairy Stone Creek and the old post office, past the factory, to a mill end shop to buy cheap sweatshirts, to visit a cousin who edited a newspaper, and to visit another whose daughter was soon to get married. That house was prosperous, with a lawn of Astroturf around its swimming pool, and a basement full of wedding presents, which were all to the bride's taste except for a set of matching luggage. The going-away suitcases weren't quite the right shade of blue.

I guess all the Philpotts will go away someday. I guess their sherbet-colored suitcases will bounce down conveyor belts in distant airports, unpacked in frantic and smelly places far from Henry County. I guess maybe this has to happen, but I'm not pleased at the prospect, and I can see why Patrice isn't, either. Just before it was time for me to head north myself, I went for a walk in the family cemetery with her and her sisters Laura and Jamie—Laura English Philpott, named for her mother's people, and Susan Jamison Philpott, named for the paternal side. We walked among the tombstones, marked at the feet as well as at the heads, while horses named Sundance and Apple and Spirit cantered and neighed on the hillside above us, and locusts droned around us.

"I feel sorry for only children," Patrice had told me earlier, "because they have more troubles than those of us who were raised up in families." I have always felt that way too, I told her. But the Philpott sisters, like my own and I, had their moments of discord. As the four of us walked over the bones of their Philpott forebears, Jamie unthinkingly broke a family rule, for which her sisters scolded her at once.

"It's *gross*," they told her, "to stand on graves"—a belief held in many times and places outside Bassett, Virginia. "To touch a tomb with his foot, even by chance, was an impious act," Fustel de Coulanges writes in *The Ancient City*, "after which the guilty one was expected to pacify the dead and purify himself." In *Fire in the Lake*,

Frances FitzGerald tells of an old Vietnamese man who resisted evacuation, asking, "If I leave, the graves of my ancestors, too, will become forest. How can I have the heart to leave?"

Mac had a lot to say about graves, too. Mac is a neighbor of my cousin Jenny's, a short walk from the Gulf of Mexico in Mississippi. I hoped that we might swim in the Gulf the afternoon I spent with him and Jenny, but since he and she preferred the pool of his apartment complex, that was where we sat and swam and talked. Mac talked, rather, while we listened. Mac had two subjects he warmed to particularly: his work at the National Aeronautics and Space Administration, and families—his own and everybody else's.

"I kind of think that one of the most fantastic things that ever happened to the south," said Mac, "was being defeated, because defeat is what's kept the clans intact. Your basic Scotch-Irish stock, with the exception of the French influence here in Cajun country, is what settled the South and most of the rest of this country, too, and that's *very* clannish stock. The family, the clan, was everything, because in the wilderness it meant survival.

"A man would leave his wife when he went off to war, and by God he'd leave her with a gun, and if she had to be the protector, then she would be. That's what happened with my grandmother. I want to know all I *can* about my own family. I'm thirty-nine years old, and my father died before I ever had a real chance to talk to him. Sometimes when I'm confused about something, I'll say, 'Mother, what would Daddy have done?' I was born when he was forty. He was an old-fashioned man. He always said that if you saw something wrong and *knew* it was wrong and didn't do anything about it, you were as guilty as whoever did do it. He said to me once, 'Mac, when I die, I ain't gonna leave you anything—I ain't got any money—but we sure did have fun, didn't we? If we wanted to go hunt and fish or swim, we went, didn't we? I'll tell you something, Mac, there ain't no pockets in them shrouds.'

"The day my dad died I was the one went to the undertaker, because in Baptist families it's the tradition to let the youngest pick the gravesite, the hymns, and the coffin. The undertaker said to me, 'Little Mac, we want the best for Uncle Bob, don't we?' and I said to him, 'Oscar Lee, my daddy was a very plain man.' The coffin Oscar Lee wanted to sell me cost $2,700, but the simple gray steel one I liked wasn't but $740. My daddy died with just enough left for a tank of gas, but what a legacy—me and my brothers, we went through a great deal of hell-raising, but we had a great deal of love, too.

"The older you grow, the more you come back to that sort of thing. The older you grow, the more you come back to the family." Saying this, Mac jumped into the pool, breast-stroked two lengths, and climbed out. My cousin Jenny asked him to join us at her house for a drink. Juleps, she had promised, for my sake.

"I'll be right over in ten minutes," Mac said as he dried his head. "First I want to call my little boy."

Another afternoon, in Louisiana, I talked with a mother of another little boy. She was disappointed in her son. But before she could tell me exactly how, she had to say what it had been like to be a child herself, thirty-some years earlier in a small town. As she talked, I sat spellbound:

"I can remember the day my innocence was shattered," she said. "I was fifteen, in an inner tube on a lake, when a jet suddenly and audibly screamed across the sky. I was *offended*, deeply. Before that, everything had been clear in the small town where I grew up. You knew what your status was, and everybody else knew too, but nobody dwelt on it. I had a closer association with black kids than with mill people.

"Blacks are purer down where I grew up," my hostess went on, "though crime in small towns is very bad and getting worse, and most of the criminals are black and young. When I was a child it was rumored there was a black nightclub over in the woods. My cousin, whom I grew up with, and I went out one day looking for that nightclub. He was from a large family that had a lot of money. Their house had real columns, not the cardboard kind. That meant real security. Everybody, blacks and whites too, knew our family. We could go anywhere around there and not be afraid.

"My cousin and I had some idea of where that nightclub was, and we found it. It was called the Golden Goblet and it made me think of *To Kill a Mockingbird*—going there was a real adventure. Late that Saturday afternoon my cousin and I parked our jeep in front of that place, held hands, told each other not to be afraid, and went into an enormous room, with silver gardenias everywhere and pictures of all the movie stars, a jukebox, a bar. We ordered Cokes.

"The bartender knew who my cousin's father was, and made us admit that nobody in our families knew where we were. 'I'll serve you the Cokes,' the bartender said, 'but I don't think you ought to stay here.' Over in the corner was this absolutely stunning black girl, with hair plaited just like Merle Oberon's, wearing tons and tons of bracelets. I became intrigued with her and smiled at her. She smiled back. She was the first person I ever knew nothing about whom I felt, literally *felt*, from way across the room. I looked at her, in her elaborate dress, and wanted to touch her. She had a very soft voice, not thick like some black voices are. She noticed I'd been watching her and could tell I didn't want to leave. I wanted to stay there and go ask her to tell me about life.

"The man at the bar told my cousin and me to go, said he wouldn't tell our folks we'd been there if we would just leave. We got in the jeep and I looked back. She was standing in the door. I turned around and looked at that girl for as long as I could, and she looked at me, and I silently prayed, Please, don't let there be a curve in the road. And I said out loud, *very* loud, 'I'm going to be just like you someday,' and you know, for two or three years of my life, I *was* just like her. All my life there've been split seconds when I've *felt* that girl.

"I never saw her again and didn't want to. I wanted her to remain an illusion. I had to tell my curiosity that it couldn't go any further. She was eighteen or nineteen then with an innocent look, but I *knew* her—maybe it was some soul-sister kind of subconscious understanding. She must have understood, too, otherwise she wouldn't have got up and walked toward the door to watch, as my cousin and I drove away.

"That's the kind of thinking the south breeds, because down here absolutely everything is seeable, feelable, and I was hoping my son and his friend would realize that, when I took them down to the town where I came from, a few weeks ago. But they did everything so quickly! They looked at the lake the same way they'd look at a TV set. They didn't *associate* themselves with it at all. Nothing in our whole trip down there just overwhelmed or drew them, the way it had me when I was a child. Maybe that's the trouble with watching so much television—kids who watch it as much as all kids do now forget how many other ways there are to spend time—if indeed they ever knew. Maybe it's our fault, for not teaching them.

"Me, every time I go down home, I just *run* to the lake, but for them there was no such abandon. It's not just them, it's their whole generation.They don't even know what it means to think of free-falling without a net. They didn't know what I meant when I told them to 'get out there, it holds you, *it* tells you, if you'll listen.'

"My mother was a good spinner of tales. She'd sit with a rifle in her lap—she was a good shot—and tell stories. But in the city now these boys have no one, nothing like that. They have too much information, and no ability to forget what they've learned and known. When I took them to the old grist mill and the old cemetery, they didn't even want to play hide-and-seek. I thought if I could run and leap around the lake and draw great big pictures in the sand, they might get the idea and at least physically imitate me, but these boys were so cautious, so tiptoeing, always asking, 'Is it safe?'

"They didn't even make big footprints the way I did, and if there's one thing you should *always* do, it's leave a trail behind you. I told them that. But they didn't listen."

These southern family arias nourished me far more reliably than azaleas or grits. They were delivered in places and by people I would least have expected. Once I heard such an aria in a bar outside Athens, from a television crew member who just had finished filming part of a series on campus. He was about to pay for his drinks and leave when the word "family" was mentioned. He began to tell of his clan in western North Carolina. "Anyone of my generation could name every one of their great-great-grandfathers," he said. "Now my people are scattered all the way from West Virginia to Florida, in search of work, and the clannishness is gone. Two great-uncles, who were twin brothers, got rich in Sarasota, so I guess now everybody's middle-class. My mother lives now with a double first cousin in Sarasota, because Uncle Hugh and Uncle Lew went there in the Depression. Their sister, my Aunt Leona, had gone there first and established some roots.

"But when I tell our kids we're going *home*, they know I mean Carolina, even though they weren't born there themselves. I go back there even though it makes me very depressed to see what has happened, the way the topography has changed so drastically. I guess the North Carolina highway department did to us what we did to the Cherokees a hundred years earlier, when the Trail of Tears deed was written with a quill pen in 1836.

"In the middle of the 1950s came such a road-building mania, that my people got surveyed and paved flat out of existence. Now a huge four-lane road runs through that valley, and all that's left is a church on the top of a hill, and the damn drag lines, scoops, and pans. Their road-building equipment is awesome, and what they use it for is awesome too—to buy out the people and move them to the small towns, cities, wherever they'll go.

"My grandmother's first cousin lived in a log cabin all his life, with no electricity. He'd set there on the porch in the peak of health at age 89, but when the highway came through, tearing down that little house of his, he died within six months. My grandmother's birthplace house is still standing, and so is her father's, up in the hollows, but they'll get to them sometime, too. Madisons, McAlisters, Snows, Conklins—at least a dozen family names go back to these people. The total clan I'm talking about had three or four hundred people, each of whom knew how he was related to all the others.

"Any great-aunt or great-uncle of mine had the same authority over me that my own parents had. We all went to the Pine Valley Baptist Church. Aunt Jodie lived in a log house on the original site, the original 1830 log house, until she was in her eighties when she fell off a ladder. She fell off a ladder and broke her leg, and she wouldn't let the doctor remove her dress to set it. He had to cut her dress to do the leg. She left her land to the church but said that if ever a stringed instrument was played in that church, the land would revert to the heirs, who now number something like five hundred. How we'd divide it up, or how she'd know, I can't say, but I known for sure that if it's at all possible, I'd like to be buried in that church graveyard where nearly everybody is my kin.

"Those highway people committed cultural genocide. I've got two uncles and half a dozen first cousins left there, but they're all scattered in the mountains and hollows. The highway department killed my great-aunt, too. She threatened to shoot a bulldozer operator with a rifle, because she had an apple orchard the creek flowed through. They blasted rock in that ruined creek and said, 'We're gonna have to cut a new creek bed,' one that would flow through what was left of her apple orchard. They offered to compensate her, and the man very patronizingly asked, 'How'll we get the rocks out of here?'

" 'Same way you got them in,' she said. 'I don't know what way *that* was, but *you* must know.' She laid a 30-30 Winchester rifle across her lap as she sat there in her rocking chair and said, 'Go down and tell your men they may drive the bulldozer *into* my field if they want to, but they won't be driving it out.'

"They had to get a flatbed lowboy truck to haul a crane and go a hundred miles round-trip, picking the rocks up one by one. They did put them back where they were, too, like she wanted. She was eighty years old, my great-aunt was, and she said it didn't matter what happened to her because the bulldozer operators knew that she really *would* shoot them.

"Those of my family who are left sit around of an evening talking of remarks that were made, hell, seventy years ago. They don't just tell of how in 1957—that was when we first got electricity and plumbing—they bulldozed a water-wheel owned by my great-grandparents. They tell of Pete Conklin, a very peculiar man who never married, and how he had his hair cut once a year on the same day. He grew a long beard that always had flour and corn meal in it, and had a sack of corn and a sack of wheat and drank whiskey at the mill all day long.

"At least a dozen houses there were owned by people I called Aunt or Uncle or some kind of cousin. These were all old people by the time I was ten or twelve; then came my mother's generation, then my own. They tell of a hound dog and a calf who sort of fell in love, named Trouble and Hard Times. They tell how Aunt Maude demanded to be baptized, at age seventy-plus, having decided she'd go to hell if she wasn't immersed in water. They lowered her into the water in her wheelchair, then she read the Bible one more time and came to the conclusion that she should convert from Methodist to Baptist.

"I had two distant cousins, old ladies who lived with Uncle Jared, who died at the age of a hundred and three. He was a leather craftsman, mystic, and prophet. He'd cure our warts. Once, so help me God, he took a wart off my elbow. Not until World War Two did these people have any communication with the outside world. I rode horses to the water-wheel mill and lived pretty much a nineteenth-century life myself, till I was almost in my teens. You see people now trying to rough it, ordering all these mock-rustic catalogues —what they're looking for is what we had—a constant steady flow of spring water piped down through hollow logs and channeled into what was called a spring house. We had vineyards and ice-cold bulk butter and blackberries and strawberries and applesauce and smoked meat—all the stuff my wife gets at the supermarket today, only a lot better.

"My uncle's been screwed every way you could imagine," this man told me as we walked toward our cars in the bar's parking lot. "His land was paved, his river is polluted, his son came back from Vietnam in bad shape, his company laid him off, and now in his middle fifties, he's out of work, diabetic and faced with the prospect of the government building a four-lane highway through his property. All our land of more than two thousand acres is now prime asphalt and gravel.

"The families, the families just aren't there anymore."

But I think he is wrong. I hope he is, anyway. Southern families may not be easy to locate or to connect with, but they still are there, and if they decide to reduce the 25-year trial period before they relax with strangers, then maybe those of us who pass through the south will fare better. I should like, on my own next visit, to meet people like an 84-year-old father I read about, who refers to his nationally distinguished 61-year-old son as "the boy."

It would be illuminating to hear his answer to the question I asked the social scientists at the conference: "Just what *is* it that makes a good family?"

The 7:40 A.M. ferry for Patchogue leaves Watch Hill in five minutes, and it's clear I won't be on it. It's clear I seem to need the sun and brine. I wasn't even planning to stay overnight; I thought I'd catch the late boat after the soy-soaked mackerel, the squash melange and the brownies. But the others asked me to stay; they said it would be good for me to get my mind off families.

For a while it worked. For a while Dave and Sue and I played Scrabble, achieving nice words: ORBS, BALSAM, VIXEN, REAPING. But then we talked and what did we talk about? What does anybody ever talk about?

Tom told how depressed he had been since the death a month ago of his much older brother. Now, at 51, he is obliged to become his family's patriarch, a role he never sought and does not relish but must assume, because his niece, in her thirties, asked him: "Will you be my father now?"

George tells of his parents: of his father who died when George was quite young, and of his mother and her sister, who both were aristocrats who married men they considered diamonds-in-the-rough. Each of the sisters had just one son. The boy cousins were raised as brothers until a seething feud developed between their mothers. The feud concerned an aged aunt whose most fundamental needs, rotated between the two sisters, were smelly and inconvenient. Each sister thought she did all the work. They stopped speaking. George and his cousin finally decided on their own that the feud was silly and need not concern them. When their mothers don't know it, they get together. Their friendship has resumed.

Loretta is still asleep on the other tiny narrow bed in the room she and I share. She fidgets. She dreams perhaps of her older son Eric, who at age twenty-three lies newly conscious in a Connecticut hospital. For six weeks he had been in a coma resulting from a motorcycle accident.

Loretta and the nurses all despaired of Eric's ever wakening at all, or regaining his intelligence, or speech, or motion, but the latest news was good: he had brushed his teeth! Not only that, but when Loretta had looked down at Eric, after he woke from his coma, to ask if he knew who she was, he looked up at her and smiled.

"I'd say I knew you rather well," he told her.

And I came here to get away from talk of families.

A Question of Scale

Inherited wealth is a real handicap to happiness. It is as certain a death to ambition as cocaine is to morality.
　　　　　　　　　　　　—Willie K. Vanderbilt

Superior worth is felt to inhere in blood which has been associated with many goods and great power.
　　　　　　　　　　　　—Thorstein Veblen,
　　　　　　　　　　　　The Theory of the Leisure Class

How restricted is the life of people who have the fewest restrictions? . . . How secluded the life of people who range farther and wider than their countrymen?
　　　　　　　　　　　　—Robert Coles
　　　　　　　　　　　　The Privileged Ones

IT'S NOT EXACTLY a storefront church, St. Oswald's. You don't hear a lot of clapping and wailing from inside, nor are its parishioners much given to the taking up of serpents or the washing of one another's feet. The charismatic revival, to date at least, has passed them by. Pew for pew, it would be hard to find in all the five boroughs of New York City a more elegant, privileged, and restrained congregation than this one. The faces at St. Oswald's made me remember reading somewhere that a man's education, like his nutrition, begins 250 years before he is born.

Before I met the Druytens, I never had been to St. Oswald's. I seldom go to church at all, much less on the East Side. I must fight being bigoted about the East Side the way some people are bigoted about French Canadians. Three or four friends of mine live there, friends whose company gladdens my soul, but I usually try to lure them westward rather than visit in their part of town. Their part of town seems to me stuffy and pinched and intimidating. But generalizing is dangerous. One recent Friday, at a party on of all places Park Avenue, I met a roomful of people who despite their evident wealth weren't stuffy at all. They were lively talkers. Among them was a woman who declared she was "sick and tired of all the clichés about poor little rich kids, and how sinister privileged families are.

"Some families with money," she insisted, "are exemplary. They not only have brains and wealth and looks, but they're magnificent people besides."

"I'm on the lookout for families like that," I said.

"You ought to meet them," she said. "All the *wrong* rich people get the attention. The ones who deserve acclaim shrink from it. The best family I know in this whole city is the one that minds publicity the most."

"Who are they?"

"I can't tell you. They wouldn't want me to. Their motto is 'Those who talk most say least.' Too bad, because if you did know them, you'd see how ideal a family can be."

"But if they're all *that* great, the world ought to know about them."

"It does, for the wrong reasons."

"Maybe I could tell the right reasons if I changed their name?"

"Maybe," the woman said. She'd see. Could I write a letter explaining what it was that interested me about families? If I could drop such a letter off at her building the next morning, before she flew off for a fortnight in Rome, she would make sure that my letter reached her nameless friends.

On Saturday I rose before daybreak to list in my letter some of the questions that had been on my mind: "What can shattered families learn from those that endure? What stereotypes about families ought to be abolished? Is blood still thicker than water? Can friendship replace kinship? Should the terms 'clan' and 'tribe' be redefined? How important to a family are ritual, myth, and religion; sense of place, property, history and purpose; elders, founders, networks of outsiders? To what extent do adversity and guilt keep families together?

"Sometime quite soon," I said in concluding this letter, "I must decide on a privileged, intact, and somewhat prolific family interested enough in these same questions to let me pay it a few visits within the next month." With luck, such visits would not only let me sample the texture of privileged family life but teach me a few tricks about making sense out of a profusion of options. If I thought I had trouble with too many choices, how must it be for people like these?

On Sunday my telephone rang. "You don't know me," began the voice at the other end, "but I'm Susan Druyten." So! The mystery family! A famous name, Druyten. Streets, dormitories, wings of hospitals were named for this family. I had seen the name on museum plaques and on the lists of symphony patrons. It had been a big name since the time of Nieuw Amsterdam. The first Druytens, I later read, came to this continent in the late 1600s, from the Netherlands, to buy and farm vast tracts of land. Some of this land had been sold by the original Druytens' heirs' sons' heirs' sons, to invest in tobacco. The name's renown seemed to spring half from philanthropy and half from avarice. The family seemed to have two subspecies: the stewards and the squanderers. Just now the stewards were in the ascendant. Years had passed since any Druyten had caused a gossipy scandal. Stewards never make much news.

Susan Druyten, she told me, was at work on her doctorate in abnormal psychology, so as to become a more informed trustee of two hospitals and two schools. Belden, her husband, had retired ten years earlier from the family tobacco business, and now spent most of his time on a task force to improve the city school system. Celia, their eldest daughter, was halfway through medical school, newly married at age 25 to an orthopedic surgeon. Phyllis, a year younger than Celia, wasn't really Susan's daughter but her niece. She and Caroline, her younger sister, had been adopted when their parents and two brothers were killed in a plane crash. Phyllis had married a lobsterman in Rhode Island. Their life was arduous. They rose at five to tend to their pots and traps. Rachel, Phyllis's age, was a librarian who lived in rural New Jersey with her ecologist husband.

Gail was a senior at Beloit. Caroline, Phyllis's sister, was in Madrid for her junior year abroad, on leave from Smith. Pamela was a freshman at Bowdoin and Helen in her junior year at Exeter. Belden's and Susan's nest was empty for the first time, but they were both so preoccupied with their projects that they scarcely noticed. Susan had several tests and papers looming at graduate school, but my topic interested her. Families, her own and her husband's and most others, seemed to fascinate her as much as they did me. Lunch Wednesday?

Lunch Wednesday, I agreed, and spent Monday and Tuesday

thinking about such rich families as I had known before, wondering what generalizations, if any, might be made about the way they raise children. There are rich families, of course, and rich families. There are Boston Irish patriarchs who give each of their children a million dollars, "so they can tell the world to go to hell." There is feudal old money, and there are *arrivistes* who hire press agents to wangle debuts for their daughters. There are Houston oil couples who drive twin Rolls-Royces and say things like "We've just had a *keen* idea for a trip! What about a horse ride through Hungary?" There are Boston stockbrokers who think it such a keen idea never to throw out old clothes that a visitor in a new shirt feels a parvenu.

There are Chicago orthodontists and Montana ranchers. There is a Delaware manufacturer who no more questions chartering a plane to fly his children to their New Hampshire ski house than I would question investing in an Add-A-Ride on a crosstown bus. Some rich families raise their children to pick up checks with what one clan I know calls the "dispenser mentality"; others rarely carry cash. A millionaire's wife I once knew in Ohio proudly wore "hand-me-ups" from her daughters. "Our children are much richer than we are," she told me, "because my husband's father never wanted me to have access to his mythical wealth." Her husband's mother never wanted his daughters to have summer jobs. "Nice people," she told them, "don't work."

I knew one rich family whose Fourth of July custom it was to spit watermelon seeds at one another across their Regency dining-room table, and another so timid they rarely said anything except in the passive voice. Instead of announcing "I tied the knot!" they would report that the knot had been tied. I used to know another man whose parents, word had it, "own half of Nebraska, and his wife's people own most of what's left." That wasn't too much of an exaggeration, apparently. In his bachelor days, before he turned thirty, this man had a brownstone building all his own in the East Seventies, and employed a live-in manservant to keep his shoes polished and to drive him around town. In his wallet was a picture of a baronial-looking house outside Omaha.

"Can you imagine?" he would ask, showing the snapshot. "We *live* in that!"

Another man I know used to take walks on the beach at Cape Cod with his dog. One day while he and the dog were walking on the beach, a teen-age boy jogged by them. The playful dog ran alongside the boy and took a playful nip at the boy's leg, just above the ankle.

"Ow!" said the boy, and limped off to tell his father. His father swaggered up to the man with the dog, demanding his name. The man with the dog said his name. The jogger's father said nothing more, and walked away.

The man with the dog had a daughter, who asked, when he took her to restaurants, "Do I have to have chicken or do I get to have steak?" When the daughter was eleven her family went for a skiing vacation to a resort she said was "so fancy that everyone else there, if you can imagine, was even richer than *us!*" Hearing her say this, her father beckoned her aside for an urgent talking-to.

Another father I know forbade his son to go on a long-awaited camping trip, because the boy had lost a sweater. "Never mind," the boy said thirty years later, "that my dad could have stocked several department stores with new sweaters without noticing the cost—he wanted me to know what a lost sweater would have meant when *he* was a boy, before he'd made his pile. It was as if he were saying, 'You ungrateful whelp! *I'll* teach you to take your heritage for granted!'" That boy was coached to deny being "rich"; if the subject had to come up at all, the terms preferred were "well-off," or "fortunate," or "comfortable."

That boy told me how he used to crouch in the back seat of the family limousine when the chauffeur would drive him to school, so his classmates wouldn't see him arriving in such style. The only child I ever have heard of who felt otherwise was a chauffeur's daughter. She sat tall and proud in the back seat, behind her visor-capped father, on mornings when he could sneak time off to drive her to parochial school. That girl did well in school; in later years her father would boast: "Our Kate, she's got more degrees than a thermometer!"

Once, for a while, his Kate worked as a fund-raiser. Her task was to call up everyone she could think of who might have access to money. At a party she had met the son of a manufacturer, many years dead. She phoned the manufacturer's son, to ask whether he knew who was in charge of philanthropic disbursements at the firm his father had founded.

"I have *nothing* to do with that place!" the manufacturer's son told her, and slammed down the phone.

Every rich family, I guess, is rich in its own way.

Susan Druyten's Wednesday lunch was boiled hot dogs, watercress and avocado salad, and Lipton's tea. Our digressive talk lasted most of the afternoon. "Belden's father always told us it was not a good idea to have too many homes," she said, "and sometimes even *two* houses seem one too many, especially now with all the girls gone." It was odd: seven vacant Fifth Avenue bedrooms, overlooking the Central Park Reservoir. It seemed even odder to reflect on the often total emptiness of the Druytens' other house, on the family's 65-acre compound a two-hour drive up the Hudson River. But the absent Druytens were there in pictures: photographs, silhouettes, oil portraits, watercolors, enlarged snapshots, group and individual wedding pictures, graduation pictures, and huge reunion pictures, taken under a row of elm trees, of all 37 living members of Belden's branch of the Druytens, at their annual gathering. All these pictures were framed in silver or leather or gold, like icons. They were icons. This apartment was as much a shrine to the notion of family as any dwelling in all America.

"The families Belden and I grew up in were very different," Susan said, "but we were both brought up to believe that families were more important than anything. My own parents were constantly at each other's throats, and I vowed that the things that came between them would never come between Belden and me. Not that we haven't had troubles in *this* family," she said. "If there's anything I can't stand it's those third-person Christmas cards that make everybody's life sound so idyllic. Every family *I've* ever been close to has been meted out a certain amount of misfortune, if not outright tragedy. People are very private about these things, but they're there all the same."

Susan's creed, as bits of it emerged in our talk, seemed classically and winningly old-fashioned: "I'm not one for wild embraces but I *do* like deference; I could never think of going through a door before an older person. Most of the rules of etiquette boil down to plain common sense." By temperament she is an archivist, a compulsive keeper of scrapbooks and journals, and a saver of all old correspondence "except the letters Belden wrote me from Germany just after we'd been married—he made me burn them because they were just too personal." She is also an enemy, futile though she knows the fight to be, of the telephone.

"But, Mum," her oldest daughter once complained, "everybody else in this whole *school* calls up their families on Sunday."

"Too bad," Susan replied. "That's not the way *we* do things."

The Druyten way is to write frequent letters and save mementoes to be glued, and extensively captioned, in the giant monogrammed leather scrapbook each girl gets when she goes off to college. "I *hate* doing these scrapbooks, especially now that graduate school takes up so much of my time," said Susan, "but I do think it's important for the girls to have records of their own history, and in context, too." By "context" she meant the headlines she had clipped from the *Times* about hurricanes, the moon landing, and Nixon's resignation. Nixon's name, I later learned, was never allowed to be mentioned at the Druytens'. So much for clichés about the politics of Fifth Avenue Episcopalians.

"Aristocracy" is a word that all her life has made Susan cringe. So has the phrase *"noblesse oblige."* "We used to have to shake hands and say that every Friday night at the bonfire, at a French camp I was sent to in Canada. Even then I couldn't stand it, it sounded so condescending." For what I gathered were similar reasons, she rejoiced in the Revised Standard Version of the Holy Bible. "Isn't 'faith, hope, and love' so much more to the point than 'faith, hope, and charity'?"

" 'Charity' is probably a more loaded word in a household like ours than among welfare recipients," Belden said when he joined us later. "The household I grew up in minded it even more." Belden was born, as was Charles Lindbergh's first baby, in 1930. When the Lindbergh boy was kidnaped, a bodyguard was hired to sit all night outside the windows of Belden and his older sisters. No sense taking chances. Spared, Belden learned at the age of five to kill a chicken, at the age of twelve to shoot a rifle, and by the time he was fourteen, to drive around leaving calling cards all over Washington, D.C., where his father then held a federal post.

"Mom! Dad! Watch!" most children shout as they leap from diving boards or attempt any other new feat. Belden probably never was like that. At school, and later at Princeton, Belden won all the awards there were to win, for prowess in athletics and in that ineffable thing called "citizenship." These awards gave him little pleasure and were never even alluded to at home; undue praise might go to a child's head, and was as out of place as undue affection. Competition and achievement were as much taken for granted as trimness of physique. Whoever it was said you can't be too rich or too thin, and that for a long race you need a lean horse, might have had the Druytens in mind. Belden's abundant hair turned white in his thirties, the way his father's did, and Susan's is not as startlingly blond as it looks in early photographs, but they both seem to embody what Thorstein Veblen in *The Theory of the Leisure Class* called the "dolicho-blond temperament"—long headed, fair-haired people of "gentle blood" who tend to take great pride in, among other things, their lawns.

I thought of this a week later, when I saw the Druyten lawn my-self: an astonishing expanse that rolls for a full and well-manicured mile back from the road to their house, and goes past a stable and a swimming pool and a tennis court before it slopes down to the river. Kempt green lawns, to paraphrase Veblen, comfort dolicho-blonds, the way well-grazed pastures comforted their primitive ancestors. The houses on this Hudsonville compound looked reassuring, too. The place isn't as elegant as the Rockefeller retreat at Pocantico Hills, or as formidable as the Kennedys' at Hyannisport, but it too was clearly dedicated to the proposition that the best place for fami-lies to be is together.

Belden's sisters and brother and their families have houses half a mile or so from his, beyond his widowed mother's place, where she and her nurse and cook and driver sometimes spend weekends. His mother's place is bigger than Belden's, which has ten bedrooms, but not nearly so big as the one that used to stand on the exact same site, before Belden's father had it torn down. He tore it down, as a child might a tower of bricks, because it had got too big. His chil-dren were grown up and married and in need of houses of their own. Families expand, Belden's father used to say, and families contract; that's their nature. Houses go up, houses come down. No sense look-ing back, except to middle distance or farther. It is permissible to contemplate such books as *Colonial and Revolutionary Families in America,* but not to dwell on one's immediate history. "At an ad-vanced age when many men care only about the past," Belden re-members, "my father never even wanted to talk about it at all.

"That's partly why I was able to leave the tobacco business with so few regrets ten years ago. Just because my ancestors had been in that business for such a long time was no reason I had to stay in it myself, if there was something I would rather be doing." There were two things he preferred: a St. Oswald's program to raise funds for housing in the South Bronx, and the citywide task force to improve the public school system. Belden now spends about half of each week in the South Bronx, and the rest of his time directing a pro-gram for volunteer remedial reading teachers in public school class-rooms. "It's very hard to reverse the image these children get of themselves," he said. "Cynics say these projects can't possibly do enough good to matter, but I like to think each one can be a beacon of hope—if these beacons burn, they can keep hope alive until some larger effort can be made."

"Retirement really changed Daddy," one of his daughters told me. "He got much more relaxed, and became more aware of the rest of the world. He'd take us up to Harlem on Tuesday afternoons, to help with a remedial reading program, and to help with the campaigns of politicians he believed in. He began to laugh more, too. I think he and Mum started spending time with nicer people. And he stopped grinding his teeth so much. He used to grind them all the time. Once, when he was driving us all up to the country, we *timed* him, and it turned out he ground his teeth every five seconds! I'm not so sure he ever liked the tobacco business at all."

So that Belden could learn that business, he and Susan spent the first five summers of their marriage under the same roof with his parents, at Hudsonville. When the Army sent Belden to Germany, Susan and her two babies lived in Hudsonville year-round. "I resented terribly having to live so close with my parents-in-law," she says now, "but in retrospect I'm grateful. I could never have understood Belden so well if I hadn't known his father. And it meant so *much* to his father to have Celia and Rachel around. He died just before Gail was born, and when he knew his own end was near he made sure to go to the jeweler to get presents to be given to the girls on their eighteenth birthdays. It never occurred to him that this might be eerie.

"He was tyrannical, but we had fun together, too. We'd play seven-letter Jotto, without even using a paper and pencil. He'd quiz me about math, too. He was terribly impressed that I'd graduated *cum laude* in mathematics from Barnard. The first question he ever asked me, the first time we met was 'What part of three is two-thirds of two?' I must have answered correctly, because he was taken with me. He had already given me his blessing sight unseen, which was something that in a Boston family like mine could *never* have happened. If Belden wanted to marry me, he figured I must be all right, so we'd better get busy and start with grandchildren."

When Belden and Susan announced their engagement, the senior Druyten gave the young woman a ring. She was so touched that she kissed him on his cheek. He and all his family were astonished. They talked of this gesture for weeks. Imagine! She kissed him! (It must be for people like the Druytens that the bumper stickers ask "HAVE YOU HUGGED YOUR KID TODAY?") Druyten sisters greet each other, even after absences of a year or so, with hurried little pats on the shoulder. Druyten menfolk greet Susan, even now that she has been in their clan for a quarter of a century, with affable handshakes. They sign their letters "Sincerely."

Belden's father died on Susan's birthday, a month before the third child was born. "He was terribly interested in this new child who was coming; he'd always admired a woman who was pregnant, and it was no secret that he hoped we'd have a boy this time. In the middle of the night, four weeks after he died, I went to the hospital, because the baby was overdue. Belden took me, and then went home. At two in the morning I went into labor—and believe me, they call it that for a reason. It was evident that I was about to go to the delivery floor.

"Just then Belden appeared. I was amazed. I asked, 'Who called you? How did you know to come here *now*?' He said, '*You* called me,' but I hadn't; he must have dreamed I had. Still, when he woke up he saw his own kneeprint on the pillow, where it would have been if he'd reached for the phone. I think it was his father who caused this to happen, who wanted us to be together for the delivery. I think God works through people you love who have died. I have a very strong sense of my brother Daniel, who drowned in 1950—I've just always felt that when I've had decisions to make and actions to follow, he's been there beside me, in a loving relationship, almost as clearly as Belden has."

Susan's own father died just recently, at 96, in a nursing home in New Hampshire—a far more inviting place, he had decided himself, than those more convenient to his Boston home. Susan had taken him to tour nursing homes as conscientiously as she and Belden had driven their daughters around to inspect boarding schools and colleges. When neighbors accused her of uprooting the old gentleman, she felt resentful: "*He* was the one who wanted to go there, and it was a *much* nicer place, maybe because it's run by country people. They seem to be better at that sort of thing."

The morning of Susan's father's fatal attack, the nursing home tried for two hours to phone her, and kept getting a wrong number. Whoever answered that other number got more and more irked with each ring. Finally, through a series of calls to Belden's office and Susan's classroom, word reached her to call the nursing home, which she did from a pay booth. A doctor there said he would need her permission to take "extraordinary measures" to maintain the old man's life. "Let me put it this way," the doctor told Susan, "to keep him alive we'll have to be *very* aggressive."

"I can't make this decision alone," Susan told the doctor, "I'll have to consult with my sister, in Scotland, and I'd rather call her from home than from this pay phone. Can I call you back in an hour, after she and I have talked?"

"That might be too late," said the doctor. So from the same booth Susan broke the news to her distant sister. Both daughters wept, "knowing how much Pater had always loved that next breath, no matter what," but decided that if his life were so marginal it ought to be allowed to end. But her father had already died when Susan phoned the doctor to tell him this.

"Wasn't that wonderful?" she asked. "It meant I didn't have to decide after all to end his life! His memorial service was more than anything else a celebration. We've had so *many* reasons to celebrate this year—Belden's and my twenty-fifth anniversary, Celia's and Tim's wedding, both our divorced sisters' remarriages, Pater's wonderful life. We're really terribly lucky."

Lucky and organized. If the Druyten daughters have a plaint about their upbringing, it is that so little was left to chance, so many hours were structured. The scrapbooks prove this. Each one begins with the plastic bracelet given babies in maternity wards. Soon after the telegrams of congratulation from each daughter's relatives and godparents, and snapshots of early birthday parties, come invitations to this and that series of classes, with single-spaced and greatly detailed report cards from every institution concerned: "Helen dances into nursery school every morning and curtsies like a little fairy princess." "Gail has learned the Apostles' Creed, but should take more part in class discussion." "Pamela is much less self-conscious this term; her progress has been heartening, particularly in history." "As a winner of the Makawe Award, Rachel is eligible to be one of next summer's Trusted Waterfront Monitors—an activity which, we might add, is looked on with favor by college admissions officials." "Phyllis seems far more troubled than she was last year; I wish we could do more to guide her through these shoals." "Caroline's follow-through on her groundstroke carries around to her head . . . her racket should follow the ball toward the opposite backstop."

Saturdays in the city were educational, doggedly so. Whoever thought of the most interesting and out-of-the-way new museum might win an Elton John record. Dinner hours were didactic; everyone got handed a card with five new words on it, and dessert wasn't served until the new words were used by all present, in proper context. "We've always encouraged games," Belden says. "They teach patience and courtesy." At school, meanwhile, the Druyten girls were learning to walk tall, strive for A's, and not lose the dollar-a-month bus passes the state of New York issued to all students who lived a mile or more from school. They learned to write italic script, remember which final consonants were silent, and to send prompt and imaginative thank-you notes: "Dear Pater, thank you so much for the money. I realy needed it. I was almost broke. Thank you again. Your so kind. Love, Pamela."

"You will be happy to hear that I no longer consider human nature basically evil," Celia had reported home from boarding school her junior year. Later she wrote that "I hope you will be pleased to know that I got 108 on my physics exam. There was an extra credit question worth ten points." That news was pasted at once in her scrapbook. Much that happened, of course, could not be so enshrined. The children confined their drug experiments to the lawn. Belden and Susan had strong suspicions about who slept where when the older girls were away, but when male visitors were brought home the boys occupied the guestrooms and that was that.

Celia was the only daughter who consented to a coming-out party. For her sisters it was entirely possible, Jane Austen and the famous beginning of the twenty-ninth chapter of *Emma* notwithstanding, to do without dancing—that sort of dancing, anyway. Phyllis, six years after it happened, finally reacted to the death of her and Caroline's parents with what she now calls her "stage"—forewarnings of which had come each afternoon when she would rush home from school to change into pants and try not to let Susan cut off more of her deliberately scraggly hair. Susan always won. Phyllis went to Bard college for a while but it didn't seem to be the place for her, and she drove off to California in a van, picking up every hitch-hiker she saw. She ignored all Susan's letters, even the one with the St. Christopher's medal enclosed.

When Phyllis finally came back, she chose a time when the largest possible assemblage of sisters would be on hand "as a buffer zone." Most, if not all, was forgiven, on both sides. "Phyllis never seemed to know how much we all loved her," Susan said. "I guess she never got over the feeling of being on trial with us. She and Caroline must always have wondered how their lives would have been if their real parents had lived. So we took great pains to do two things: remind them of their real parents, so they wouldn't forget them, and try to make them feel how much they were a part of our family."

Phyllis's sister Caroline, away in Spain, had always been more docile. "Sometimes it worries me," Susan said. "Caroline's never had anything like Phyllis's 'stage.' Awful though that period was, I almost wish she would—I hope she isn't bottling up all her resentment so that it will explode someday. It's something of a comfort to read her letters from Madrid. She seems to be having the *most* heavenly time."

When they heard of the death of Phyllis's and Caroline's parents and brothers, Belden and Susan rushed to Los Angeles. It never occurred to them to return without their suddenly orphaned nieces. "Families are *made* to stretch," said Susan. "When I was a girl, my parents adopted the daughters of some friends of theirs who had drowned. There was no reason in the world why Phyllis and Caroline shouldn't become our girls' sisters, the way those girls were mine. As for Belden, the first thing he said was he'd always wanted to have seven children."

But first they had a fight on their hands. Phyllis's and Caroline's maternal grandmother thought that she herself was the one best-suited to raise the girls. She said such mean things about the Druytens and Susan's late brother that Susan found it difficult to turn the other cheek. "It was a terrible time!" Susan told me. "I don't get angry very often, but I certainly did then. I had to force myself to remember how the most disarming weapon, when others are being belligerent, is respect. It throws people off balance as nothing else can." The grandmother quit her fight only when her daughter's will was found, naming the Druytens the children's guardians. "You *do* seem to be family people," she admitted to Belden and Susan. "I'll say *that* much for you."

That was a grudging version of the sort of compliment the Druytens have been collecting all their lives. "What a nice family!" customs officials would exclaim, when all nine Druytens disembarked from the S.S. *France,* or a 747 Pan-Am airliner. Never once were they asked to open a single suitcase. "What a nice family!" hotelkeepers would marvel, showing the Druytens to their most commodious suites. "You'll like the Druytens, they're a *nice* family," the elevator man on Fifth Avenue told Nanny Ferguson, the first time she went there. She had come to interview Susan Druyten, about a job helping with the children. Nanny was hired and stayed for fourteen years. "When Mrs. Kennedy went to the White House and said how she needed a nurse, I almost felt it was my patriotic duty to send Nanny," says Susan. "I said *almost.*"

Nanny joined her employers on their frequent trips to Europe, sometimes taking the younger girls with her to visit her own family in County Wickford while the older Druytens and their parents ventured farther. Belden's father had ruled that one expensive hobby was permissible. Travel, Belden and Susan had early decided, would be theirs. Abroad, exploring neutral territory together, they discovered the closeness which families like the Taylors of Gary, Indiana, have no choice but to take for granted at home. "Our trips, more than anything else, have kept our family as intimate as it's been," says Susan. "It's on trips that we achieve a togetherness we never can seem to find at home, with everyone off to lessons or parties or friends' houses." One of the first photographs that caught my eye in the Fifth Avenue library was a cheerful one, framed in red leather, of all nine Druytens gathered around and on top of the van they rented in 1969 to drive through the Cotswolds.

"That was the first time all nine of us went abroad together, and when we hit on our secret formula for successful family travel: the older girls could go off all day on whatever adventures they liked, within reason, but everybody had to be back for a family dinner. We announced this rule in advance; whoever didn't want to abide by it could stay home. They all came." All nine went to the Cotswolds and on other occasions to the Aegean and the Rockies and the Alps. The family snorkeled in the Caribbean, toured Yosemite and Disneyland and Colonial Williamsburg and Historic Savannah and a dude ranch in Wyoming, and sent cards to their friends from The World's Most Crooked Street in San Francisco.

In high school years the girls went to special camps and on organized bicycle tours of Europe, keeping in close touch with home by mail: "Our hotel is in a part of Paris called the Latin Quarter," Gail reported, "perhaps similar to Greenwich Village." "Did Cher really get married for only four days?" Pamela wrote. "That sounds crazy! Maybe it was just a publicity stunt! What do you think, Dad?" The older sisters tried not to resent the younger ones their easy rapport with Belden, who in earlier years had been much less approachable.

"I never once saw Mum and Uncle Belden kiss each other," Phyllis said, "or any of us, either. That took some getting used to, because one of the things I remember most clearly about my own parents is how they'd scream and fight, but how on Sunday mornings they'd scoop all four of us kids into bed so we could read the funnies together. Mum and Uncle Belden—I call him that because I had such a case of hero worship for my own father—weren't like that at all. I don't suppose they meant to seem so aloof, though. I know they care. I still get tears in the corner of my eyes every time I talk to Mum, no matter how mundane the subject is. And Uncle Belden knows so much! I wish I felt I could ask him for help in figuring out our finances. I'll bet if I asked him to, he would."

Belden and Susan are fond of all their sons-in-law: Jacob Martin Blackstone, a leather worker who became a Rhode Island lobsterman after he married Phyllis; Robert Michael Chelski, an ecologist classmate of Celia's who never had worn a black tie in his life before her coming-out party, where he met his future wife Rachel; and Timothy Southgate Holmes, M.D., an orthopedic surgeon whom Celia admits first having admired because he looked so much like a Druyten. He and she each had thirteen wedding attendants, and got so many presents she was still busy writing thank-you notes five months later.

"Tim's godmother gave us some sheets, for twin beds, which turned out to have cost three hundred dollars," Celia told me. "I took them back to the linen store and traded them in for quite a few other sheets, double size, still the no-iron luxury kind. Mum was appalled; she thought I should have got table linens *everyone* could see and enjoy. She disapproved when I used my Tiffany credit for stationery, too; she thought I should have completed my crystal instead." I was almost relieved to hear that "Mum" isn't perfect. So she can be a martyr and a bit of a martinet. So Belden is, or at any rate once was, capable of teeth-grinding, "vein-bulging" anger. So Rachel and Phyllis still fight and scream when they get together, just as my sister and I do. So Pamela hasn't a flair for languages, and Gail still can't sight-read. How refreshing: the Druytens, then, are just like everybody else?

Not quite. Only a minute percentage of American brides have to figure out ways to downplay the disparity between their own enormous trust funds and their husbands' modest salaries. "I had to implore Rachel not to get their stove on the installment plan," Susan told me. "Rachel has always known exactly what she wants. When we gave her a birthstone necklace for graduation she asked if she couldn't *please* have a Rouault instead, so we took the necklace back and got her one." All the girls are given gold watches, Gucci loafers, and fur coats for their sixteenth birthdays, and a houseful of furniture, or its monetary equivalent, when they marry. They get $2.50 a week spending money until they are fifteen, when the sum jumps to $50 a month and becomes a "clothing allowance."

I learned this lore in visits to Celia's four-room apartment on Washington Square, Phyllis's house overlooking Narragansett Bay in Rhode Island, and Rachel's modest farmhouse, with a mailbox outside it reading DRUYTEN-CHELSKI, in rural New Jersey. All the daughters greeted me with hospitable eloquence. So did their husbands. Phyllis, helping Jake to salt down junkfish to use as lobster bait, was far and away the most informal.

All the girls said they hoped to have children someday. Phyllis said she'd adopt a Korean or Cambodian if she couldn't have her own. None seemed likely to raise a houseful of six, or ever to lose touch with her sisters. Phyllis wished somebody had urged her not to get married so early. "In these five years Jake and I have *never* been away from each other for so much as a week! Maybe we should just get divorced, but still live together, most of the time."

A pickup truck drove up her driveway as she spoke. Two lobstermen emerged, with down vests over their T-shirts.

"Where's the boss?" one asked, seeing no sign of Phyllis's husband.

"Oh, come *on*," Phyllis said. She'd been through this before. "You have no *idea* how macho it is up here," she had told me. "I really have to hand it to Jake; when other fishermen ask him a question, he says he'll have to talk it over with me first, which is more than they'd ever do for their wives. I guess they think we're pretty weird, we trust-fund hippies."

Trust funds, it became quite clear, are not unmixed bonanzas. They can cause guilt, the sort of guilt that inspires some rich students to drop their final g's and otherwise disguise their class accents and say, as a former subdebutante I know once did, "I tink ya gotta rebuild neighborhoods, create alternatives and tax de hell out of de rich—revolutions's de only ting dat's big enough." Others band together in foundations to give inheritances away to deserving causes. "I'd never do that," Celia told me. "I don't think any of us would. We may not have mentioned Nixon's name at our house, but we're not Maoists, either. But I know how it is to feel guilty about money. I felt guilty all through the sixties. I sort of groveled and pretended to be poor, until I realized how phony that was. One weekend when I came home from Princeton needing a new hairbrush, I found one at a drugstore a few blocks away and took out my checkbook to pay for it.

"When the clerk saw my name and address printed on the check she went, 'Boy, you live right *on* Fifth Avenue? You must be just *filthy* rich!' You know what I said to her? I said, 'You're right, I am,' and to myself I added, 'and I love it!' What's the use *not* loving it, not trying to use it to make life simpler and nicer and maybe better? Money creates new problems, sure, but don't forget how many old ones it solves, too. Don't tell Mum or Daddy I talked about this though. They think it's crude even to mention that sort of thing."

Families with serious money seldom do mention it, even among themselves. "I don't know how much Belden has and I don't *want* to know," Susan said when I finally steeled myself to bring up the subject. The subject is embarrassing. We don't talk about it, children are told, any more than we talk about our underwear. It's not discussed. It's there, mercifully: it allows us to do all kinds of things other families can't even think about doing. But it also sets us apart from other people and makes us forever wonder: Do they like us for ourselves, or for it? Worse yet, money makes us conspicuous, which we can't abide being.

Mutedness is not merely a taste; it is a principle. We adorn ourselves and fill our rooms with the more subdued colors from nature— not the nature of the tropics or even of a deciduous forest in autumn, but of the bluish-greenish-brownish-grayish coastline of New England. ("Take that thing *off!*" Belden's father once yelled at his fiancée—the only time he ever shouted at her—when she met him once wearing a scarlet coat.) The passive voice is preferred to the slightly less understated active. Voices aren't raised; doors aren't slammed. Sounds are muffled and goods protected. There's a hotpad between each plate and the placemat beneath it; a blanket cover separates the quilt and the bedspread. Such people modulate their voices and favor sixty-watt lightbulbs, margarine, reasonably priced toilet paper, public transportation as opposed to taxis, and order. They never leave the oarlocks in the gunwales. Frozen or even canned orange juice will do when fresh fruit costs too much. Aren't there more dishes to wash in these nice fluffy hot suds? We can't go to bed yet; the fire's still burning. What do you mean you're throwing out those beans? We can put them in the salad tomorrow, to be served on the Meissen with a glassful of something in the Steuben. Who says any family's balance of economies and extravagances has to make sense? What family's does? And who can blame privileged people for finding such antidotes as they can against what seems to me their special malaise, a kind of spiritual agoraphobia, a terror of the consequences of an absence of limits. There is, after all, a question of scale: it is possible to have too much space, too many rooms, too many choices.

"How do you deal with this problem?" I asked Celia. "Isn't the freedom to do anything you want, go anywhere, buy anything, see anyone you want—isn't all that freedom just as constraining as slavery?"

"You don't understand," she told me. "If you're born a Druyten, you see, you're *not* really free. Being a Druyten brings with it all *kinds* of inborn limitations."

Money and power generate dynasties, but other forces can keep them going. Belden Druyten, whose ancestors came here three hundred years ago, might or might not agree with the old Quaker adage that if the first generation *does* well, the second one *marries* well, and the third one *breeds* well, then the others can take care of themselves. But Belden, this slim and humble heir of patroons and robber barons, isn't a Quaker. His wife calls him "a Pindarian—I was just reading Edith Hamilton about Pindar, and it occurred to me that Belden's the same sort of person: he's above suspicion, incorruptible. Pindar prayed: 'With God's help may I still love what is beautiful and strive for what is attainable.' "

Belden would not presume to call himself anything but an Episcopalian. He is kneeling now next to his wife on a russet velvet pillow, toward the end of the eleven o'clock service at St. Oswald's, and they join in the prayer on page 829:

> . . . knit together in constant affection those who, in holy wedlock, have been made one flesh. Turn the heart of the parents to the children, and the hearts of the children to the parents; and so enkindle fervent charity among us all, that we be evermore kindly affectioned with brotherly love . . .

My own grandfather would have approved the processional hymn, on page 576, "Come, Labor On."

The families we have just finished visiting are founded on, buttressed by, and sometimes all but enmired in their own legends. The most striking thing about them is their trenchant sense of tradition and, in most cases, of place. Now we are going to visit another set of families whose strengths are of quite a different nature. But first I want to tell of some encounters I had along the way, encounters that seem to signify.

In Pacific Palisades, south of Los Angeles, I met two doctors, a married pair in their sixties who live in a secluded house surrounded by eucalyptus trees. The house has a swimming pool and a lawn where the doctors play croquet. These doctors are vigorously liberal and unhappily childless. After the riots of 1965 in Watts, they spent weekends doing volunteer work at a community center, where they met, and grew quite fond of, three black children.

This couple invited the black children over, to play on their lawn and swim in their pool, and the black children came. They came often. The doctors began to wish they could adopt the black children, but an odd shyness prevented their even asking whether this might be possible. They wanted very much not to be patronizing. They weren't even sure that the children returned their affection, until late one day after a swim, when they and the children had changed into slacks for a barbecue supper and hung up their suits and towels to dry. One of the children, an 11-year-old girl, looked up at the woman doctor and said, "How come you didn't hang my towel between yours and his, so I could feel more part of the family?"

In Pennsylvania I met a man who works at a dogfood factory. The factory is part of what is called the "pet accessories industry." The man and his wife would often say to each other how ironic it was, to think of all the money and love people spend on animals rather than children. They wished very much that they had children themselves. At the state fair, they had visited a booth advertising children in need of adoption. On television they had seen commercials advertising "Baby of the Week." Maybe, they thought, they could adopt a child themselves. They went to an agency, which showed them videotapes not of babies but of growing children, some of whom in their short lives had been in as many as nine foster homes.

"Adoption," the social worker told them, "is like marriage; it's like falling in love. You're not going to want just any old child, and any old child isn't going to want you." The trouble with many of the children available for adoption was that they were visibly and dishearteningly handicapped. So few people wanted to adopt them that standards for adoption had been relaxed—people who were unmarried, or homosexual, or over the age of 35, or atheists, or who had been to psychoanalysts were at last being permitted to adopt children. The social worker thought this relaxation of standards was long overdue. "None of us would be allowed to be parents," she told the couple, "if we had to meet criteria like those."

But the dogfood worker and his wife did not wish to adopt a handicapped child. They wanted a child who was healthy and bright. The social worker said no such children were available, except for a set of four—two brothers and two sisters—who had already lived in five foster homes, who could only be adopted as a package. "If you guys were willing to take all four," the social worker told them, "you'd have a real good chance."

So they did adopt all four, although both their own sets of parents warned them not to. "Our folks panicked at first," the wife of the dogfood worker said, "but now they treat the kids real good. In a way it's almost easier with four—one kid might pout for five days if you jump on him for not cleaning his room, but with four they have a distant early warning system among themselves; they look out for each other.

"We've really lucked out with no medical problems," the adoptive father said, "and we're just starting now to pick up on how smart Debbie is. The other day, when I was looking for something I'd misplaced, she remembered which closet I'd put it in three months ago."

"Adoption works in stages," his wife said. "First there's a honeymoon, but when it's over, is it ever over. There've been times when one of the kids has said, 'I want to go back to the foster home,' but we've just said, 'Uh-uh. We went through too much to get you. You're stuck with us. You're home now.'"

On a ferry between Woods Hole and Martha's Vineyard one rainy day in early June I sat next to a dental hygienist who seemed to feel like talking. That day, she told me, was the fourteenth birthday of a son she never had seen in his whole life, not even when he was born. She hadn't been married when she had borne that son, and had agreed during her pregnancy to give him up for adoption.

"Giving him up was the stupidest mistake I've ever made in my life, and I've made plenty," she told me. "The doctor said it wouldn't be so bad, that it was impossible to love someone you never even saw, and that I should just think of the whole thing as an operation, as some surgery. But after he was born and taken away I ached to see and hold that boy with my whole being. I ached so much that I sobbed for three days. The doctor said I should never tell anyone who might ever love me that I had had that baby. That was the way the thinking went then: that it was all a sin. It makes me so mad to think all this happened before the social climate changed."

"Yeah, I'd like to be a father," a man in his early twenties said one evening. "I think I'd be a good one; I'd be compassionate, honest, concerned. But I don't even have a relationship. No one I know has a relationship. Sometimes I wonder who is ever going to have families in two hundred years—twenty years, even. It gets into social Darwinism: the scary thing is that the people most opposed to having kids seem to be the smartest ones."

A young woman I had taught in a class once, but never known well, amazed me one Sunday afternoon with a phone call from three thousand miles away. Since it was Sunday the rates were low, and she needed someone impartial to ask: Should she have her tubes tied? Should she become voluntarily sterile?

"It's hard to find a dude who'll respect a woman's freedom," she said, "and birth control is such a hassle! But I'm real squeamish; I don't even like to visit people in hospitals, much less be a patient myself." Don't do it, I told her. Don't have your tubes tied. Someday you might want a baby.

Another student, herself from a family of six, volunteered one day after class that she was "not into the physical thing of having a baby.

Maybe I'll adopt an Asian one, or two—being an only child would be a drag. Or maybe I won't have any at all. I might not be cut out for living with other people. Maybe even just living with a dude, let alone getting married, is a copout. Maybe I ought to live in a collective instead."

Not for these people—not yet, anyway—the implicitness cherished by a friend of mine who said what he liked best about being married was "not having to talk all the time about Our Relationship and where, if anywhere, it is going. Now we have a vested interest in not talking about it. It's no longer an issue of 'Can we go on this way?' We simply do go on."

A boy I know unwrapped a gift jar of Old Spice cologne on his six-teenth birthday, opened it, and said, "It smells just like Dad." Such comments won't often be heard in the families in the chapters that follow. Many of the children in the chapters that follow will come of age with little scent or sense of their fathers, without knowing what Philip Roth in The Professor of Desire calls "the perplexing propor-tions of tremendous closeness and tremendous distance between my father and myself." The people in some of the chapters that follow don't think resident blood fathers are of central importance. They like to tell how many mythological heroes were foundlings, brought up by nursemaids and shepherds and wizards, not for years to wrest the swords from the rock where their fathers had left them. One of them referred me to a passage in Jane Austen's early novel Love and Freindship [sic]:

> Our mothers could neither of them exactly ascertain who were our fathers . . . This is however of little conse-quence, for as our Mothers were certainly never married to either of them, it reflects no Dishonour on our Blood, which is of a most ancient and unpolluted kind . . .

Perhaps because I am myself the product of patriarchies I am not quite so sanguine about fatherlessness. Nor do I applaud the way new families blur other old lines. I admire them, though, for the valor of their imagination. I agree with the anonymous author of an angry New Republic *article called "Confessions of an Erstwhile Child" that "there ought to be more than one way a youngster can enter adult society with more than half his sanity left," that the idea of child as property is obscene, that custody by natural parents ought*

*to be regarded as a privilege rather than as a right, and that some
people simply aren't fit to be parents at all.*

*Two of the families in the chapters that follow are devising new
variations on the old theme of parent or parents and child under one
roof. Others, experimenting with communitarianism, disdain old
ideas about the merit of roofs and even about children. These are
families with short histories and uncertain futures. What they lack
in continuity they have in energy and curiosity. They reach toward
one another and out toward the world with an open ardor, and their
instinct for family and tribe can match any family's in the section
preceding. Their common and refreshing hope, in some cases a conviction, is that there are ways and ways of achieving kinship, of
which birth is only the most obvious.*

Just Think: Nine Years

*Some people think that the amateurishness of family
life is the most widely distributed human beauty.*
—Harold Brodkey
"A Largely Oral History of My Mother"

"Hey, Mom, do unicycles cost a lot?"

"I don't imagine they're cheap."

"Could I get one someday?"

"Someday, maybe. Soon, no."

"Are we poor?"

"Well, our ship hasn't exactly come in."

"You ought to know—you work at the marina."

"Very funny."

"I heard Grandma tell Grandpa we were poor when I was visiting them."

"We'll do all right, Buzzy."

The beach is too windy this Memorial Day, so Angela Lydia Larson Olmquist and her 9-year-old son are sprawled sun-bathing on towels in the yard behind their apartment complex in Montauk, at the tip of Long Island. So am I. After two months in this apartment, their seventh home together, they don't much like it. After one night in the thin-walled, three-room place, neither do I.

They are thinking of moving to a huge reconverted house a few miles to the west, with eight other single parents and six other children. Someone at the marina where Angie works told her about a vacancy in that house. This afternoon we are all going to have a look at that big house and its occupants. I'm betting that Angie isn't going to like it.

"You're the last person I would ever expect even to *consider* communal living," I tell Angie, whom I have known since we were freshmen in college.

"I guess I am too straight, in most ways, to be typical of the—how many single parents did you say you'd read there are in this country?"

"Nine million, some say fourteen million." In theory, at least, I know more about such matters than Angie does. Angie shies away from theory. She does not read *Momma: A Sourcebook for Single Mothers*, or subscribe to *Single Parent News: A Journal for the One-Parent Community*, or belong to a chapter of Parents Without Partners, or go to "workshops" with titles like "Put the Elf Back in Self." If she did, we probably wouldn't have kept in touch off and on all these years. We usually differ about politics, but her stubborn refusal to be pigeonholed is one of the reasons I like her. She never marched for peace or went to a consciousness-raising session, and if she had to ally herself with some cause it might even be the Right-to-Life League, so great is her aversion to abortion, but I can't picture her parading in front of some state legislature with a bottled fetus, either.

The third and last daughter of a retired brigadier general in the United States Army, Angie was brought up with a respect for authority and an appetite for changes of scene. I had to put a whole new page in my loose-leaf address notebook to keep track of her moves. Several times, when I have acted on the impulse to phone her, nasal-voiced recorded announcements have advised me that her number was not in service at this time, or had been disconnected, or had been changed and would I please make a note of the new number. She gets around, Angie does, partly in the wake of men who attract her. Since she and Buzzy's father parted, before the boy was two years old, there has nearly always been some man at the edge of her life, if not at the center. These romances don't last long, nor do the intervals between them. Women friends, Angie tells me, are scarcer than male ones; talk is harder to come by than sex.

Professionally, too, her life has been episodic. What a résumé she could print: elementary teacher at two schools, one in a ghetto and one for the daughters of the most privileged families in Cleveland. Tour guide at a bird sanctuary in Florida. Cocktail waitress. Secretary. Liquor salesperson. "Recreational aide" at a nursing home. Once, between Angie's jobs, a rich woman going off on a vacation paid her $800 to spend a month living with her poodle. All she had to do was keep the dog company, take it every week to a pet grooming salon to be clipped and shorn for $20, let it sleep at the foot of her bed, and walk it.

She came to Long Island from Florida to be near an airlines pilot who since was transferred to San Diego; she didn't want to follow him there because San Diego is too near Seattle, where her parents live. Her parents send for Buzzy every summer, but they and Angie don't seem to get along, or want to see each other. I refrain from asking why. It is almost refreshing to find someone enigmatic about family matters. Of late I have been feeling like Cora Taylor, who said, "I carry a lot of secrets."

"Did you ever think of going back to teaching?" I ask Angie.

"Not really. Kids are terrific four or five at a time, but a whole roomful of thirty of them can drive me up the wall. They *need* so much, or at least they did in my two schools. What they need isn't teaching, either. It was amazing how the posh kids seemed just as neglected at home as the ghetto kids did—both places they'd just *cling* to me—those whose parents left them with governesses and those who found their parents slumped over bottles of booze."

"Not all kids are as lucky as Buzzy, I guess."

"With a mom like *her*? You call me *lucky*?" Buzzy is kidding. "Hey," he asks later, "did you ever know my dad?"

"Just a little, a long time ago."

"Did he look like me?"

"He wasn't as blond, but I guess his hair must have been lighter when he was a kid. His nose was the same shape, sort of."

"I look a little like my grandpa. Every summer I go to Seattle to see him and Grandma and Aunt Dodo and Uncle Pete. Aunt Dodo's an accountant. Uncle Pete's a basketball coach. They have three kids. The kids are pretty nice. I have another aunt, too, but she's in Hawaii and we don't hear from her too much. Once I met a man on a plane who lived in Hawaii. He didn't know my aunt. I made friends with him. I always make friends on planes."

"Buzzy makes friends wherever we go," says Angie. "You should have seen him on this all-day fishing excursion. Everyone on that entire boat was telling him their whole life stories. He ought to be a shrink when he grows up."

"I wonder what happened to that guy Roger, Mom," says Buzzy. "Remember Roger, from the boat? The divorced one you thought was cute? He said he'd take me hang-gliding. Do you think he's forgotten?"

"Maybe not. Maybe he'll call. Hey," Angie warns me, "careful with that city white skin. If you haven't been in the sun since last summer, this sun is dangerous, even though it's not even June. You'll get a third-degree burn if you don't watch out. Buzzy, pass her the cream, but first you'd better let me smear some on your back, too."

"You know what you could call this cream when you put it on me, Mom? You could call it *son* cream, S-O-N, get it?"

"I get it," says Angie, as she lights a cigarette.

"Don't you think it's a good pun?"

"Sure." She doesn't sound convinced.

"Are you feeling uptight? Is it time for your period?"

"It's just that we stayed up too late talking. I could have used a couple extra hours' sleep."

"You never sleep enough. You smoke too much, too. You ought to be more careful, Mom."

"When I want your advice, young man, I'll be sure to let you know," says Angie.

"Be nice, both of you," I say, "or you'll spoil my illusions. I've come all the way out here to see the perfect two-person family."

"Give the lady another lemonade," says Angie, passing the Thermos.

"Ladies, plural," says Buzzy. "Here comes Mrs. Himple." From the back door of the apartment building, with an aluminum walker and a stuffed mesh bag, comes a neighbor whom I already have met: an 81-year-old with no grandchildren of her own who follows Buzzy around as a puppy might follow its master.

"I hope I'm not disturbing you," Mrs. Himple says as she settles into a webbed plastic chair next to our towels. "I just thought you might be hungry for some of these grapefruit rinds I've just candied."

"Oh, Mrs. Himple, how nice of you to bring them all the way out here," says Angie.

"What's this you're reading," the old woman asks the boy, "a book about Abraham Lincoln?"

"Yeah. He must have been neat. He was my kind of person. I bet if we'd been kids together we'd have been friends."

"I'll bet he wasn't as good a speller as you are," Mrs. Himple says. "Want to try some new words?" Having no choice, Buzzy agrees. He gives "cacophony" one "a" too many, but guesses right on "eucalyptus," "meretricious," "culinary," and even "hors d'oeuvre," then misses on "concupiscent."

"I don't even know what that word *means*," he says.

"It has to do with—well—cravings," the old lady says. "Your mother will explain to you." Angie restrains a wince. Mrs. Himple, she has told me, keeps careful watch over her visitors, few of whom are female.

"French is much harder than Spanish," says Buzzy, as if to change the subject, "but it's fun. You know what my mom's initials spell, in French? Hello! A-L-L-O is French for 'hello.'"

"I've been thinking of dropping the 'O' and just using my maiden name," says Angie.

"Wouldn't that be confusing for Buzzy?" asks Mrs. Himple.

"It might be," says Angie. "I haven't decided for sure."

"Think it over carefully, dear," says Mrs. Himple. Next she has another quiz for Buzzy. Does he know which countries have as their capitals Tegucigalpa? Prague? Canberra? Phnom Penh? Teheran? He does. She is about to drill him with still more questions when the ringing phone gives him an excuse to run inside.

"Such a *bright* little scamp," Mrs. Himple says to Angie. "That father of his must really have been a whiz."

"Oh, he was," says Angie.

"We'd better get on inside, too," says Angie. "This sun is brutal, and I'd like to wash the salt out of my hair before our excursion this afternoon."

"Are you going to streak it again, dear?"

"Not this time."

"Good. It looks so much nicer when you wear it the natural way, even if it *is* going gray. Look, you know I wouldn't tell you these things if I didn't have your best interests at heart."

"Clever of her, to figure out where Buzzy's smartness comes from," I say to Angie back in the apartment. "She's really a shrewd observer of genetics."

"You can see why I want to get out of here. I love the idea of different generations together, but that woman is a *trial*. My own mother never carried on that way about streaked hair."

"Do you still hold your wet head out the window of a cold winter's night so you'll catch cold and sound sexy like Tallulah Bankhead?"

"I only did that once, when I was fifteen. Do *you* still hide your dirty dishes in the oven? Or was it the bathtub?" Our friendship is a cobweb of such frail legends.

"You know what Mom does when she doesn't want to hear the phone ring?" Buzzy asks. "She hides it in the icebox."

"Makes it cool and nice. Know what Buzzy did once, when he didn't want to go to school? He put the thermometer under the hot water faucet, so it would read 104° and I'd keep him home."

"Another time I swallowed fourteen of Mom's birth control pills," says Buzzy. "I thought they'd taste like candy. They didn't. Boy, were they awful. This guy Glenn was around then, and he drove me to the hospital, where I had to have my stomach pumped. Hey, what happened to Glenn, Mom?"

"I think he moved to Key West."

"He looked kind of like John Wayne. Did you know that John Wayne's real name is Marion Morrison?"

"I had no idea," I say.

"My mom didn't know that either. She's not dumb, though. She could work in real estate, if she wanted to. She passed the test on her first try. She's really a lot smarter than Mrs. Himple thinks."

"Lucky you, to get to live with her."

"I know. What would make it perfect would be if she would quit smoking, and take better care of herself, and marry either a lawyer or an athlete or a TV announcer—one of those guys who say things like, you know, 'Walter Cronkite, CBS News, New York.' Only not as old as Walter Cronkite. That would be the neatest of all, an announcer. Maybe she could find one who would take me fishing. I found out when we went on that all-day excursion that my mom's not so good at fishing. If she'd find a man who could fish, and who had a couple of kids of his own, for me to play games with, that would be cool. Hey, want to play hand hockey?"

"I'm not good at games like that."

"It isn't so hard. I'll show you. It's sort of like a pinball machine. My grandpa sent me this game for Christmas. See, that's him over there on the wall, with my grandma. He was in World War II. He fought in Japan. Maybe someday he and Grandma will come here to visit us. They don't like to leave Seattle, though. See, here's how you play this game. You stand at that end, and I'm here, and we both try to shoot this puck up to the other guy's basket with these lever things, then keep score. See?" I see, and I try, but I'm no match for Buzzy.

"A brother would be the most fun to play this with, or a dad. Hey, do you think my dad will ever come back from Venezuela?"

"Is that where he is?"

"We think so. Either there or in Brazil."

"I guess you shouldn't count on having him come back."

"Would my mom like it if he did?"

"That's a question you'd better ask *her*. I'll bet you *have* asked her."

"He has," Angie says, back from the bathroom with a towel

around her head. "I've told Buzzy many, many times that his dad and I are better off apart. We found out that we didn't love each other, the way a lot of kids' parents don't."

"But did my dad love *me?*"

"How could he not?"

"Oh, Buzzy," says Angie. "We've been over this so many times. Of course he did."

"But if you love someone, don't you like to be with them?"

"Most of us do," I say, "but some people are more complicated."

"You know someone who's *not* going away? *You're* not, Keith William Olmquist, Junior. You couldn't get away from me if you tried to." Angie grabs her son from behind and wrestles him to the floor. Writhing loose takes all the boy's strength and makes him grin.

"Is this commune place in the same school district?" he asks.

"You know it isn't. Why? Does the idea of transferring bother you?"

"No, I sort of like it."

"But that's one of the things that worries me, you transferring so much. Don't you get sick of always getting used to new people, so soon after we've moved here from Ronkonkoma?" The boy says nothing. "Is something wrong at school?"

"Not too," says Buzzy.

"Come on, something *is* wrong," says Angie. "What is it?"

"It's one of the gym teachers," says Buzzy. "He acts sort of weird sometimes."

"Weird? What kind of weird?"

"Not as bad as that guy we saw at the beach who asked, 'How do you like my hair this way?' when we'd never seen him before in our whole lives, but that same type. He looks at me funny, the way Tod did."

"Oh, Jesus," says Angie. Tod, I learn, was an assistant soccer coach in one of the towns where Angie and Buzzy once lived. He took an interest in Buzzy, and planned so many hikes and outings and excursions that after a while Angie wondered how he ever had time for anything else. Once, when she had to cancel a weekend camping trip Tod had planned for Buzzy, without checking in advance with her, Tod grew furious and said something about "apron strings." Another time he got angry when Angie phoned from her office to see whether Buzzy was home. That in turn made her angry. "One of the things a lot of single parents don't do," she told me, "is keep track of where their children are, and make sure the kids know where to reach *them*. A lot of them go out two or three nights in a row, too. I never do that. My rule is one night out, one night in. Anyway, this Tod got to be just too much."

"How do you mean too much?"

"One afternoon Buzzy came home from school and said, 'I'm kind of glad Tod's not my real dad,' and when I asked why, he said, 'Because real dads don't hug their kids that way, I don't *think.*'"

On the train to Montauk from New York I had taken a gray manila folder labeled "SINGLE PARENTS," which I had been filling for a year or so. The last addition to the folder was a letter from a woman in Maine whom I know very slightly, telling about her 16-year-old son.

> I'm no believer in institutionalizing children, but Eric's emotional problems and learning difficulties have *got* to be treated. His father has abandoned him and refused financial help without a court battle, so my only avenue to treatment is through his father's group insurance policy. It won't pay for a school, but it will cover 80 percent of the cost of an accredited psychiatric facility . . . I've been looking into all this, and I'm horrified by the total absence in this culture of affordable facilities for these kids, and the incredible cost of decent ones. Some charge $50,000 a year, *base*. I guess the children of the poor, and those with no access to an insurance policy, just end up lost, or jailed, or dead.

Maybe they do at that. Or they take to smearing car windshields with grease, as two teen-age boys did to mine at a red light the week before my Montauk visit, obliging me to pay them a dollar to clean the grease off. Or they drop rocks from footbridges onto the roofs of passing cars. Or they take control of the loudspeakers in subway cars, like one fatherless boy I heard about, to announce that he was going to blow out the brains of everyone there. "He didn't mean it, of course," said the social worker assigned to that boy's case, "but how were *they* to know?"

"Would it have made so much difference if those boys had fathers?" asks Angie.

"I've been reading books that strongly suggest it would have," I tell her. "Societies without fathers breed childish people. No sooner do revolutionaries symbolically slay one father than they take on another, stronger one—Stalin followed the Czar; Mao came after Confucius. The weaker the fathers, the more totalitarian the governments tend to be, the more vulnerable individuals are to the state. The more a father's authority gets transferred to institutions outside the family, the more inadequate people feel, both fathers and children."

"I'm not going to let Buzzy grow up and join the Hitler Youth, don't worry."

"I guess you teach him a lesson or two now and then along those lines."

"Not now and then. Every day. Like he wanted to sneak two free birthday dinners from the pizza parlor; I told him he only has one birthday so he just gets one free dinner."

"Do you wish you didn't have to do all those lessons alone?"

"Of course I do. You have no idea how much responsibility it is, to have someone entirely dependent on you, emotionally and intellectually, and let's not forget physically. For the first six years of Buzzy's life he and I were never apart for one single night. Much as I adore that kid, it got to be a bit much not *once* waking up without him in the same or the next room. My parents had been making half-hearted noises about having him come to see them, so when he was six I decided okay, here's their chance, I'll send him to them, and have a whole two weeks to myself. So guess what happens the day before he's supposed to fly to Seattle? He falls off his bike and breaks both arms."

"Maybe it would be easier to be a single father."

"I think it would; men who have custody of their kids get a lot more sympathy than women do."

"Lots of men *do* have custody. I know several men myself who have their children."

"I'll bet they don't get accused so much of running 'broken homes,'" says Angie. "What a loaded phrase that is. It really pisses me."

"It ought to," I tell her. "It's a stupid stereotype. It's not new, either. I've just read an article pointing out how many widowed and deserted people in this country brought kids up alone in the eighteenth and nineteenth centuries, not to mention during World War Two. And if you want to feel that there's a little history behind your situation, read classical mythology. There are more single mothers in myths than there are in Santa Monica, which for your information seems to be the single mother capital of the world."

"What am I doing here in Montauk, then?"

"You never were one to follow the herd. Besides, who says you have to stay here? Why don't you and Buzzy move to the city?"

"How would we eat?"

"You could check the phone booths for stray dimes. Have you ever tried to track down Keith to nail him for all those back child support payments? He must owe you many thousands of dollars."

"He does. That's why he's gone to South America. I have such mixed feelings I don't think I'd want to see him if he turned up here right this minute. He put me through too much."

"I never knew him that well."

"His looks were what got me first. Those lizardy eyes—I've always gone for eyes like that. That special kind of lean physique. He was a terrific dancer, too. And smart. Once he told me he had an IQ of 171. I believed him. And could he sweet-talk! I had to really force myself not to go back with him after I'd made him leave. He'd call up at all hours of the day and night, before I had the phone unlisted. I had to keep two lists, one in my purse and one by the phone, of reasons why I shouldn't let him back into my life, no matter what."

"You never did tell me what the trouble was. Maybe you don't feel like it."

"No, I still don't. Take it from me, it was trouble. Fatherhood scared him, that was one part of it."

"What was Keith's own father like?"

"Poor. Drunk. Very big with the sacrifices."

"I've just been reading a book about that sort of thing." I show Angie Richard Sennett's *The Hidden Injuries of Class.* "Let me read you two passages I've underlined: 'Isn't betrayal the inevitable result when you try to endow your life with a moral purpose greater than your own survival?'—"

"That's what Keith did, I guess, he betrayed his dad—"

"—and, later on, 'the tragedy of loving as sacrifice is that those who are pushed to feel grateful cannot.'"

"That makes sense. This Sennett must be a smart man."

"He is. I met him once at a party."

"You go to a lot of parties?"

"Too many, sometimes, especially during the holidays."

"I know what you mean, but I've also had holidays when I didn't go anywhere at all. Keith finally left just a few days before Christmas, when Buzzy was a year and a half old. We were in Fort Lauderdale then, where I didn't know one single person—at least not well enough to get invited for Christmas. You know what I did that Christmas? I thawed a frozen turkey leg, and roasted it, just for Buzzy and me. It was leathery and stringy and awful. I cried."

"Where were your parents?"

"In Seattle. I didn't want to tell them Keith had split. I was too proud, I guess. They never did approve of him. The next year, or was it the year after, I hired this guy to come over dressed up as Santa Claus to bring Buzzy a bunch of presents. Buzzy loved it, depressing and ridiculous though it was. I've often thought he's the only thing in my whole life that's ever made any sense at all."

"Somehow or other you seem to be doing things right," I tell her. "That kid seems to be turning out fine. Maybe it's enough to have one terrific parent. Anyway, lots of people who *do* have fathers seem to have rotten ones. Let me read you from another book:

". . . fathers fulfill neither their 'human' conciliatory, emotional role nor their second role of setting a visible example of how to deal with things, how to live in their civilization. The consequence is the great army of neurotic climbers and the host of 'forgotten' men who search in hordes for surrogate satisfactions."*

"That's some folder of cheerful research you've got there," says Angie. "What you've said and read to me is all true, but I think you might be missing the point about what single parents really need."

"What? Money? Is it true, do you think, that only fifteen percent of men pay what the courts order them to?"

"It probably is true, but money isn't what I mean. I mean friends —the sort of friends you can call up and say, 'I don't care *what* you're doing; you have to come over here right this minute to keep me from throttling my little boy'—and mean it, and they would, they'd be over. But people like that aren't so easy to find. If they were, I wouldn't have to resort to you."

"Thanks, pal," I say.

"But really, I was telling you before, men really are easier to find than women friends. Don't you think so?"

"I've been lucky. Maybe if I had a child, or a husband, it would be harder."

"I haven't found anyone of any sex to confide in the whole six months we've been up here from Florida, unless you count Buzzy."

"I do count him. You could have a worse confidant."

"But one isn't enough! I'm greedy! I need several!"

"You mean you need what one of these articles in my folder calls a 'primary community'—a sort of network of friends."

"For a network of friends, even if it had to be called a 'primary community,' I'd give—I'd give a lot."

* Alexander Mitscherlich, *Society Without the Father.*

"And that's why we're going to the commune?"

"The commune! I almost forgot! We'll be late if we don't get going right this minute. Buzzy!"

My guess had been right. Angie and Buzzy didn't like the commune. I could tell they didn't like it long before we got back into their car to drive home to Montauk.

"Wasn't that a weird guy, the one who was playing the gong in the living room?" asked Buzzy.

"What was his daughter like?" asked Angie. "You met her out in the yard, didn't you?"

"She was vague. She hadn't been living there too long. She told me she spends six months with her mom in Indiana and then six with her dad here. For a while she lived with her aunt in Illinois."

"Jackie did say something about these people having 'checkered pasts,' " said Angie. It was Jackie, her colleague at the marina, who had told her about the commune in the first place. Jackie arrived late for our appointment. She had a blond Afro hairdo, a Levi's pantsuit, the longest fingernails I had seen in quite some while, and no apparent sense of irony. Her preferred adjectives seemed to be "fabulous" and "dynamite." She made me feel as if I were back at a social science conference.

"I'd have got here sooner," she told us, "but I've just been to a Making Relationships Work workshop, and I got into such a mellow space that I hung out later to rap with some of the trainers. It was *dynamite*. Shep went with me, Angie, can you believe it? Shep," she explained to me, "is this ex-Jesuit I've been seeing. He has so much trouble with intimacy in public that he won't even hold hands, but let me tell *you*, that priest is one fabulous fucker."

"Buzzy, why don't you go see the back yard?" asked Angie.

"Does my language make you uncomfortable?" Jackie asked. "Our kids here aren't uptight about stuff like that. It might be really good for you two to move to a scene like this, you know? The two-person system, under stress, is the least stable form of any human interaction. We single parents have to teach our kids a two-part message: one, that they can always depend on us, and two, that they can get along without us, too, if they have to. One problem is the Domino Theory—these kids have the subconscious feeling that since one parent left them the other might leave, too."

"I have had that feeling about Buzzy, sometimes," said Angie. "Sometimes he pretends to like friends of mine more than I think he really does, so I won't be upset by his not liking them, if you follow me."

"Do I *follow* you," said Jackie. "That's one of the things we try to work through here. Shep's been helping. When I was married, I controlled my boys *way* too much. We were such a cliché. When they and their father and I would go out to some restaurant to eat, I'd wish people wouldn't even look at us."

"My family was like that, too," said this commune's oldest member, a woman who looked about fifty. "Our kids hated all the weekends when my husband made us do these perfect 'familial' things. I hated them too, and it turned out even my husband didn't like it. There we'd be, all locked up together all day on a boat, pretending to be having fun. Or we'd go on these camping trips where nobody could figure out how to put up the goddamn tent and nobody even *cared*, but somehow we felt we had to act out the whole charade."

"The way we work things here," said Jackie, "is that no matter which sex the parent is, the idea is 'Mother, don't smother.' The gender revolution, you know, is the biggest thing since the Bolshevik. The more people you can get input and feedback from, the more karma you can work through. Our dinner conversations here are dynamite—we cover the whole spectrum from astrology to numerology to the importance of sharing. Maybe you could stay for dinner tonight?"

"I don't think we'll be able to," said Angie.

"Too bad, because you could get a better idea of what we're all about. You could talk to Luigi, the lifeguard, and Kurt, this other *really* nurturant father who's into photography. We like to have people who *do* things, who are into personhood. That matters more than yin and yang, don't you think?"

"Mmm," I said.

Jackie gave us a tour of the house. Each adult had a private room, sharing a bath with two others. The basement was divided into two big bedrooms, one for boys and one for girls. Everybody used a huge common kitchen, dining room, music room, and library. "On the first Saturday of every month," said Jackie, "we all stay home for at least four hours, to clean our own Room Consciousness Area. The idea is to add to the consciousness of the house. Less than four hours isn't enough time. And every seven nights one adult has full responsibility for everything—shopping, planning the menu, cooking, cleaning up, helping the kids with their homework, and seeing that they get to bed on time. I was on last night, so now I have a whole week free."

"Doesn't it confuse the kids," asked Angie, "to have someone different in charge every night?"

"They love it," said Jackie. "Most of us here are really close. We're mostly earth signs—we have fabulous birthday parties, by the way. You and Buzzy are Cancer and Taurus, right? You'd fit right in. The lady who just left the house was Gemini, moon in Sagittarius, and that wasn't so good. She was pretty much into privacy."

"I think I'm pretty much into it myself," said Angie. Soon afterward we were heading back east toward Montauk.

"What bothered me most," she said, as we stopped at a clam bar for supper, "was the sign on the icebox that said, 'Initial here if you know who took the bacon.' And I didn't like the idea that they all seemed to turn on all the time, either. Not with kids around. What if some kid were to get hurt while they were all stoned, and needed to go to the hospital? Who'd sign the medical release? Maybe they don't even *know* about medical releases. And what would happen to a kid who had that many people to take orders from?"

"Some doctor I read about said he thought every child ought to have four different 'parent figures.' "

"Four different *regular*, steady ones might be fine," said Angie, "but a different one every night? By the age of four a kid might be so intimidated he would listen to anyone. Boy, a 'broken home' might be better than that."

"That woman I was telling you about, Isolina Ricci, she ends her article saying the definition of a family comes from within—if you *think* your home is broken, then it is. If you *think* you and Buzzy are a family, then you are."

"I *do* think we are," said Angie. "I might even go see my own parents. Maybe it's a mistake for me to sort of boycott them, the way I've been doing."

"But Mom, you said you and they drove each other bananas."

"We do, but maybe I ought to give them a chance, anyway. It's stupid, after the age of twenty-five, to hold that sort of grudge."

"How many years past twenty-five *are* you, Mom?"

"That's my business."

"You're kind of mean today."

"I know I am. That's why I wish we had other people to live near, if not with, so that there'd be somebody for you to turn to and say, 'Wow, she's really being a witch today, isn't she?' and not think it was all your fault when I was in a bad mood. You wouldn't need to take it so personally."

Back in the apartment I looked more closely at the tinted portrait of Angie's parents. Her father looked strict in his uniform, and I wished her mother's eyes smiled as much as her mouth did.

"You want to see our family album?" asked Buzzy.

"Sure I do. I love family albums." The one he brought was the thinnest I ever had seen. He was always smiling, in all the class pictures, all the birthday party InstaMatic snapshots, in Montauk and in Florida and in Cleveland. As the pages went on he got younger. On the last page of all was a picture of Buzzy as an infant, being held high in the air in the arms of a man whose back was to the camera.

"That's the only picture we have of my dad," he said.

"Let's take some more pictures tomorrow," his mother said.

"Pretend you're having fun, you two," I said the next day as I focused the camera. They both made faces, standing with their arms around each other.

"We *are* having fun," said Buzzy. "Just think, Mom, nine years together and we still love each other."

I always have a hangover after hearing jargon like Jackie's at the commune. Her line "the two-person system under stress" stayed with me until the next time I met a single mother with her child. That next "system," though, really consisted of three people, of whom the third was not nor ever could be anyone's father.

Supermarket Checkout
Clerk of the Year

"IT WAS one of those classic misunderstandings," Doris is telling me. "Eileen thought *I* wanted a guinea pig when we moved in here, and I thought *she* wanted one, and it turned out neither one of us really wanted one at all—but look at us now."

I'm looking. Doris is feeding special pellets to three furry, caged creatures whom she has named Jeffy, Miss Mouse, and Fatso. "They're Abyssinians," she tells me. "They look like a mass of cowlicks all over, don't they?" In a corner doze two mongrels named Woody and Bruce. Bruce, Eileen tells me, is "on loan—*permanent* loan, it looks like—from two friends who've moved away." The only absent member of this household just now is Eileen's 4-year-old daughter Denise, whom neighbors have taken to prekindergarten at the Methodist Sunday School. When Denise comes back, in an hour or so, we'll all have the sauerbraten Eileen is fixing in the kitchen.

The kitchen is cheerful, big enough for us all to eat in, with movable magnetized letters on the icebox door arranged to spell D-E-N-I-S-E. A dentist's appointment card is tacked to a bulletin board, along with a list of phone numbers and a couple of cartoons. The apartment has two other rooms, a living room with Denise's bed and dresser screened off in a corner, and a bedroom just big enough to hold Eileen's easel along with the bed. On the bathroom sink, next to the standup shower stall, are two big toothbrushes, one small one, and a bottle of Bay Rum cologne.

"This sauerbraten recipe," Eileen tells me as she grates the potatoes for the side dish of dumplings, "is the only thing good I ever got from Fred's family."

"Unless you count Denise," calls Doris. Fred, whom these women are pleased not to have seen in several months, is Denise's father.

"The sauerbraten smells wonderful," I say.

"It even *looks* good," says Doris. "Eileen's lentil stew now, that's another matter. If you saw that, you'd think it was something to patch a road with. The first time she made it, I said, 'You don't expect me to *eat* that, do you?' She very meekly, in that way she has, said 'yes.' So I ate it, and I was glad. And I still am glad." The two women who are in their early thirties, exchange a smile. It is quite a smile.

Eileen, a lapsed member of Weight Watchers, has straight black hair hanging thinly to her shoulders. She bustles around the kitchen in terrycloth scuffs and a turquoise corduroy caftan with a floor-length gingham apron over it. Some would say that the map of Ireland, where her ancestors came from, is written all over her face. The maps of Austria and Wales are less discernible on Doris's. Doris is an imposing presence, with searching, startling blue eyes and prematurely silver curly hair. She sits with her knees two feet apart, holding her cigarette between thumb and index finger, wearing Levi's, work boots, and a gray sweatshirt.

"Someone asked me once how come I never wear a dress," Doris says, "and I said, 'Probably for the same reason Katharine Hepburn never does.'"

"Nobody better mess with Doris," Eileen says. For two years now this pair has lived in these rooms, a flight above a beauty shop in a tiny hamlet in central Michigan. From their living room window you can see the post office, and one of the town's two groceries, and a few of its rundown houses. A short drive away is the restaurant-hotel where Eileen works as hostess and waitress. "It's a funky place with a repetitious menu, but the food's not bad, and sometimes people come here all the way from Detroit," says Eileen. "The ones who act like they had money usually turn out to be asses. The ones I like best are the guys who drive back-hoes—*they're* the gentlemanly ones, the ones who tip. The lady who runs the place, unfortunately, is out of her gourd."

"She's got plastic grapevines in there, instead of real plants," says Doris. "I happen to detest plastic plants, but when I volunteered to get some real ones for her, and even hang them there, she looked at me as if I was crazy."

"As I recall, she and her husband were punching each other out in the kitchen that day," says Eileen. "They do that a lot, while I smile and greet people at the door."

"That husband of hers," says Doris, "is one of the snidest little weasels I've ever seen. I usually think of people as animals—Eileen here, for example, is a possum—and if there was ever a weasel, it's him. But we have to earn our living somehow. Delivering phone books had its moments, but it only took a week and paid a grand total of $73. We don't want to go on welfare, but it's tough. I once worked at a cheese processing factory, but got laid off. Eileen would like to be a painter, but for now she's a waitress. I'd like to raise my own Irish wolfhounds, but for now I work in someone else's kennel."

"I gave her an *Encyclopedia of Dogs* for her birthday," says Eileen.

"Me and Eileen are book freaks," says Doris. "Neither one of us went to college—in fact, I'm a high school dropout, but we sure like to read. See these shelves? She cowed me into building them, and we put the maple stain on together." The eclectic library includes the *Better Homes & Gardens Cookbook, Walden, Walden II, May Craig's 14-Day Shape-Up Program, Everything That Rises Must Converge, Woman Plus Woman, The Exorcist,* and Dr. Spock's *Common Sense Guide to Child Care.* A book I wrote myself, in fact, is the reason I am here today. That book told in part of random visits to households around the country, and when Eileen and Doris read it they decided to invite me to theirs. The letter came in Eileen's startlingly clear, even hand. It said that if I ever should be in Michigan, and ever had wondered about lesbian motherhood, they'd be glad to see me.

In fact I had been wondering. Court battles over the custody of homosexuals' children were much in the news. Somewhere I read that 2½ million such cases were pending. Experts debated the "fitness" of gay parents to bring up their own or each other's children. "Male Role Models," I read, either are or are not necessary figures in a child's life. Gay households, I read, either are or aren't wholesome breeding grounds for new generations. An atmosphere of love and trust, never mind gender, either is or isn't all that counts. Conclusive studies had yet to be made. In one sampling of 21 children of lesbian mothers, 19 out of 21 chose "gender-dimorphic" favorite toys—girls, that is, would tend to choose dolls, and boys cars. ("It's hard," the social scientist in charge confessed, "to know how to rate a kite.")

I know some mothers who I assume are lesbian, but they never have seemed to want to talk about it. I know several pairs of women with grown children and ex-husbands, who together have established what looks like amiable and intimate housekeeping. I know a number of settled male couples whose homosexuality is neither denied nor ever discussed. During my term at the University of Georgia, the campus gay activists organized "Blue Jean Day," when the wearing of jeans was taken as a declaration of gayness. Many men went around in heavy tweedy woolens on that quite hot day.

Two single men who rented a four-room house together outside Detroit were evicted by neighbors who had never even met them. This pair's presence, the neighbors complained, would ruin the "family atmosphere" of Grosse Pointe Park. Since a town ordinance forbade "occupancy of a single-family home by persons not related by blood, marriage, or adoption," the eviction was legal. A British journalist who told in the *London Evening News* of six artificially inseminated lesbian couples found her home attacked and spray-painted with the slogan: "HERE LIVES A GUTTER REPORTER." Demanding legislation to stop such unorthodox pregnancies, a Member of Parliament said that "to bring children into this world without a natural father is evil and selfish. This evil must stop for the sake of potential children and society, which both have enough problems without the extension of this horrific practice." The subject of homosexuality clearly makes almost everybody a little nervous. Most people would rather not dwell on it. But here, in the wholesome middle of America, were two women who were eager to.

"One thing I like about Eileen," Doris says, "is the way she's learning to be so upfront. The day we moved in here, she got on the phone and told her mother. Her mother said, 'You're not living with Doris *that* way, are you?' and she said, 'Yes I am, and we're in love.'"

"A couple of months later," says Eileen, "my mother had a nervous breakdown. They gave her a woman psychiatrist, who I don't think has done her much good. My brother explained to this doctor that 'my father died, my sister broke up with her husband and now is a lesbian,' and my mother, sick as she was, broke in to say, 'Oh, don't tell her *that!*'"

"Maybe that shrink was well-intentioned," says Doris, "but I'm not sure you can dispense mental health in fifty-minute doses."

"See, my mother always thought marriage was something you stick with no matter what. Even if it isn't perfect, and I'm not sure hers and Dad's was, you make do. Security is what matters to her. Take no risks, be responsible, pay your bills, keep your job: that's what she thinks. That's why I'd never want to go on welfare."

"Me neither," says Doris.

"How'd you two meet in the first place?" I ask.

"Through Fred, oddly enough," says Doris. "He and I worked in the same chocolate factory. At first he thought I was a big bull dyke and I thought he was a snotty little creep, but he liked the way I stood up to the women in that plant. There's nothing more cruel than a pack of heterosexual women, and they gossiped viciously about me and Karen, my lover then, who worked there too. I finally said, 'Look, I'm a lesbian and Karen's a lesbian and we live together, we're lovers, okay?' and that ended all the gossip. Fred admired me for that.

"We'd have lunch together, and we made friends when we discovered that we both liked animals. We also both liked old people and babies, better than those our own age. I usually figure that people in between can take care of themelves. So he asked me to come over and meet the wife. So I did. Right off I liked Eileen very much, but it wasn't mutual, not at first. I didn't come sneaking through the woods after some man's wife.

"Then I started finding out stuff about Fred that wasn't so nice. He told me he was cheating on Eileen, that sexually they weren't compatible. He had this girlfriend named Bambi, and when he went with her he'd tell Eileen he was spending the evening with Karen and I. Sometimes we did all have drinks together. I told him, 'Fred, I really like your wife,' and Fred told Eileen I dug her. Next time we all had drinks together, at the tavern in town, I got to talking to Eileen about health foods—you know, carrots and stuff.

"She asked, so help me, 'Would you like to see my pattypan squash?' She had this giant squash in the back of the pickup she and Fred had driven to the tavern in. So I went back to see it. 'Doesn't it feel good?' she asked. It did. We discovered we liked each other, and went for a walk down the road, and came back with stars in our eyes. She was really attracted to me, in a way she never had been to Fred."

"Fred got angry," says Eileen. "He wanted to play a swinger game, not break things up. Doris told me if things ever got bad I should come and move in with her, so one day I picked up Denise and did."

"That was after I broke up with Karen, and Fred started really carrying on with Bambi."

"Fred used to want us to get Doris to babysit, can you imagine?" Eileen asks. "He'd say, 'She's so *nice*, even if she is a dyke'—but now he's got a real hate on for her."

"Why'd you marry Fred in the first place?" I ask.

"We both worked in the same dime store. I was nineteen. He was sexy, in a greaser sort of way. We had some laughs. I wasn't crazy about the courses I was taking in college. It seemed like the thing to do. We didn't have such a bad time. He came on like super-daddy, off and on, with Denise; when she was a baby he'd take as good care of her as I did. We tried to have another baby but somehow never could.

"At first, in fact, I didn't want my marriage to end, even when I found out that Fred was in love with Bambi. I had a whole empire built with lots of ego props around me, and even though I was dumfounded, I didn't want a divorce. The way I'd been brought up, I figured the thing to do was hang in there and try to keep things together—"

"—and drive me crazy," says Doris.

"By that time Doris and I were in love, but I thought maybe we could all be sort of swingers, for Denise's sake. I thought Fred and I could keep on living together and he'd see Bambi sometimes and I'd see Doris sometimes, but that was insane."

"Eileen, you have to remember, once won a Supermarket Checkout Clerk of the Year award," says Doris. "Her cousins are podiatrists and secretaries. Mine are bank robbers and welfare recipients. My mother's been married three times and, let's face it, she was a whore. She was a carhop, and she drove my own father away when I was still a baby. When I was five, and she told me she was getting remarried, I said, 'Yippee, I'll have a father like the kid across the street,' but what I got was an asshole. It was like being raised by two kids.

"When I came out and told her I was a lesbian, I was fourteen then, my mom said, 'Oh, you're just like Bubbles'—Bubbles was the poodle she'd just had spayed—and I said 'No, Mom, it's different, I'm not like a spayed bitch.' Mom messed around for several years before she married her third husband, the one she's still with. He's the one I wish was my real father. He's a big, burly 200-pounder who kisses his sons and plays with the dogs.

"All I ever wanted myself was a family-type atmosphere, but I sure never found it at home. My own family's scattered all over the whole goddamn world. None of us knows what the others are doing. So the only family that matters to me is the one right here in this house."

"My mom's kind of gotten used to us," says Eileen. "When we first went there together, on Thanksgiving and then Christmas, she'd get out extra sheets for the sofa the way she did when I went with Fred. Fred thought the bed was too narrow for us both to sleep on. Doris doesn't think so. By Easter, Mom accepted reality."

"I don't care much for Eileen's brother Jim," says Doris. "I don't like the way he badmouths his mom—it makes me mad to see a woman beaten down."

"But now that Dad's gone, Jim's the man of the house," says Eileen. "And at least he's accepted Doris and me, that's something. Other relatives are supposed to think she's a friend and roommate. Aunt Sue, she's my mother's skinny, grouchy, hyper sister, 'knows,' but she's not *my* idea of a role model. Her daughter Donna, has boyfriends who wear leisure suits—big hulks with pomaded hair and white patent leather shoes and belts."

"Aunt Sue's cellar doesn't have a single spider in it," says Doris. "A kid could never have any fun in a cellar like that—it looks more like an operating room."

"She thinks it's utterly reprehensible that my mother's kitchen is so small she has no place to put the dish drain except the sink," says Eileen. "Last summer, we were over at the lake in her vacation bungalow, and she finally figured out the relationship between Doris and me, and said, 'You're forbidden *ever* to come to this house again.' She said that to my mom, too. If my mom had the ego, she'd say, 'Fuck off.' "

"First time I ever had dinner with that clan, I said, 'Never again,' " Doris remembers, "but what can you do? It was Thanksgiving at Aunt Myrna's. She said, 'Thank God we all have our health,' and Aunt Sue said, 'Yes, not like Happy Rockefeller,' so then there was a discussion of mastectomy and retribution—Happy was a bad mother, see, so she deserved to have her tits cut off."

"I always have a pounding headache with those aunts," says Eileen. "I wish I could say to my mother, 'Here you are at age sixty, you live with your son, you hang out with these awful women—why don't you build a life for yourself?' She used to work for Grant's, and you know what happened to Grant's. That's her luck. She just says, 'Oh, I'm so nervous, I can't do anything else.' "

"If you're locked up in a cell," says Doris, "you have to get used to it."

"Marriage was a kind of cell for me," says Eileen. "I guess one of the reasons I got married in the first place was to rule out a lot of choices that now, all of a sudden, are opening up to me. It's scary, in a way."

"It's *very* scary," says Doris.

"But I do know some things I want. I want to paint. I want a house in the woods, because the woods give me a feeling of cosmic serenity. I want to travel, too, and see what dynamic currents are

going on in this land today. A lot of people are having things *happen*
to them. I wish a few things would happen to me."

"What about the chase?" asks Doris. "Wouldn't you call *that* dynamic?"

"What chase?" I ask.

"Is there time to tell her before Denise comes home?" asks Eileen.

"We'll send her out to play, if not," says Doris. "The sauerbraten
will keep."

So. The chase. My hostesses describe it in the present tense, inviting me to picture it. It happened six months ago. They're driving
through the year's first blizzard, heading from Ann Arbor to Kansas
City. With them are three lesbians they have only just met, who represent the Ann Arbor section of an unofficial gay underground whose
chief purpose is to reclaim kidnapped children. Denise, five months
earlier, had been kidnapped by Fred, and taken to Kansas City. At
least that's where they think she is. Their new friends from Ann
Arbor think so, too, which is why the carload of five is driving
through the snow, all night, playing Ghost and Twenty Questions
and Password to try to keep awake.

"He took her away the day before Father's Day," says Eileen. "He
called that morning to tell me what time he'd be by to get her, and
on the phone he sounded so nice and sympathetic, like his old self,
like the Fred I married. I told him how my mom was looking for-
ward to seeing Denise on Father's Day, this being the first Father's
Day since my dad was gone—and he said, 'Oh, how *is* your mom,
give her my best, won't you?' I felt sort of sorry for him—after all
he'd been on unemployment, fifty-one dollars a week."

"But such subterfuge!" says Doris. "Fred comes here with his
friends Steve and Mimi, who'd never been nice to us, and I thought,
Gee, maybe we can all be friends after all. Mimi asks can she come
upstairs to wash some rhubarb. That floored me: always before she
treated me like shit, now she's asking me a favor. So I think, That's
cool, and lead her upstairs."

"Meanwhile, out in the yard, Steve gets me to show him where
I've planted the tomatoes," says Eileen, "so I do and the garden's
behind the beauty shops, and all of a sudden I hear this big roar of an
engine, and when I look around Fred and the baby are gone. Mimi
runs downstairs and gets into the car with Steve and they drive
off—it turns out Fred had someone else parked around the corner in
a getaway car."

"He couldn't drive himself," says Doris, "because he'd had his license revoked for drunken driving. I was furious. I said to Eileen, 'You stupid-ass fool! I *told* you never to turn your back on that sneaky creep snake, and you did, and now the baby's *gone!*' "

"I should have known," says Eileen, "that whenever Fred felt his foundation crumbling, he'd grab that child to prove he was a man. He was and is an insecure greaser, from a big, loving, violent Bavarian family. I guess he was sure I'd come crawling back to him after a while with Doris, and when I didn't—when I actually preferred her to him—he was fit to be tied.

"It wasn't so much that he wanted Denise; there were times when he hardly paid any attention to the poor kid. But he'd been having trouble with his new girlfriend, with all the custody agreements. I guess it was idealistic of me to think we could work out visitation rights. Fred was so erratic about seeing her, even before all this happened. He'd talk big—he'd say he was taking her on a two-week vacation with his whole family—but then never show up, because he'd found some chippie to screw or smoke grass with."

"Custody still isn't figured out for sure," says Doris. "But think of the absurdity of having custody decided by one male judge—it all depends on his whim, and *he's* never been to the house, he can ignore all he hears. My old lover Karen was raped a few years ago, by a black man who lured her to a field, but when they tried him, he cut his Afro and wore glasses and looked earnest. Never mind that he was a stinking, lousy, cowardly rapist, the word 'lesbian' carried more weight—it was used, in fact to set him free. 'Everybody knows lesbians are deviates, they'll do anything,' is what we kept hearing."

"Doris could have cut Fred's legs off if she'd found him after he took the baby away," says Eileen. "I think she was madder even than I was."

"I was full of rage and self-pity to find Denise gone," says Doris, "because in a way she'd become my daughter, too. At different times I'd feel different ways toward her. When she made me a Mother's Day card, I felt like a step-parent, and I can always tell, just by listening to the way she cries, whether she's hurt or in pain."

"How'd you find out that she was in Kansas City?" I ask.

"It took five agonizing months," says Eileen. "Fred wouldn't say, his friends wouldn't say; we finally had to 'borrow' a Master Charge bill out of his mailbox, and in it we found a receipt from some health spa near Kansas City. I figured that was where he'd taken her, because his cousin Frank lives outside of Kansas City."

"We really did detective work," says Doris. "Then someone told us about this underground lesbian network in Ann Arbor. Talk about sisterhood! Talk about family! Those women never even heard of us, but they cared more about us and did more for us than our own relatives."

"Those were an awful five months," says Eileen. "It took all my energy to keep myself together at work, so when I came home I'd cry and scream and have fits. It almost drove Doris and me apart. All my life, see, I'd loved babies. I wanted to have another child—I still wouldn't mind having one—and if I hadn't had Denise, I'd have felt awful. I always loved dolls, wanted a baby of my own long before I even knew where babies come from. I *liked* being pregnant, and once Denise came I was with her all the time."

"When we finally got to Kansas City," says Doris, "the Ann Arbor lesbians had lined up a place for us to stay, through the Daughters of Lesbos in Kansas City, with this Jewish lesbian named Sandy, who lived in the Romanelli district off Ward Parkway. That Sandy was a trip. Before she'd decided she was gay she had three sons. What a trio. The oldest one was a liar, the middle one a screamer, and the youngest one a grunter—he'd grunt the whole theme from *Batman*. Ida, from Ann Arbor, she'd put towels around those boys like Batman capes, and we all played with them. They acted surprised. They had very few of what you'd call the social graces. They had the manners, in fact, of young wolves. I ended up smacking one kid's backside, and made him take a bath. That little gremlin. Then we all went to have enchiladas and Carta Blanca—quite a lot of Carta Blanca—to check over our plans."

"That was Sunday night," says Eileen. "We'd already tricked the 411 operator into giving us Frank's address, in the Gladstone neighborhood. We decided not to phone and say we were doing a special market research survey on baby soap—that was our first idea—but to go right to the scene of the crime. So we drove there, to Frank's house, and guess what we found: a FOR SALE sign."

"The sign said not to come in without calling the real estate agency first," says Doris, "but Sandy has an idea. She's Jewish, right? So she'll come on like this pushy Jewish bitch, househunting for her husband who's about to be transferred to Kansas City. So we're all sitting in the car, she's putting on eyebrow pencil. We get everything all rehearsed. We wait in the parking lot behind a bar while she goes in."

"She comes out after a while; she tells us Frank's in there, a little boy's in there, and so's Denise—'Your daughter is beautiful,' she tells me—and she asks Frank if Denise is his too, and he says no, she's his cousin's child.

" 'Oh,' Sandy asks Frank, 'is your cousin a widower?'

" 'No,' he says, 'it's a weird story. Her mother found herself a girlfriend to play with.'

" 'Doesn't the mother want the child?'

" 'Look,' Frank says, 'she knows her husband has a cousin in Kansas City; if she wanted the kid she'd be here to get her.' So then, like we've planned, Sandy puts her lipstick—lipstick, isn't that an inspired touch?—behind a pillow so she'll have a reason to get back in, and comes back out to the car to tell us. We figure that if Denise is in there, and Fred isn't, this is as good a time as any for the reabduction."

So the posse of women marched to the door of Cousin Frank's house. Only Sandy rang the bell; the others hid behind a bush. "Sorry," Sandy said, "I think I left my lipstick in your house." She went in first. Then the five other women followed, before Frank had a chance to close the door.

"He must have thought at first that we were a bunch of college girls looking for a small German man to play with," says Eileen, "because he said, 'Oh man, cool, yeah, come on in.' But then when *I* march in his expression changes. He goes: 'Hi, Eileen.'

"I start running around looking in all doors but one; he's blocking that door with his body. I dart in, though, and find Denise. She's asleep but she wakes up and starts crying. I say, 'Look, Frank, I don't want to call the police, but if I have to I will, and you'll be arrested for kidnapping.' "

"It's a Liliputian-sized house," says Doris, "and I make it my business to look around. The living room and dining room are all open, and straight ahead is a doorway. Frank draws himself back against a little alcove there and pushes Sandy aside. By that time I'm feeling a lot of sisterhood, and I don't like what he's doing to my sister, and I guess I got to look pretty angry, too, because Frank asks me, 'Who the fuck are you?'

"I go: 'I don't want to hurt you and I don't want you to hurt me, but I want Eileen to get her daughter back. There's police out there, Frank, and they'll get you.' Just then Eileen floats by with the baby. Frank asks me, 'Do you want to talk about this or ain't you got the guts?' Ida says, 'Maybe we *should* stay and talk,' but Sandy screams, 'No, there's someone at the back door!'

"Can you imagine—Eileen with her ass still hanging out of the door of our car, and Fred at the back door? Fred and Frank, we forgot to tell you, like to play with G-U-N-S, it makes them feel good—"

"Denise isn't here; you don't have to spell it out."

"Anyway, we get the hell out of there and we finally make it back to Sandy's, all of us, congratulating each other, calling our mothers, calling the lawyer who tells us to quick quick quick get out of Missouri."

"How'd Denise take all this?"

"First she cried for her daddy, and she cried for Sweetie, her doll—she wept, 'My baby, my baby, she doesn't know where I am,' and I couldn't blame her. But by the time we got back to Sandy's she was fine. She hopped onto the toilet by herself, which she hadn't been big or coordinated enough to do when she was taken. And we asked her, 'Remember Miss Mouse? Remember Woody?' And she turned to me and said, 'I love you, Mommy,' and tears came to my eyes—I thought, Oh God, how many times I've dreamed that she would be back, and here she is."

"For a while we hid out, with some Ann Arbor lesbians, and then with another friend," says Doris. "We laid low and played it cool. I kept thinking how when I was a kid myself my mom would leave me alone, and no matter who she'd board me out with, I'd never forget her. Once she told me, 'This will be your mommy now.' That confused mommy stuff is no good."

"I panic all over again when I think how close we came to missing Denise completely," says Eileen. "Fred, it turns out, was just about to take her to Hawaii. If he managed to get her that far away, we'd never have found her at all."

"Doesn't Denise miss him?" I ask.

"Look," says Doris, "if he'd been a good father, it'd be great for her to see him. But just because his sperm activated the egg doesn't mean he has the right to haunt this child forever. I'm not saying he would willfully chain her to a bed, or feed her bread and water, but there are worse things. If when she's eight she asks, 'How come I don't have a daddy like Jeanie down the street?' then we'll have to try to explain things to her. For now we say it's better to be with us and that he has to stay away, and she seems to accept it."

"Are there any men in her life?"

"Well, the guy who runs the laundromat, Mr. Hoffman, gives her piggyback rides, and Jeanie's father, from down the street, the one who's taken them to Sunday school, is nice to her, and the fellows who left us Bruce—this dog here, they used to hang around—"

"Can I ask *you* a question?" Eileen says to me. Fair enough. "Does all this make you nervous?" she asks.

"I guess it does, a little," I tell her. "I guess I'd prefer that Fred be a decent, responsible man and that you and he could have worked things out." I tell Eileen and Doris of the French historian Amaury de Riencourt, who I once heard say in a speech that polarity leads to vitality, that the drive toward sameness "might end up by creating a third gender, a neutral type comparable to the sexless workers among ants and bees." Most of each sex's complaints about the other, de Riencourt added, revolve not so much around "cruelty, aggression, or tyranny but passivity and indifference." To make light of the famous "difference" between the sexes, he went on, "does more to destroy the inner core of the family than anything else." What, I ask Eileen and Doris, did they have to say in response?

"There's *plenty* of difference between the two of us," says Eileen.

"There are ways and ways of differing," says Doris.

"Do you think gay people are inadequate parents?" Eileen asks me.

"You two are probably far more adequate than a lot of straight couples," I say. "You have humor, for one thing, which isn't nearly as commonplace as I wish it were."

"But I'll bet you're wondering what's the moral of this story, aren't you?" asks Doris and she is right. "You're thinking, What does it all add up to? Never leave your daughter alone with her father? Never trust a German if you think you're going to fall in love with his workmate from the chocolate factory? Beware of cousins in Kansas City?"

"What I'm also wondering," I say, "is what'll happen to Denise when she grows up—where'll you take her for family reunions? Who'll be her aunts? The lesbians from Ann Arbor?"

"Maybe they will," says Eileen. "One of them did send her a doll for her birthday."

"And what about her own—uh, gender?" I ask. "Do you want her to grow up and be a lesbian?"

"God no," says Eileen. "I pray she won't be left-handed and I pray she won't be queer."

"And what's she supposed to think about *you?*" I ask Doris.

"I don't want her to think of me as a daddy, or a big sister, or a pal, exactly. I don't know—surrogate mother, maybe? No, that's jargon. What counts is she shouldn't think I'm a jackass when she grows up. I'd rather she'd hate me than that. You have to be consistent with a child. A child needs not so much a role model as someone stable. And I think I will be stable, as far as she's concerned. I have an instinct for that kid like a mother bear, and when she asks who I am I say, 'No, I'm not your other mommy, I'm Doris.' Whatever the hell that means."

"What if she'd been a boy?" I ask.

"I guess it would be harder," says Eileen. "But I wouldn't mind finding out. Maybe someday we'll adopt a boy."

"We do see ourselves as a family," says Doris. "Lots of kids are raised unconventionally these days, after all; ours isn't the weirdest household I know of. Besides, think how many closet bisexuals have been parents all through history."

"What about Fred?" I ask.

"I guess we'll have to worry about him till Denise grows up," says Eileen. "We'll have to move, to keep away from him. He might always try to kidnap her again."

"Maybe we should move to a lesbian community," says Doris. "Those dykes in Ann Arbor were absolutely lovely. Some of them have kids, and they seemed to be doing fine. On the other hand Sandy's boys, in Kansas City, were a mess."

"But so are a lot of straight people's kids," says Eileen.

Footsteps sound on the stairway outside.

"Look who's back!" says Doris, and lifts Denise up to the ceiling. Instead of hugging or stroking the child, she pats her, gingerly, as a man might do. Not glissando, staccato. Denise has a straight nose, like Eileen's, and blue eyes and blond hair, presumably like Fred's. After ten minutes or so, when she gets used to me, she shows us all the pictures she has crayoned at Sunday school and asks if she may go for a walk with her dogs.

"Not just now," Eileen says, "we're going to have dinner first." And so we sit down, the four of us. We don't say grace, but gratitude is in the air all the same.

"This sauerbraten is dynamite, Eileen," says Doris. "I'll never leave you."

"Me neither," says Denise.

Denise has held true to that promise. Doris has not. A couple of years later, Doris left Eileen to go live with another woman on the Upper Peninsula. Eileen was crushed, for a time, but she reasoned that gay unions are no more durable than heterosexual ones, and started looking around at experiments in communal living.

In their search for new living quarters she and Denise had better luck than Angie and Buzzy did in the chapter preceding. Eileen and Denise found a household to their liking, a lesbian collective, and moved right in. They had seen five or six other places before they decided on this one, and learned that communes can vary at least as much as marriages do.

Shark Meat, Peacock Feathers and Soybeans

I SIT ON THE BALCONY of a twelfth-floor apartment on Turtle Creek Drive in Dallas, a few days after the summer solstice. At nearly nine the sky is far from dark; it makes me think of the Magritte painting "Empire of Light." Several of us are out here passing around a pipe of hashish, admiring the view of Revershon Park, listening to a tape deck of Gato Barbieri. Others are inside, dancing with futuristic abandon. Two women sit staring into each other's eyes, as they have been doing these past twenty minutes. The women, Betty and Sue, both look to be in their thirties, and they both live in this apartment. So do Doug, who is close to fifty, and his nephew Jeff, who is sixteen. All four have their own rooms. Doug is sort of involved with Betty, but not too much. He is also sort of involved with five or six other women in other informal Arica households around the country; Betty is sort of involved with a couple of other Arica men.

Arica, named for a village in northern Chile, is an eclectic and elaborate system of mental and physical exercises designed to lift humanity out of the morass in which Oscar Ichazo feels that most of us too long have been enmired. Ichazo is a Bolivian student of mysticism and science. His systems, geared to nine "levels" and four "planes of existence"—physical, mental, emotional, and spiritual—are said by his followers to point to the "possibility of global awareness and agreement," and "a full journey, available for the first time in human history, to total freedom of consciousness." Ichazo's techniques, as synthesized in the village of Arica and transplanted all over the United States, are taught in "programs" which can last from one hour to and beyond a forty-day, $600 "training." The programs earn his foundation about $1 million per year gross. Some 50,000 Americans are alumni of "the training," which an Arica brochure says is meant "to free us from negative associations surrounding our past, thus converting our experience into wisdom."

The "training" so affects some Aricans that they choose to forsake their former living arrangements and move into group Arica house-holds—actual houses in some cities, high-rise buildings like this one in others. This large apartment house is not entirely Arican, but three or four of the spacious places in it are, as are several kindred others a walking distance away. Aricans are sociable; they like to visit back and forth. Several neighbors have stopped by here tonight. One, who flew south last weekend for a fishing trip off Padre Island, caught the shark we fileted for dinner tonight. I wouldn't order it again, but it tasted okay. My contribution was the boysenberry sherbet.

Before this evening all I had heard about Arica was that its fol-lowers swore by a dramatic-looking 25-minute daily series of exercises called "psychocalisthenics," which I had seen done on some Long Is-land beaches, and that it hadn't much use for conventional families. On this last point my source was an orchestra conductor who, as he put it, had "lost two wives—one to Scientology and one to Arica." This man housed and cared for his children by both sundered un-ions, and his view of Ichazo's system, as of L. Ron Hubbard's, was understandably prejudiced. In any case I had been meaning to check out Arica for myself when, by chance here in Dallas, I ran into Doug, whom I had not seen in fifteen years.

Doug, last time I saw him, had been a lawyer and poet, but that was before he had heard of Ichazo or taken the "training." Now Doug was a trainer himself, and looked more engaging than ever. His deep thick auburn hair had grown much longer, and there was some-thing even more hypnotic than there had been before about his gaze —perhaps, he explained when I remarked on this, from having so often done *trespasso*, the eye-locking Arica exercise I now see Betty and Sue trying. When I told Doug the rumors I had heard about Arica being an anti-family institution, he gave me a dashingly patient smile and denied the charge. "Arica *is* a family," he said. "It's helped me to have a better relationship than ever with my own ex-wife and children. Why don't you come by and see for yourself?"

So here I am, talking to Doug and his nephew Jeff, whose hair is also auburn and whose eyes can also impale, and who is remarkably assured for a 16-year-old. As we talk the phone rings. It is for Jeff. His conversation lasts less than a minute, then he disappears.

"That was Lucille, upstairs," Doug explains when Jeff is gone.

Lucille, he adds, is 44, and her man has been in Mexico for a fortnight, which is why she has taken to "ordering Jeff up, like a pizza.
Jeff thinks it's a gas." Nothing stuffy about Doug's views. He thinks
that polygamy, "which is practiced furtively by who knows how
many adulterous Americans, is about to come out into the open, and
high time. The Mormons did it, the Moslems do it, so why shouldn't
we? It works."

"Is this Arica's theory?"

"No, it's my own, but just think about it: it makes sense."

"Wouldn't jealousy be a problem?"

"Not after women get used to it. When women get used to sharing a man, it's no more of a big deal than passing the bread." He
says nothing about the possibility of men sharing a woman. "As the
gross national product shifts from manufactured goods to services,
you see, the whole sexual ethic is changing. The only problem with
making it with more than one person is the danger of infection."

"It's not confusing for the kids?"

"We don't *have* all that many kids around here," says Sue, who
finally has quit staring into Betty's eyes. "Kids interfere too much
with our process here, which one way or another is to stay high, have
our full capacities realized. We don't have much time: if pollution
continues the way it's doing now, there won't be any more plankton,
and we'll lose seventy percent of our supply of oxygen."

"Not the sort of world you want to bring a kid into?"

"That's partly it. Little kids are okay when you're tripping or playing, but on a day-to-day basis they bring you down too much. Anyway, I've been in a child space myself this whole week."

"Me too," says Betty, as she shoves a new tape deck into the
stereo. "Just now, at thirty-seven, I'm finally learning to play, which
is far *out*, but the child space isn't all fun by any means. It's painful
to remember how much of my real childhood I spent chasing after
my older brothers trying not to be left out."

"You're right to get in touch with those memories, though," Doug
says. "That's a lot of what Arica is about, speeding up each other's
process, filling in the holes. If your own father wasn't really available
—as mine wasn't even though he was around all the time—then what
you need is *new* fathers. I find new ones all the time in Arica."

"That's what families are for, isn't it?" asks Sue. "Arica families,
anyway. Families should give all their members whatever it is they
need to get more balanced. Arica doesn't threaten families. It makes
them better. Only the weak ones fall apart. It's Darwinian."

"My kids know that wherever they go in this country, they'll find an Arica house with a community of shared ritual, shared warmth, and shared concern," says Doug. "Want to dance?" We all get up and dance around the room, not touching.

I am drawn to the idea of communal living. For one who has spent the better part of her adult years alone, I am drawn to it immoderately. It can be glum to walk into a room where there is no one to give a glance of acknowledgment, much less the applause we all secretly crave. But time has taught me self-protective tricks. When last I came home from a two-month trip I phoned some neighbors, twenty minutes before being dropped off at my front door, so they would be standing there to give the illusion of welcome.

Energy, to use one of this past decade's more tarnished words, is not always ignited in company, but for me it often is. The simple prospect of sitting down at a table set for ten, with hunks of paper toweling for napkins, can lure me to travel long, soggy distances. The prospect of having soulmates close at hand has led me to consider knocking down the wall between my apartment and the one next door, or building a spiral staircase to the one below. All my life I have doodled floor plans of houses, and waked from dreams of empty rooms—rooms suddenly mine to furnish and people with, if not a usual family, then some less orthodox replacement.

Such families of course are not really new at all. Their attractions and dangers have been known since long before Aristotle cautioned in his *Politics* that communes might be a less than ideal way to raise children: "We say that each man has a thousand sons, but these are not one man's sons; any one of them is equally the son of any person. As a result, no person will concern himself very much about any of them . . . two impulses, more than all others, cause human beings to love and care for each other, 'This is my own' and 'This I love.'"

Throughout history, ownership and love have been defined ambiguously. Never for long have we settled on a solid answer to the question of where and in what manner and with how many others we ought to live and raise our children, if in fact we are parents. The fashion for communal families has never vanished for long. One of its great resurgences occurred in this country a century ago, and although only nine of those that bloomed then lasted for more than a generation, their collective legacy endures here today. In fact it thrives. Those who thought that the sudden vogue for communes was another hectic symptom of the sixties were mistaken.

Such families thrive, here and elsewhere, in part because the human soul craves a certain amount of order, a commodity in short supply of late. Many people in recent years have come of age without ever shedding that state of mind the Japanese psychiatrist Takeo Doi calls *amae*—a pronounced and childlike need to be passively dependent, which can last far beyond childhood. *Amae*, Doi suggests in *The Anatomy of Dependence* (Kodansha, 1973), springs from a pronounced and widespread lack of authority. It blurs the distinctions between subject and object, adult and child, male and female. It accounts, in part at least, for the worldwide epidemic of student rebellions whose hidden message Doi thinks was: Give us a father, give us some guidance, tell us what to do. It also accounts, I suspect, for the new profusion of communal extended families, particularly those I think of as ashrams.

Ashrams, technically, are hermitages, religious retreats for colonies of disciples who revere a common leader and agree on a common ideology. Arica, it seems to me, is a secular network of such ashrams. The commune in Grittleton, Wiltshire, where Princess Margaret went when her marriage broke up probably isn't an ashram, nor are the collectives to be discussed in the next chapter, most of whose sole guiding principle is that their members like each other well enough to save money by living together for a while.

Ashrams offer their members structure, system, ritual and, if you submit to their authority, infinite comfort. They also cause trouble. Their recruiting methods are sometimes hard to distinguish from kidnapping. Ashrams of this sort have given rise to a whole new vocation, not quite listed yet in the Yellow Pages but vigorous all the same: deprogramming. If you think your child has been brainwashed by his abductors, you hire a deprogrammer to remind him, perhaps with force, of the good sense he has forgotten having once learned at your knee, and to bring him home. Your child and his new church, of course, may not see the matter this way at all. Neither may the American Civil Liberties Union, which has been involved in a number of court cases supporting the right of young people to join whatever religious groups they like. At issue in such court battles is that most entrenched and esteemed of American values, freedom of choice. In theory, of course, we want our children to grow up with a spectrum of options, the like of which their grandparents could never have envisioned; isn't that what this country is all about? But who ever thought our children might choose to shave off their hair and paint their foreheads and walk the streets as changing mendicants?

"Conservatorship laws," in most states, allow one person to take temporary but total control over the affairs of another, if the other is aged or disabled enough to need such protection. Lately, and quite controversially, such laws have been applied to the children of members of new groups with names like Citizens Engaged in Reuniting Families. A judge in California awarded "conservatorship" rights to the parents of some people past the age of 21 who had become enthusiasts, to say the least, of the Reverend Sun Myung Moon and his Unification Church. "The essence of civilization," this judge reasoned, "is a father, a mother and a child, even if the parents are ninety and the child is sixty." A higher court overruled, but such battles, which can cost the parents as much as $15,000, are far from finished.

Not to say that all ashrams are sinister or insidious. Some, from what I know, sound exalted. Given time, I would want to learn more of Dorothy Day's Catholic Worker Farm in Tivoli, New York, and the other outposts of her movement, and of the three radical Christian intentional communities run by the Society of Brothers, whose motto is "We're prepared to die for each other, but to live for each other is something much harder." I would like to look into the Chabad houses run by the Chasidic Jewish Lubavitcher movement. What I saw ten years ago in California of Charles Dederich's Synanon, for reformed drug addicts, impressed me. So, I assume, would the "families" of ex-addicts organized by the drug therapist Judianne Densen-Gerber, who believes, with many others, that "if you're not born into a loving family, you have to make one." Victor Paul Wierwille's The Way Foundation in New Knoxville, Ohio, which a number of former teen-agers from places like Rye, New York, have made their ashram, interests me rather less, as do the Reverend Moon's establishment and outposts of the Hare Krishna movement.

All this, of course, is a matter of style as well as of substance. Ashrams, like people, attract or repel me by their syntax. Many ashram people talk too earnestly, for my taste, of "process," and of the "space" they are in. I heard about one ashram whose residents were so militantly vegetarian that they would no more wear animals' hides than eat meat. A friend of mine happened to have canvas tennis sneakers on when he visited this place, where someone came up to him to say, "Thank you for not wearing leather."

In some of these places there is so much prating of everybody's unceasing quest for "personal growth" as to make one long for the company of emotional dwarves. Growth, unless some intelligence guides it, can be cancerous, just as freedom can be chaotic. Ashrams do not always appear to value such intelligence. Ashrams are nearly always overfond, for my taste, of the verb "share," whose metaphorical use I would like to see retired for five years at least. Ashram people go on way too long about their need to "share" their "gut feelings," and to say how interchangeable we all are or ought to be, how childish it is of us to brood over lost loves and other attachments.

Attachments, such people like to say, are dangerous, leading as they do to pain. The important thing, such people like to add, is to know how to let go of loves, of weekends, of involvements. What they say isn't wholly untrue, but their emphasis makes me gag. What needs all the emphasizing it can get, instead, is our need to cherish and build on our meager common histories. The German philosopher-sociologist Theodor Adorno wrote:

> A person can only be said to love if he has the strength to hold on to his love. . . . The person who is taken in by the lure of unreflective spontaneity, who proudly thinks of himself as honest in listening only to what he supposes is the voice of his heart, and in running away when he ceases to hear it, is, for all his sovereign independence, in fact the tool of society. Passive, without knowing it, all he does is accept whatever cards the interests of society deal to him. Love which betrays the beloved betrays itself. The obligation to fidelity imposed by society is the opposite of freedom, but it is only through fidelity that freedom can set up a rebellion against the dictates of society.

"Does he mean that holding on is more rebellious and courageous than letting go?" I asked Tony Scherman, a young writer and philosophy student who called Adorno's lines to my attention.

"That's it," said Tony. "I think he's right, too. It takes real guts to be constant. *Everything* in this society militates against constancy. The nature of work, of entertainment—most people I know who aren't in school don't read books anymore—of friendship, of love. You were asking me if I thought the importance of permanence is *exaggerated?* Hardly. Quite the reverse."

I agree. If you tell me that you, whom I have just met, will do nicely as a substitute for the man I have been thinking about all week, or that the department store saleswoman over there is interchangeable with my sister—any more than I am with hers—then forget it. I don't want even to visit your ashram, especially if I would there be serenaded with songs like:

> When I'm good to my planet
> My planet will be good to me.

Of course it will, but who needs to say so? Ashrams, organized around people known in the trade as "charismatic leaders," tend to belabor the obvious. That is one of the big reasons why, for all my communal impulses, I never stay long in them. I try to keep an eye on them, though. Now and then I come across one so exotic I feel I ought to need a passport to get in.

Two hours now I've been sitting here with crossed legs. My knees hurt. They hurt a lot. They hurt in an ache that has just become a throb. The throb becomes so unbearable that I stretch my legs out before me. At once I am chided by the woman on my right. "*Never* show the soles of your feet to the guru," she whispers harshly. "That's one of the sixty things you're not supposed to do in a temple."

"But the guru isn't *here* yet," I whisper back.

"He's coming now," she says, and so he is. Here comes Baba with his tambourine. See Baba walk down the aisle, with the men on his right and the women on his left. See Baba beam. Smell Baba's incense. Hear Baba talk. Or rather, hear Baba's translator interpret, since the eleven languages Baba is said to know do not, even after a good while in this country, include English.

Baba Muktananda is appealing, up there on his powder-blue velvet throne. No question that he dresses colorfully. Today he isn't wearing the orange wool ski cap he sometimes has on, even in midsummer, but he has put in his false teeth, which subtract a good three decades from his 68 years. His orange shirtlike garment is hiked above his crossed knobby knees, revealing his high orange socks. (Orange is clearly the favored and sacred color for habitués of this ashram.) Beside Baba is his wand. His wand consists of perhaps twenty resplendent peacock feathers, bound together with a burgundy velvet handle. To get a swat from that wand, in a new kind of laying on of hands, is to be blessed beyond imagining. Male peacock feathers are said to have amazing medicinal value: "The male peacock has so much power in his eye that he needn't even touch the female to sire a child." So say Baba's followers, of whom several hundred are here today for this Father's Day Intensive weekend. (Intensives, at this ashram, differ from regular weekends in that a physical touch from Baba, or his wand, is guaranteed. "I want to thank you all for your energy," someone says during a break. "This is my first Intensive, and it's really intense.")

Bless us, Baba, we chant in Sanskrit, as we sit here with crossed legs. If we have not yet memorized the Sanskrit syllables we read

them phonetically, from a mimeographed sheet. Kindle our hearts'
flame with thine. Show us the god in ourselves and in each other.
Welcome us all with love. *Om namah shivayah.* Six syllables in *om
namah shivayah.* Prufrockian Westerner that I am, it crosses my
mind that it must take us five minutes to drawl out those syllables,
to the tune of sitars and a lone violin. Nothing hasty happens in this
giant meditation hall. Not now. It must have been different when
this hall was a nightclub, called the Penguin Room, of a Jewish
resort named the Hotel DeVille, and before that the Nemerson.
With Baba here, the nearby village of South Fallsburg, in the Cats-
kill Mountains 75 miles northwest of Manhattan, feels at least as
Hindu as it does Jewish.

Baba's ashram is, among other things, a floating family, a movable
commune. A couple of hundred of his several thousand disciples in
the Siddha Yoga Dham Foundation do their best to go where he
goes—California, New York City, South Fallsburg, London, Rome,
or the home ashram at Ganeshpuri, northeast of Bombay. Tens of
thousands more followers keep the faith at 200 other centers, around
the world, among them residential ashrams in Oakland, Ann Arbor
and Boston as well as in New York. To hear these disciples talk you
never would know there were any other gurus, any other holy men,
any other saints. Wherever they go they enshrine Baba and his
teachings. They paint gigantic, innocent pictures of sacred peacocks
and elephants. They letter signs that say "KNEEL TO THE GOD IN EACH
OTHER," which is the essence of Baba's creed. That, and leave your
ego at the door with your shoes. That, and heed the teachings of the
guru, hear his parables. And don't forget, especially this week, that
"Baba *means* father."

I keep looking for signs that if Baba is our common father, then
we all are siblings, a family. What, Baba asks rhetorically, is better
than a family? God, Baba tells us, loves families. Children need parents. Husbands need wives. The way to make your family better is to
be better yourself, which means hang in there, keep on meditating
and chanting and lining up for *darshan. Darshan* is the long line we
form when we all queue up, two by two, to offer Baba the pieces of
fruit we have either brought from home, as a kind of hostess present,
or bought at a convenient stand just outside this meditation hall.
When we finally reach the head of the line we bow to Baba, touching our heads to the carpet at his feet if we want to be orthodox, and
place our fruit in a great big basket. As soon as the basket is full it
gets whisked away, for all we know to be resold. If we wish, we can
then hand Baba some jewelry or a child's toy or whatever else we

would like to have him bless with his touch. (All this reminds me of an audience I and a few thousand other people had in 1960 at the Vatican with, rest his soul, Pope John XXIII. The people here are no less excited by Baba.)

Some, when they get to the head of the *darshan* line, give Baba bottles of whiskey and beer, packages of cigarettes, joints of marijuana, cans of corned beef hash, contraceptives, or other emblems of renounced poisons. Such trophies are displayed in glass cases that line the hallway outside, where our shoes are filed. Not that Baba tells us individually to give up such evil things—he rarely has anything like a personal encounter with anyone here—but, as a follower puts it, "Just to be in the same ashram or the same *continent* with that cat can work a powerful magic."

The magic is most intense when the lights are dimmed and someone up near the altar takes the microphone. In a style drawn equally from the spiels of television shows' warmup men and airline stewardesses, we are asked: "At this time will you please remove all glasses and contact lenses." (At this time, indeed.) We comply because there is no telling whose eyeballs Baba might feel moved to touch, as he makes the rounds of all several hundred of us in the darkened hall. Everyone here is guaranteed at least a stroke from the peacock wand, but some get more—Baba might rub your eyeballs, knead your shoulder, or, best of all, breathe into your nostrils—"and if there's *ever* a time in your life to inhale," as the warmup man tells us, "that's it."

Eyes naked and closed, we sit there meditating in the dark, trying not to wonder where in the vast room Baba is. Sooner or later comes the swish of his wand in our section of the room, and softly though he treads, we can hear his barefoot steps coming up right behind us, and we never know what he'll feel moved to do. Maybe because he knew I was a writer, I was much blessed: I got not just the peacock swat and an eyeball rub but the breath up the nostrils, and I must say, though no stranger or even loved one had ever previously breathed up my nose, it felt oddly good. I did remember to inhale as deeply as I could. I didn't have dramatic *kriyas*, though. *Kriyas*—physical responses to the *shaktipat* that floods one when Baba uncoils one's *kundalini*—are as various as reactions described in the *Hite Report*. *Shaktipat* is energy, and *kundalini*, coiled at the base of your spine, is to your body what your mind is to your head: invisible, but all-important spiritual energy. Unleashed *kundalini* can lead to *kriyas* of moaning, sobbing, whinnying, shaking, and wild fits of laughter. It can be fairly weird, sitting there in that dark room hearing all those *kriyas*.

Baba disappears when he is finished uncoiling all our *kundalini*, and there follows a sort of question-and-answer, show-and-tell session, of testimonials to him. If three disciples have just survived a small plane crash, it is clearly because Baba was not yet ready for them to "leave their bodies." (If they had died, that presumably would have been fine, too.) If a dentist from a suburb of Chicago recovers from a nearly lethal heart attack, and loses fifty dangerous pounds of fat, that is also Baba's work. If a follower from Montana finally achieves her long-postponed dream of opening her own beauty shop, her luck can be traced to the swat from the peacock wand. Another woman, who looks around fifty and sounds as if she came from Brooklyn, tells how "when Baba touched me today it was like an explosion of joy, as if we were dancing madly around in the forest—I had to say to myself, 'Down, girl!'" Then a black man rises to declare, "When Baba touched *me*, he made me realize I had to create a space in my life for my *own* father, and give Pop a whole lot more love than I'd ever found time to do before. It felt so *good* to get that out of the way."

"*Sadgurunath maharaj ki jay!*" shout the other disciples as each testimonial ends, meaning, approximately, "Amen!" or "Praise the Lord!" Not for a moment do I suspect that the connection between Muktananda and each of his followers is feigned. Deity or not, this guru is remarkable. But I don't sense much going on among his followers. The lines are all vertical, between them and him, not horizontal. Each of them venerates him, but they don't have much to do with each other, which is why all this seems too simple to be a family. These people don't seem to have much to say to each other in the dining hall, where vegetarian casseroles (surprisingly good ones) are ladled out under signs that warn commendably, "DON'T TAKE MORE THAN YOU CAN EAT." The lines stretch a city block in that dining hall, but there's no restive chatter the whole time we wait, with distinctly un-American patience. We can't chatter because we are chanting. Chanting is my favorite aspect of this whole ashram—I like to hear it and I like to do it—but now and then I get sick of the same old tune and start to harmonize. Sally Kempton, who told me about Baba in the first place and who sees to it that I get where I'm supposed to go around here, frowns when I harmonize. "It isn't traditional," she says. Sally, whom I had known slightly before she became a disciple, is as loquacious about her new life as anyone could possibly be, telling at length how she never before had known such peace and joy. Other people I meet here are less forthcoming, both with me and with each other. All they ever talk about, as far as I can tell, is Baba. Some of them don't seem to talk at all. But there's one exception: the playwright Arnold Weinstein, once of the Yale Repertory Theatre and now very much with Muktananda.

"A lot of people come here," Weinstein tells me, "because they need a family and don't have a real one. A lot come from regular families that can't get their ass together to save their face. Almost all their stories are the same—the families they left behind are a mess."

"Any special kind of mess?" I ask.

"What's the difference?" retorts Weinstein. "Why bother with details? What's the good of all those *factlets*—all those pounds and pounds of information in the Sunday *Times?* You know what factlets do? They pollute."

No doubt they often do, but I'm partial to the odd factlet myself. I'm somehow gratified to know that Baba Muktananda was born to a landowning family in South India on May 6, 1908, and that he left home at 15 to become an ascetic. After 25 years of wandering, he became a disciple of Swami Nityananda at Ganeshpuri, 39 miles from Bombay. Nityananda made him a swami in 1947 and when Nityananda "left his body" in 1969, Muktananda succeeded him at Ganeshpuri. Nityananda, to judge by the vast portrait of him that hangs like a billboard from the ceiling above Baba's throne, was a bald fellow with a quizzical expression who wore what looks like a G-string and had a huge, pregnant-looking belly. Baba has a smaller version of that belly, too, maybe because being a guru is such sedentary work, or maybe because it often involves seeming maternal. Gurus, I am told aren't just fathers. They are whatever their disciples need them to be.

After this Father's Day Intensive, I make a second visit to the ashram. I am persuaded to return for the big weekend of the weddings. Baba is going to marry no fewer than sixteen couples, in the grandest celebration of his whole visit to America. Big it is: the ashram is crowded to the point of bursting, with confused-looking parents and kinfolk of the 32 principals, wellwishers from all kinds of other places ("NEED RIDE TO BOSTON," a bulletin board notice says, "AM BEDDED IN N.E. CORNER OF SWIMMING POOL, WITH CLOCK-RADIO") and at least three visitors from central Illinois—my sister, her son, and her daughter. They are here because they are my guests this week; they have to go where I go. The kids think it's funny. Ann, never much of a one for incense and sitars, is appalled. Whatever gene I inherited that prompts my own affinity for such things is missing altogether in her. The church she goes to now and then is a no-nonsense place where the sermons tend to be about subjects like jogging. She is also most emphatically a carnivore. As soon as we arrive here, just in time to queue up for vegetarian supper, she grabs the keys to my car and whisks her kids off to South Fallsburg for a kosher hamburger, rare. If they had it she would order steak *tartare*.

Artichoke soup is our menu. I eat it with Sally Kempton and Arnold Weinstein, watch fireworks, and the next day admire the costumes of all the American fiancés, newly renamed Manu and Gayatri and Govinda. Normally Baba's followers wear simple Indian shirts and saris, with the women adding red tika dots to their foreheads and pinning their hair up in demure topknots. But for the wedding, pearls surround the brides' eyebrows, and they wear tiaras of roses and baby's breath, and carnation leis long enough to be slipped over the heads of their grooms. Thus entwined, the couples march three times each around a sacred flame (providentially none of their flowing chiffon garments gets caught in the fire), and then up to the altar. There Baba blesses them, marries them, gives them turquoise-covered books and *prasad*, refreshments, in this case oversweet fudge. They feed each other the cookies and pose, just like the Presbyterians some of them probably once were, for photographers. The photographers, as at most weddings, really run the whole show—the act of picture-taking long since having become more important than the picture itself, or even the ritual. Somewhere along the way, I once heard, we gave the camera the right to form our memories of the event. A several-tiered multicolored wedding cake is borne to the altar, and the rest of us are passed *prasad*. (The hardest thing for these disciples to renounce must be sugar.) We all get handfuls of yellow rice and red rose petals to toss at the newlyweds.

Ann can't wait for the wedding to be over, nor will she allow her children to succumb to the temptations of the gift shop, which include buttons and mirror-backs showing Baba's sandaled feet as well as his face: with and without a smile, with and without false teeth, with and without the ski cap, with and without glasses. The shop also sells posters, pamphlets, books, and a cassette called "The Nectar of Chanting." I feel an urge to hang around and talk to the parents of the brides and grooms, to try to get more sense of their children's allegiance to the place, but Ann—who is, after all, my guest and my blood sister—begs me to get her out of here.

"These bliss ninnies are no more a family than a convention of hairdressers would be," she declares. "I'd far *rather* go to a convention of hairdressers, to hear them talk about whether or not the wedge cut's going to be a big deal next year."

"But there'd be that awful smell of hair spray."

"Anything," she replies, "smells better than incense. And if this place is so familial, where are all the children?" I look around, and—come to think of it—don't see many. That perhaps is this ashram's flaw. That, probably, is what makes any family a family—the promise of a new generation, the sense of diagonal and horizontal as well as of simple vertical connections. I think of the time someone said that there's a woman in India "for whom Baba is a *baby*, isn't that far out?" No, it isn't far out. It makes sense. Baba, it suddenly strikes me, is everyone's child. Strolling from his house to the meditation hall here, on the most mundane of errands, he invariably and instantly attracts a swarm of cooing admirers who act like ancient relatives from a faltering family line which only he, an infant, can be expected to keep alive. It's as if he were a clever child doing handsprings, instead of an elderly toothless man out for a walk in the humid Catskills air.

They don't talk about *shaktipat* or *kundalini* at Stephen Gaskin's Farm in central Tennessee, outside the village of Summertown. At The Farm—capital T, capital F—they call it juice. The 1,760-acre Farm's 1,100 residents are meant to be "juicy" all the time—to be juicy and telepathic as they "develop a cheap and livable and graceful life style," that being "one of the most important and heavy things that we can pass on to mankind, as a teaching to everyone." The things they aim to learn, Gaskin says, include "how to get along together, how to think beautifully and accurately, how to learn to govern ourselves.

"A third of the planet," Gaskin also says, "is starving . . . We want to show, by being loving together and having a good time together in close enough proximity to share these goods, that a bunch of people can be together, with a lot of love, without requiring a tremendous area of territory for each person to keep from fighting with each other." These aims are not modest, nor is The Farm's eight-year history. Since 1970, when they left the Haight-Ashbury section of San Francisco on the journey that led them here to Tennessee, they have built up a system that allows each one of them food, shelter, education, health care and travel expenses for no more than a dollar a day.

They also have established a medical and dental clinic in La Paz, Baja California, where they hope also to set up a soy dairy, as "a cot-

tage industry for a low-income neighborhood where protein foods are
lacking in the diet," a center for the relief of earthquakes and urban
distress in Guatemala, other city centers in Denver, the South Bronx,
and Bangladesh, and satellite farms in California, Florida, Michigan,
Missouri, New York, Ontario, and Wisconsin. Musicians among
them give concert tours. Farm people also write, print and market
their books and pamphlets—on birth control, on vegetarian cooking,
on Citizens' Band radio and on "spiritual midwifery," by natural
childbirth, which they teach at a Home Birth Center. Farm "ladies,"
as grown females are always referred to, are urged to breed all the babies they can. Videotapes of "Spiritual Midwifery" are sold for $15.
Of the 800 or so babies thus far delivered on The Farm, more than
half were born to mothers from outside. Other people's children are
cheerfully welcomed too, as are escapees from nursing homes. The
Farm needs all the hands it can get to help, because through a program called PLENTY it aspires in time to raise enough food to ship
to all the world's hungry.

If all this sounds audacious, as it surely does, then so did the notion of The Farm in the first place. Probably the biggest and most
thriving extended family ashram anywhere, The Farm began in the
fall of 1971, when a caravan of one busload and 70 carloads led by
Stephen Gaskin reached central Tennessee. They decided, rather as
Brigham Young's entourage had decided on Salt Lake City, that this
was the place for them. They were tired of California, where they
had lived for some years, tired of seeing and being hippies, tired of
hard drugs. The time had come, they felt, for them to till the soil,
smoke only marijuana, and practice what Gaskin had been teaching
in his Monday night classes—informal gatherings which quickly became a Berkeley ritual. Considering themselves "a family monas-
tery," they wanted to find a place to settle where their religious be-
liefs would not seem "weird." The fundamentalist country south of
Nashville seemed promising, so they pooled their savings to buy their
first 1,000 acres of Lewis County soil for $70 an acre, a price which
has since nearly sextupled.

Their use of marijuana, sacramental though they considered it, got
them into trouble. Soon after their arrival, Gaskin and three other
Farm men were arrested and charged with growing marijuana. Three
years later, Gaskin served eleven months in jail. His good cheer
behind bars and all the industry on The Farm won the neighbors
over. The Farm is, after all, an impressive place, and Gaskin, a
bearded blond in overalls with bespectacled and searching eyes, is an
impressive man even to those who do not regard him as their own

charismatic leader. Since he came to Tennessee, weighing 120, he has gained 55 pounds. He has also gained—if he ever needed it—a contagious assurance. "Everybody here has got to get a chance to be as heavy and responsible as possible," he tells his followers, "because some of you, later on, are going to be running farms a lot bigger than this one.

"It's impossible to invent a religion," Gaskin also says. "Religion is something that exists, like electricity. You study it and learn about it, the way you learn about electricity." He himself was an English professor at San Francisco State College, a protégé of the semanticist S. I. Hayakawa, and the husband of Ina Mae Middleton, by whom he has three children. Ina Mae and her brother and two sisters were frequent guests, my Aunt Martha remembers, at Homelands Farm in Iowa: their mother would bring them over in the morning from Marshalltown, where the Middletons lived, and they'd stay for lunch and supper. "They were an *outfit*, kid," my Aunt Martha assures me. Ina Mae's and Stephen's family today live in one of The Farm's fifty households, which have between twenty and sixty people each, housed less and less in tents and huts, and more and more in brandnew wooden houses.

I first heard of The Farm from a young man half my age named Tom, who happened to be in the same Transcendental Meditation class I signed up for in Iowa City, in January of 1975. Both of us, it turned out, had severe doubts about the grandiose claims made for TM by its zealots, but we reasoned that if even a tenth of those claims were to prove valid, the price of a mantra—a secret word to repeat to ourselves while meditating—would be well worth paying. Tom and I talked of all this once after class, walking through a bitter night. Even in that subzero cold Tom wore nothing on his head but an old cotton bandana. That bandana, he said, brought him luck. He had taken it to a lot of places. It had been burnt in campfires, faded by the sun, washed in the ocean. In his two decades Tom had been around plenty, and wondered aloud to what end fate had fetched him up here in Iowa. Ostensibly, he had come to take courses in Chinese history and German, but was that what he really wanted to do? Might he not do better to go back to The Farm?

"The what?" I asked.

"The only place I've ever been," Tom said, "where I really felt I knew where I was at." He elaborated. "Everybody at The Farm is so telepathic—they all know what everyone else is thinking, because they've all got rid of their egos. I never realized till I spent some time there myself how much trouble my own ego has got me into." Tom and I both came of "egotistical" backgrounds: his parents, he said, were liberal, academic, scientific, and suburban. His grandfather had willed him a cello which he had not been encouraged to play on The Farm. "If I go to The Farm," he said, "there'll be no skis, no cello, no art. What you do there is eat, sleep, work, open up your senses, smoke dope as a sacrament, work more, and love each other. It's monogamous. You have one wife, and she stays home while the man is out working."

Farm people, Tom said, were purists. They were such strict vegetarians that they didn't even wear down-filled jackets, or leather shoes and belts. Nor did they eat honey, considering it "too heavy on the bees." He was called Thomas there, not Tom, because the place doesn't hold with nicknames. Milk comes from soybeans, not cattle, because to produce milk cows must be pregnant. People there have a besetting sense of purpose. "They work their asses off all day doing what they're meant to do," and if there's any question what that might be, they just ask Stephen.

"I guess I'd better have a look at that place myself someday," I said, and a few months later I did. My friend Charles made a deal with me: we would meet for a weekend together in Tennessee, and he would go with me to The Farm if I would stop with him at the Jack Daniel's distillery, an hour or so to the east.

"Capitalist imperialist boozer," I said.

"Bliss ninny," he replied.

We went to both places, and both beguiled us. Just before reaching The Farm's gate we stopped for barbecue sandwiches at a Summertown luncheonette, expecting drab gruel once we got to The Farm. We were wrong.

First, like all the 20,000 people who annually visit The Farm, we had to be sized up by a welcoming committee. If they had thought we looked like narcotics agents or that our hearts for whatever reason were not in the right place, they would have told us to go back to the world. We passed, but where were we to throw our sleeping bags, on what turned out to be so crowded a weekend? The word went out over Beatnik Bell, The Farm's primitive phone system, that "we've got an older couple here needs a place to crash." Older? Us? A pair of kids just barely out of their thirties? We fell asleep in someone's otherwise vacant loft, and woke to find several other couples who had been sent to join us. A groggy minuet of handshakes ensued: Hi, I'm Jane, I'm Charles, I'm Doak, I'm Frieda, I'm Ruth, I'm Ivan. Ruth and Ivan, it turned out, had come to The Farm to "soak," to decide whether they really wanted to stay. Others had come for sanctuary from uncongenial laws or to escape whatever were their demons. One man we met at The Farm, a roving silversmith, buttonholed one of our hostesses to say, "Now look, just suppose I were to stay on here," to which she replied, "Aha! We've got your gourd!"

The creed with which The Farm wins gourds—heads—is as simple as Baba Muktananda's. "Our best tripping instruction," a Farm man told us, "is first change yourself, then change *it*, the rest of the world. It's hard work, but we really truck. We take care of The Farm and The Farm takes care of us. When we move in we sign over all we have. Stephen says that living here is a sort of guaranteed poverty, but what would we do with money of our own? I had a comfortable nest egg once, but all it did was make me anxious. That's the consequence of all attachment to money and to everything else—anxiety."

Nobody seemed very anxious during Charles's and my tour of the premises. Two friendly Farm people in overalls were assigned to show us around, and did so cheerfully, leading us down fern-lined paths and over brooks into tents, huts, privies, the school, the store, the bathhouse, the printshop. Two or three single people generally shared a house with a couple. Couples were devoted; single people were advised to stay celibate until they found mates, which they should hasten to do. A few rules had been changed since Tom's time: Honey was off the proscribed list, and I heard a couple of nicknames used. The children we saw seemed impressively less bratty than many on the outside, probably because all their elders treated them more naturally, and less like puzzlements. "What this place is all *about* is bringing up kids right," someone said. "We're doing it all for the kids." It was clear that The Farm's people prized not only the gigantic family they had themselves become but the smaller ones in which they had grown up—"We write home, give them The Dogpatch News, tell them how the potatoes and onions and cabbage are coming, till they say, 'Wow, that kid that used to be such a far-out junkie, he's really gone through changes!'" They also prize, above all, the families they are breeding. So many women I saw at The Farm were conspicuously pregnant that for all I knew we might witness a "birthing" that very day.

That didn't happen, so we sat on a porch for a while and talked to a half-dozen midwives. "Come back in September," one said. "September's going to be our big harvest month—we'll be having all *kinds* of birthings then." None of The Farm's rituals means more than midwifery. "Kids have telepathy," Gaskin later said. "Lots of times I've looked into the eyes of a newborn baby and felt the vibes just coming at me crystal clear and pure. And I've looked into the eyes of a mother at a birthing and watched her pupils break up into mandala after mandala."

"We like pregnant ladies to come here five months before they're due, at least," a midwife said, "and totally trust our judgment. If we say at the last minute that ladies should go to the hospital for care, then they go. A local doctor works with us real closely. We've taught the local doctors a lot of stuff about vibes.

"We like the father to be there, too. Unless there's something wrong with the way he and the lady run their energy together, it's good for him to be there, plugged into and connected with the lady to help her out, and help the midwife. To *be* a midwife you have to be a student of Stephen's, married in a loving relationship with a man, and have had a baby yourself, preferably one delivered here. We wish the word would spread that any lady who's pregnant is welcome to come here to let us birth her baby. We'll keep it and bring it up if she doesn't want to."

"Catching, for midwives, is the highest level of karma," I heard from Stephen's wife Ina Mae, who was "sanctioned as priestess" when her husband was in jail so she could conduct weddings—weldings, they are also called—and funerals, as well as being head midwife. "Next down the ladder from catching are the ladies who take, clean, count, and make sure the baby is healthy—a lot of tricky things can happen after the baby makes it through the passage. After that, another lady holds the flashlight and does the baby oil. Babies come out all white, and only turn pink after they get the Holy Spirit.

"Before we circumcise babies, we give them a couple spoonfuls of wine. If a lady goes into labor too soon, we'll get her drunk—we're not so High Brahmin that if people outside offer us wine we won't have some with them. We've all had plenty in our systems before, so a couple more sips won't hurt."

The Farm's flexibility, I suspect, is one reason it has kept going and may well last beyond its present generation. They drink the odd sip of wine, they allow their children to watch the odd television program, they are not opposed to the idea of factlets. A copy of *Newsweek* I saw on the premises looked so dogeared I figured it was a year old, but it turned out to be the previous week's. But the most heartening stories of all concerned Uncle Bill and Aunt Tillie, both of whom I would greatly like to have met. "Uncle Bill," I was told, "is a far-out cat in his eighties who used to work in a pickle factory. We rescued him from a nursing home and now he's one of our cooks. He usually makes the appetizers; he's *real* good with turnips.

"And Aunt Tillie, she was one man's Jewish grandmother, who

died here. It was the most peaceful death any of us had ever seen. All of us read and chanted in Hebrew while she just very peacefully, after eighty-eight years, went out."

I would like to have been on The Farm that day. I would also like to be there for a birthing. Many tricky things indeed can happen after we "make it through the passage," but I can think of a lot worse families to be born in and to die in.

For the tricky part in the middle, I prefer the company of families like one I chanced to find in Iowa.

On the Slaunch

WRAP UP YOUR GIFTS. We wrap them. Shift down your gears. We shift them. Open now your pores. They're open. We open them each afternoon in the sauna, next to the swimming pool. We meet in the sauna when we're through with our typewriters, classrooms and libraries. Too much talk, too many words: we need steam. We need the steam that arises in dense clouds from the water we pour onto hot-piled rocks in this small, wood-walled room. Naked, each supine on her own birch shelf, we wait in languid layers for the steam to coax forth our sweat. Some of us sweat much more easily than others.

"Nowhere on my entire person is there a single drop of perspiration," Philippa complains one afternoon. She is six feet two.

"That's because your person is Nordic," says Barbara, who is just five feet. "We Mediterraneans are better at that sort of thing."

"Unless I'm mistaken," says Philippa, "Odessa is *not* on the Mediterranean."

"But before Odessa my people came from the Fertile Crescent."

"Whose didn't?" I ask, as droplets finally appear on my own Nordic forearm. "Everyone came from there originally, even us slow-sweating Anglo-Saxons, if you trace back far enough. For myself, I can hardly trace what I'm doing right this minute, here on this shelf in Iowa City, Iowa."

"You're here," Philippa reminds me, "because we made you promise to come for Thanksgiving." She was right. I had shortened my western visit to make it here in time, bringing tequila from Mexico and jellybeans from Oregon. "The reason you like it here so much is not only that we chose you, but we chose each other as well."

"You've stayed three extra weeks," says Barbara, "because we weren't ready to let you go."

"We're still not ready," says Philippa.

"Into the pool!" says Barbara. "Twelve more lengths before we leave!" We wriggle into our bathing suits, we swim, we sauna again, we shower. We zip up our parkas like children in snowsuits to shop for more presents for the clans we were born to, whom most of us will see next week at Christmas, and for one another, for the clan we have here become. As soon as we get home, which for Philippa and five others and me is a boxy, stolid farmhouse just outside town on American Legion Road, we wrap our presents. We vary the colors and patterns of paper and ribbon, mindful of how the packages will look under the avocado plant. We wrap them at once, because the contents of the packages matter far less than the sense of mystery and promise they exude.

The presents go under the avocado, instead of on the stereo, because that is where Mark wants them, and this is Mark's house as much as it is Philippa's. Mark met me at my plane on Thanksgiving afternoon, in his plum-colored parka. He has the kindest, bluest eyes and the most patriarchal auburn beard of any 29-year-old in all Johnson County. He and Philippa, who is two years his junior, found and leased this farmhouse soon after they found each other. She knew she wanted to live with him as soon as she discovered how carefully he put away tools. He knew he wanted to live with her as soon as he heard her use the phrases "lambent wit" and "fiscal irresponsibility" in the same sentence before she even got up one morning. Next they set about looking for the dozen or so of the rest of us to fill out their clan. Some of us in this chosen family are musicians, like Mark; several are writers, like Philippa. Not all of us live here, but those who don't come whenever we can. The house doesn't look charming: it has silver plastic strips taped to the windowpanes, peeling floral linoleum, rumpsprung overstuffed armchairs, plastic coffee mugs and no fireplace. Still, in few places anywhere have I lately felt more at ease.

"How long can you stay here?" Mark wondered when we waited for my luggage at the airport.

"Only till the turkey soup is finished," I told him. "I've got to move along, get on with my work."

"But you can't go so soon," he said. "How can you miss the First Annual Charade Classic—Earth and Air signs versus Fire and Water?"

"You can't go so soon," Barbara told me later. "You don't want to miss my Hanukkah party."

"You can't go so soon," said Philippa. "You have to wait till Nutie's leg heals, so we can go for a run in the woods with him." Nutie is her Great Dane.

"But my work," I said. "I have more people to see."

"You've seen enough," said Mark. "And you can work here in Iowa City 52240."

Fifteen months earlier, when I first pulled off Interstate 80 into Iowa City, I would never have believed I might come back voluntarily. All I hoped then was that the four-month term I had been lured to teach, at the state university's Writers' Workshop, would pass quickly. "Take plenty of synthetic fabrics," Philip Roth had warned. "Otherwise you'll never get the smell of hamburgers and french fries out of your woolens." Iowa is, as everyone knows, a cliché. Its wholesomeness is as proverbial as Texas's size. The last soldier's body shipped home from the Vietnam war was an Iowan's. Iowans are shamelessly chauvinistic, gathering for picnic reunions at tropical old-age colonies. Not for a minute do they care if ham radio operators refer to their region as "zeroland." Never mind that Iowa City's divorce rate is, as someone put it, four out of three, nor that it is modern enough to support chapters of Al-Anon and Weight Watchers and advanced classes in Transcendental Meditation. Even if some Iowans are as jittery, as drunken and as overweight as anybody else, they are on the whole purer and less given to dissembling. As someone who married one told me once, "You always know where you stand with an Iowan." So you do. I learned that early on, in annual visits to my own Iowa grandparents. When they died, and the family scattered, I developed an appetite for surprises, which I tended to find in places far away.

I was flattered to be asked to teach in the fiction section of the Workshop, but reluctant. How, never having published a paragraph of fiction or taught anyone anything, could I be qualified? Don't worry, they told me, come anyway. They insisted. I came. I came on a day so humid that envelopes sealed themselves shut, on the same day Gerald R. Ford pardoned Richard M. Nixon, on the same day Evel Knievel tried in vain to catapult himself across the Grand Canyon. The double bill at the campus drive-in was *Savage Lust* and *Heathen Sisters*. My own sister, whom I phoned long-distance for a word of encouragement, recalled something she had read about Bertrand Russell.

"He had the only peak experience of his whole life," she told me, "lying in a gully alongside the Mississippi River, looking up at the clouds."

"Surely he didn't *call* it a peak experience?"

"Whatever it was, he had one."

"Are you telling me I'll peak in Iowa?"

"I'm telling you you might."

"But you should have seen the way the students looked at me at the introductory picnic the Workshop had."

"How did they look at you?"

"With suspicion." The only thing about me that comforted those students at that picnic, I later learned, was that at least I didn't have sprayed bouffant hair or long red fingernails, or otherwise match their image of a New York woman. They looked intimidatingly bright to me. What could I tell them about the craft of fiction? Better I should have been asked to lead a seminar in metallurgy. I suffered an attack of a malaise I later heard called *verforwenheit*—a feeling of having been flung by alien forces to the wrong planet. What would I do for company? How would I pass all the long, looming evenings in the gathering gloom of winter?

"If you're not married, you won't be entertaining men here," said the manager of the Blue Top Motel, where I had just taken a two-room apartment for the term. It wasn't a question, it was a statement. "Entertaining": what a word. The manager and her husband had two towheaded crewcut sons and a bumper sticker on their car that read "NOBODY DROWNED AT WATERGATE." In my own car I set forth over the rolling roads to explore the countryside, in search of adventures. Once I followed a train of buggies drawn by trotting horses to an Amish meeting house, where people in nineteenth-century costumes beckoned me, in my yellow turtleneck, inside. The Amish women wore caps of white chiffon over their simply fashioned hair, and long dresses in plain dark colors. Men grew beards as soon as they got married. "Boys," unmarried men of whatever age, were beardless; "girls" wore dresses cut differently from women's. I shared a hymnal of German songs with a friendly woman named Mrs. Joe Junior Miller, who first asked me, "Do you want to sit with the women or the girls?" She later told me that chief recreation for the Amish was spelldowns, held in that same meeting house, by the light of the kerosene lamps I saw hung from the rafters.

The next night I went to a franchised steak house and was easily persuaded to join a traveling salesman named Walt, who no more liked eating alone than I did. Walt told of how "the women was like dolls" in Thailand, where the Army had sent him, and of how he missed his children, whom he rarely saw, since they lived with their mother.

"I guess a family's about the hardest thing to leave," Walt said later when we had a drink together at the Lazy Leopard Lounge, "and the hardest thing to stay with, too. Do you have a family?"

"Not really," I told him, "but I'm looking for one."

Strong ones were there all around me. The families I began to find in Iowa City made me think of what Rainer Maria Rilke had written about "the love that consists in this, that two solitudes protect and border and salute each other." If the climate is right, families can protect and border and salute each other, too. In Iowa, at whose borders signs read "A PLACE TO GROW," the climate is as fertile for families as it is for corn and hogs. One of the families I felt drawn to, to my surprise, was a branch of my own. My second cousin Bob Moninger, a junior high school band coach, turned out to live a short walk from the university campus. His wife Rosalie taught piano. They both were active in the Lutheran church, and had three children. We had met before, with mutual indifference, but time can make cousins more tolerant of each other, or at least more curious. We forgave each other our political differences and drank *mai tais* together before their fireplace as their infant son learned to crawl. We talked of the farms, now all sold, where our grandparents had raised our fathers.

"Midwestern families are solider than others," an Iowa City doctor's wife told me, "because they're less intruded on by the demands of society. There's a certain stability of temperament here that you don't find in other places. My own husband is a rock of stability, like the old Methodist farmer whose crops got wrecked in a hailstorm and who said, 'Well, this is a bad time, but we'll survive.'

"Good families don't just happen, though. My piano tuner son, who just moved back home, said to me, 'I'm aware for the first time of how hard you've worked to keep this family going.' Traditions are a big part of it. There was a period in their teens when you could hear my boys think, 'who needs to hear A *Christmas Carol*; it's not worth it to keep up with these customs,' but now *they're* the ones who ask for it, and quote great chunks of it with delight. And our youngest child, our eleven-year-old, you know what she did when we took her to visit her grandparents' farm? She brought home some earth from that farm in a Dream-Whip container. She said she *needed* some family dirt."

Families with such a distinct sense of themselves kept attracting me. Much more often than I needed milk or cream, I would go to a dairy farm, just off I-80, to buy products of its herd of registered Guernseys. That farm's small store operates on the honor system; you write down what you've taken and leave your money in a glass jar. I would go there hoping for a glimpse of the proprietor or his wife. He looked like a sort of rural Clark Kent, and her complexion made me think of the cream they sold. They weren't garrulous, but I liked to hear whatever they might have to say about their children and their work. On a separating day, the wife once told me, her husband's chores last from five to eleven in the morning. "The vet doesn't come any more often than necessary," he said, "and *then* it's too often."

I also went frequently to an aptly named store called Things & Things, where my purchases included a jade plant, a black wool coat, and many pastrami lunches. That store's proprietors endured a tragedy in the time I knew them. Their twelve-year-old son, who had detested haircuts and loved motorcycling with his father, was killed in the crash of a small plane. His parents reacted with an uncanny composure I shall forever associate with Iowa. "Sometimes I just get mad thinking 'Why isn't he here?'" his mother once said, "but I figure we were lucky to have him as long as we did, and how much worse it would have been if he had had a slow, wasting disease. We try to have a lot of other young boys around the house now, to fill the void."

If I wasn't yet part of a new family in Iowa, I was discovering cheer in surprising places. Tracy and John helped to ease me through the weeks before I found my clan. Tracy and John, who came daily with mops and brooms and vacuums to clean my Blue Top quarters, insisted on being called "maids" instead of cleaning persons, and in other ways too were original. The day after I gave a public reading at Epstein's Bookstore—a ritual expected of all Workshop faculty people—I found a yellow cleaning rag on my desk, on which they had typed a message that said, "WE, THE MAIDS OF THE BLUE TOP MOTEL, PRESENT THIS AUTOGRAPHED RAG TO MS. JANE HOWARD." I framed that autographed rag. As much as the applause at the reading, it made me feel less scared about not being part of a family.

Being scared, up to a point, is healthy. "It's all right to quake in your boots half the time," my friend Marjorie Martin once told me. "It's when the quaking never stops that you ought to go for help." (She also observed that "a little pain never hurt anybody." Stoic woman, that Marjorie.) The late poet John Berryman was of like mind. Berryman and I once flew together from New York to Dublin, in the course of an article I did on him for *Life* magazine. We talked of his numerous heroes, among them Sir Francis Chichester, who had sailed alone across that same ocean. The night before his departure, Chichester had told reporters that "I shall be scared stiff most of the time," a line Berryman relished so much he roared it for all the plane's passengers to hear, adding, "NOW ISN'T THAT ADORABLE?" I could see his point.

Kate Berryman, the poet's widow, lives in Minneapolis, and when I go there I stop to visit her and her daughters. One visit, Kate told me she had a "fantasy extended family"—a tribe whose members changed as often as every week, a tribe of friends who she secretly pretended were her real kin. I could see her point, too. "I'm adopting all sorts of people into my tribe," Kate said. "Some of them don't even know it—I'm too embarrassed to tell them." I told her that I do things like that too, all the time.

Once, on a bus, I met a chatty woman who said among many other things that "Privacy's okay, I guess, but once a week is enough for me." I thought she made a certain amount of sense, too. I feel disenchanted about privacy myself, some of the time. The best interludes in my own life have been those when I have had a choice between solitude and companionship. That choice is not so easy to come by. It is more of a luxury than any credit card. Somebody ought to figure out how to make it less rare. Jessie Bernard, who writes more articulately than most sociologists, has asked in print: "Shouldn't we think of isolated households as merely a relic, or just transitional to something better? Shouldn't we be seeking new ways to supply privacy without exacting such a high price?" What is needed, Bernard goes on, is not nuclear fission but "nuclear fusion." In a similar vein, at a conference I once heard the august Margaret Mead declare that "this whole country is a prison! People are segregated, stratified in developments." She is right about that. Architects ought to design new houses, or buildings, or clusters of buildings, so that people who care about each other could share kitchens and other common rooms and still be able to retreat to privacy.

The Utopian communes of nineteenth-century America were one approach to this need, and so are the "charismatic" establishments led by the likes of Stephen Gaskin and Baba Muktananda. But not all groups who live together share a cultish vision. The most exotic thing about many such households is their rainbow-colored loft beds, their profusion of plants, and the scent that betrays their fondness for cats. These are people who get up in the morning and go off to work. Theirs is a modified, bourgeois kind of communitarianism, with no thought of charisma.

"We're not charismatic, we're not even spontaneous," one man told me whose extended-family commune was about to disband after seven years, which is six years and nine months longer than most such experiments last. Five families had pooled their resources to begin this commune, in a huge old white elephant house with several outbuildings. For a while everyone had got on fine: "We gave up Triscuits and Ritz crackers," the man told me, "and were grateful for sardines. We had jolly evenings, and rituals—birthday cakes in the shape of outhouses, violins, sleighs, whatever was appropriate. We had hayrides, and evenings of parlor games." But then two of the original five families pulled out and moved away, and recruiting others to replace them turned out to be far more tricky than anyone had expected. The household split into two factions. There were the Slobs, who didn't care how greasy the stove got, and the Straights, who cared too much. Each faction grated on the other's nerves, like fingernails scraping a blackboard.

I heard other such stories. A Texas friend wrote me about a household she once had known which "went up in a blaze of sexual hyperactivity and recrimination after about a year—there were long discussions as to what would be the proper reinforcements, proper disincentives—that means punishments—and whether or not X should screw Y's wife Z. Not far away was another commune filled with people who were into being compleat Christians through social commitment, communal living, and thoroughgoing pacifism. They were militant anti-warriors, feminists, shoulderers of every burden, righters of every wrong. They were kind of depressing.

"Another group I knew then was full of people who were what they ate. They would hang around the kitchen table playing bluegrass while someone cooked up that day's carrot-bulgur-lecithin surprise cake. I'd have stayed there for dinner more often, if I cared more for alfalfa and rolled oats. That was their undoing. More and more they would sneak off with a gorgeous ten-ounce bag of some proscribed junk, and when someone discovered Frito crumbs on the bedspread, all hell would break loose."

Food is never a simple issue in such households. Long debates filled evenings in the disbanding five-family commune: Should or shouldn't they buy supermarket peanut butter? Could or couldn't they afford a new, non-electric can opener? Could or couldn't they bear to live with a pink stove, pink ones being considerably cheaper than white? Should or shouldn't they feel "comfortable" about hiring a "facilitator" to arbitrate their mounting differences of opinion? All this discord eroded what once had been a positive group spirit. Bitterness grew. Only after I swore never to say who these people were, or where their experiment had burgeoned and was fizzling, would they even consent to tell me their bleak history. I almost wished I hadn't heard it; the story was dismaying. When that household finally broke up, its members were planning to sneak off at odd times during the middle of the night. They couldn't find the words to say good-bye.

Chosen clans seem to work better when they don't try to live together. Generally these clans get started at a time and in a place when people are vulnerable, and more aware than usual of how much they need each other. One of my clans consists of people I conspired with, in the late 1950s, to figure out whether or where we belonged in New York City. Other random bunches of people and I joined forces because we chanced together to wash enough dishes, chop enough onions, or cross enough state lines, for purposes that ranged from peace marches to assaults on Mount Katahdin. But most chosen clans can trace their origins to institutions. Institutions are a sure and fertile source of clans, if they bring people together in small enough groups for specific enough tasks at regular enough intervals, and offer enough added occasions, some planned and some not, for kinship to develop.

The Iowa Writers' Workshop, whose students and teachers spend four regular and uncounted spontaneous hours together every week, has probably spawned as many healthy clans as any institution in America. The one I happened to find there had taken shape before it and I ever heard of each other. Philippa speculated on its origins in a letter:

Looking back, I think that the clan was partly a function of the farmhouses, both mine and Barbara's, environments that were in themselves familial and congenial. Doors were open, parties were relaxed, good things to eat were in the refrigerator. The Workshop afforded us an official relationship to one another—random, as in families, and somewhat ritualized. We got to be like brothers and sisters who discover that they like one another. We felt special (not all Workshop groups like one another, any more than all families do. Ours was lucky).

When I was growing up my aunts and grandparents had the strong sense that our family was something amazing, comparable to the Kennedys. "They're just like us," one aunt said of the Kennedys, making them, not us, the imitation. I think all families with any kind of self-consciousness do the same thing, and we did too, back in your Iowa days. Lots of people, I have since been given to understand, resented our becoming a family, but our doing so gave us the kind of support we needed in an environment that scared us. We did the things that families do—ate together, played together, worked together, gossiped about one another. Also, like most of the families I've ever been part of, we were oversupplied with mommies and undersupplied with daddies. Thank God for Mark.

Mark, I think, was the benign father, the guy who knew how to fix things, who picked people up at the airport. I got to be the mommy and you got to be one of the sisters. The roles, of course, were fluid; we knew how to shift from parent to child when necessary. I think, though, that play was the key to the clan—the capacity for mutual enjoyment. I also think that every group on the verge of becoming a clan needs someone who does the drawing together, who is conscious of the group's potential a little sooner than the others are.

You and I are both avid drawers-together; I have an extremely pronounced need to be surrounded by as many friends as possible and to have them reassure me that my love is as acceptable as theirs is flowing. If you will remember, I bearded you in your den and virtually pressed friendship on you.

I do remember. Philippa fell into step with me one day after the first class I taught, in which she was a student. She asked me to dinner the following week because, as she put it, "I want to make friends with you." I looked up at her in wonderment. She wanted what? In my twenties I didn't go around saying such things to anyone, much less those fifteen years my senior. Nobody did. In those constricted times it didn't do to take such chances. We played it safe, sticking pretty much to our chronological peers, and were the poorer for it. "See that girl over there?" a friend once sidled up to me at a party to whisper. "She was born in the forties!" Think of it!

The nerve of one so young, to walk full-grown among us, usurping our position as ingenues. But who would want for long to stay an ingenue? Only ex-ingenues know how age, in its way, can console: how with age we can richen our chosen families both with mentors, too young to have borne us, and protégés or apprentices, too old to be our children. Someone first to learn from, someone later to teach. Any professional passion can be the subject matter. For Oliver Wendell Holmes and the law clerks he thought of as his "sons," it was jurisprudence. For Dr. Rosalyn Yalow and the "professional children" she told of in accepting her Nobel Prize, it was nuclear medicine. For others it might be the hooking of rugs, the cutting of hair or the fixing of carburetors. The point is a shared devotion to work, a conviction that work matters as much as a child. To borrow the language of my family farm, where "slaunchwise" meant diagonal, devotion to work, whatever the work might be, can make clansmen of people from generations on the slaunch.

It was my band coach cousin Bob Moninger who reminded me of that word "slaunchwise." Bob, the archivist in my generation, keeps files and files on Howard history. One afternoon he was telling how our common ancestors spent the winter of 1853 in a cabin on a knoll not far from Iowa City, near the site of Herbert Hoover's grave. On an impulse, we piled into his car to look for that ancestral knoll. We couldn't find it, but never mind; the search did us good. By then I was also making other searches, in cars and in conversation, with my new Iowa clan.

Safely past the politeness barrier, my new clansmen and I were saying what we really thought of one another's work and plans. Should Mark become a mason or a rock star? Should Philippa study law, or Icelandic literature, or both, or neither? Should Barbara go into publishing? Should she first spend the summer as my assistant? Should I risk being the boss of a friend? I decided to try; her contagious confidence would surely come in handy. It did. Later, with similar pleasure, I ate lobster with Bob Chibka in Maine, clams with Mike Harris at Pismo Beach, and drank beer in the Rockies with Carl Schaffer. I also paid a visit to Joanne Meschery, who lives near the Nevada border in Truckee, California. Never did a one-day visit feel so much like a week, and a good week at that. Joanne decided that I needed to see a monument to the Donner party, Lake Tahoe, Carson City, Virginia City, Reno and an abandoned gold mine called American Flats where graffiti read "HIPPIES, MONKEYS, COWBOYS & NIXON" and "WISDOM IS WHERE IT'S AT."

Joanne told of camel and ostrich races in the old days, and how Chinamen's corpses were boiled and sent back to China, and how even now, in the winter, Truckee graves had to be dynamited. We talked of all this, in that one dizzying day, and we talked of and to her family—"Mom," her daughter Janai wanted to know, "is God true? I know Jesus is, but is God?" I missed Joanne's answer, maybe because it was interrupted by another question from her son Matthew, in his Doctor Dentons: "Mom, do you like me?"

"Sure I do," Joanne said as she kept on splitting logs into firewood. "I'm crazy about you. People here," she told me, "think of my three kids as a real mob."

"Would you tell Sarah can she come to see us?" Joanne's other daughter Megan asked me. Megan and my second-cousin-once-removed Sarah Moninger had been best friends in Iowa City, where Megan knew I soon would be going. Joanne and I talked of our friends there, too. Quite a clan we had there, we agreed. It was clear that not all the ties that had connected that clan's members to one another would last. A few already had frayed enough to snap. But remarkably many still endure today.

Some of the people on this clan's fringes may not even have guessed how they helped to define it. A clan, especially one without children, needs elders, and as far as I was concerned we had good ones in Fred and Dorothy Pownall. Dorothy, who once had written an advice-to-the-lovelorn column for the *Cedar Rapids Gazette*, was as spirited and earnest as any student in my last Iowa class. The following summer, at her urging, I stopped to visit her and Fred, whom she always called her "date," at their cabin in northern Wisconsin. The morning I waked up there happened to be Dorothy's eightieth birthday and she served breakfast from the same table where she and Fred had eaten their first connubial popovers 57 years before. "I think we still *have* one of those popovers around here someplace," said Fred.

If a clan needs elders it also needs at least one Unclaimed Treasure, as Valerie Lagorio had the wit to call herself. Valerie is an English professor, a medievalist by trade, who played the accordion at parties, and worried with me that Philippa might be spreading herself too thin. She also told me how she dealt with the business of being unclaimed. "When people wonder why I'm single," she said once, "I quote the old Irishman who said, 'It's manners to wait till you're asked.' Anyway, married or not, I have my family of friends. Wherever I've gone, I've made a point of setting up such a family—people who are givers as opposed to takers, or Doers, as my father used to put it, as opposed to Clunks.

"Families of friends absorb a lot of time and thought, but they're worth it. When one bachelor friend of mine got so sick he had to be in Intensive Care, where only relatives were allowed as visitors, I said, 'You'll have to let me in, because *I'm* this man's family.' One year I had him and another bachelor and two widowers and two widows to dinner on my birthday. Not a one of them remembered what day it was, and I got so mad I told them, 'I want you to eat fast and get the hell out of here, because you'd have your noses in a sling if I forgot any of *your* birthdays. You *owe* that much to me.'

"That was two years ago. Last year my birthday was quite another matter. Early in the afternoon the florist's truck drove up to my house with a dozen pink roses and a card signed 'Happy Birthday—John.' An hour later, the same truck was back, with yellow roses: 'Many Happy Returns—John.' An hour after *that* the roses were white, and I told the florist to take them back and bring me a chrysanthemum plant instead."

The winter solstice approaches. Philippa's divorce decree comes, in an envelope emblazoned with an eagle holding a shield, juxtaposed on the Declaration of Independence and the Constitution. ". . . The allegations of Petitioner's Petition are true," the document says, and "there has been a breakdown in the marriage relationship of the parties to the extent that the legitimate objects of matrimony have been destroyed and there remains no reasonable likelihood that the marriage can be preserved . . . It is therefore ordered, adjudged, and decreed that the marriage relationship . . . is hereby dissolved . . ."

The Petitioner is grading papers. The papers are about Othello. They remind her, she says, "of some idiot taking a hammer to the Pietà." And the decree, I ask? Oh that, she says: it's about as big a deal as getting a duplicate driver's license. If I'm going to Moss's Dairy will I ask if they know where to find good, noncommercial dressed chickens? And do I know where the ribbon is, because she has more presents to wrap.

The pile of presents grows bigger, under the avocado plant. The Lovely Corinne, as our resident graduate pianist is generally known, practices the Ravel for her recital, cursing when she misses a note. Jack, who brings her coffee every morning in their bedroom, kneads her shoulder by way of comfort. The pump outside the farmhouse wheezes rhythmically. Nutie lopes in the cornfields, covered now with snow. Exams and graduations loom. So does Christmas. Our departures cannot for much longer be postponed.

One night four of us sit down and find ourselves making a cake. We don't discuss making it; we just do it. We mull wine and announce a party. The party turns out to be a big one, with much eclectic singing. *Mark my footsteps, good my page, tread thou in them boldly. With angelic hosts proclaim. The belfries of all Christendom. And the moment before she died. In no other arms entwine. Mr. Bojangles was his name. Sometimes I live in the town. You make me happy when skies are gray. Is it weakness of intellect, birdie? To bow and to bend we will not be ashamed. My regrets couldn't be greater at having to scram. Should time or occasion compel us to part.*

Time and occasion resoundingly do. We are rent and torn asunder as we're drawn to different coasts. Mark and his guitar are off to California in search, as he puts it, of "national recognition." Philippa may or may not see him when she returns from her Fulbright year in Iceland, where she will find "skeins and skeins of yarn" to knit us all caps and scarves. Barbara is wondering whether to apartment-hunt in the East Village or the Upper West Side. The boxy farmhouse is soon to be demolished, and the barn that adjoins it will be split into tiny apartments, rented to people whose names we'll never know. It's just as well.

Talk follows the singing. Shop talk, mostly, concerning writing and teaching. Teaching, we agree, is as much a matter of passion as of information. When it goes well it is, among other things, a pep rally. All of us wonder whether and when we will teach again, and whom, and what we have learned from one another. For my own part I am sure that in this place I have learned far more than I can have taught, and that what we all have discovered together, only rarely in classrooms, is that the passage of years guarantees very little in the way of answers, that ambivalence and ambiguity will follow us all the days of our lives, but that words and wit and woods and food and music will endure as sources of comfort.

We have learned that surprises exhilarate, if they don't barrage us too fast, and that the quest for the proper balances between stillness and motion, restraint and excess, sound and silence, will continue, and that too much freedom—a life too much at large, as George Eliot writes in *Daniel Deronda*—can feel at least as constricting as too little. We have learned, maybe most importantly of all, to cherish the company of those who can make us laugh, who can forgive us our shortcomings, who can restore to us or evoke in us a feeling of purpose in the face of absurdity. These are the people we choose for our clans.

A Peck of Salt

> . . . it can be but a sorry and ignoble society of life,
> whose inseperable injunction depends meerly upon flesh
> and bones.
>
> —John Milton
> "Doctrine and Discipline of Divorce"

> For it seems clear to me that we were so created that there
> exists between us a kind of bond, which strengthens with
> proximity . . . with relatives nature itself has produced
> friendship, but of a sort that lacks constancy, because
> friendship is superior to relationship, in that good will can
> be withdrawn from relationship, but not from friendship.
> If you remove good will, the very name of friendship is
> gone, while the name of relationship remains.
>
> —Cicero
> De Amicitia

CALL IT A CLAN, call it a network, call it a tribe, call it a family.
Whatever you call it, whoever you are, you need one. You need one
because you are human. You didn't come from nowhere. Before you,
around you, and presumably after you, too, there are others. Some of
these others—in my view around nine, for reasons to be looked at
presently—must matter. They must matter a lot to you and if you
are very lucky to one another. Their welfare must be nearly as important to you as your own. Even if you live alone, even if your solitude
is elected and ebullient, you still cannot do without a clan or a tribe.

But where are you to find one?

What a question. For most of human history, looking for a tribe was the least of anyone's worries. Our tribes and clans were right there in plain sight, like our kneecaps. We were born into tribes, or married into them, or they enslaved us, and that was that. Our tribe kept the howling wolves at bay, and shielded us from savage aliens. It made our decisions for us. It named us, bred us, fed us, taught us how to earn a living, found us our mates, and willed us its property. It told us who we were, what we stood for, and what we might hope to become. After we died, it honored our memory. It kept us much too busy ever to question its rituals or to wonder whether some other tribe might have been more to our liking.

A couple of anachronistic tribes of this sort still survive today, but most such august and enveloping clans have long since evolved into families. Families, as all who read newspaper headlines know, are embattled and confused and irksome—so irksome that their members plot and scheme to leave them behind, dwelling at length, the while, on their shortcomings. The United States, as Rebecca West somewhere said, is a nation of middle-aged men running around complaining about their mothers. What folly. What misspent energy. However frail and perforated our families may have become, however they may annoy and retard us, they remain the first of the givens of our lives. The more we try to deny or elude them, the likelier we are to repeat their same mistakes. The first thing we have to do is to stop such efforts. Instead we must come to terms with our families, laughing with them peaceably on occasion if we can manage to, accepting them as the flawed mortals they are, or were, if we cannot.

The trouble with the families many of us were born to is not that they are meddlesome ogres but that they are too far away. In emergencies we rush across continents and if need be oceans to their sides, as they do to ours. Maybe we even make a habit of seeing them, once or twice a year, for the sheer pleasure of it. But blood ties seldom dictate our addresses. Our blood kin are often too remote to ease us from our Tuesdays to our Wednesdays. For this we must rely on our families of friends. If our relatives are not, do not wish to be, or for whatever reasons cannot be our friends, then by some complex alchemy we must transform our friends into our relatives. If blood and roots don't do the job, then we must look to water and branches.

"How are we going to get from here," Eulah Laucks was asking, "to wherever it is we want to go?" By "here" she did not mean the

Montecito patio restaurant where she and I were having lunch. I made a point of telephoning Eulah, when I got to California, because she had impressed me at our first meeting, a few months earlier, at a conference on families in Massachusetts. She had seemed to make much more sense than most people at that conference. I had admired her upswept swirl of white hair and her train of thought as well: "The idea of family extension in purely blood-tie terms," she had said, "has exhausted itself for our age, and given rise to some of the worst evils that have plagued us—elitism, suspicion, fear, competition, and greed . . . there is no help but to . . . extend the idea of family to include nonmembers in ever greater numbers." What a refreshing and promising view, I had thought in Massachusetts.

"Our suspicion of strangers isn't lessening," Eulah now was saying, over California salad. "It's *growing*. What are we going to have to do? Wait for some catastrophe like the last scene of the movie *San Francisco* for this trend to reverse?" What indeed? In my genes I know myself that water isn't really thicker than blood and never will be, but I also strongly suspect that we could do far worse than to act as if it were. For a good half of the people I know, in this jarring age of former in-laws and sudden step-parents, the faith of our fathers would seem to be crumbling.

"My *father*?" a Detroit social worker said between panel discussions at another conference. "I don't even *know* the dude!" Even those of us who do know and love the dudes in question, who have forgiven our mothers living and dead their frailties, and who cheerfully accept the charges for collect calls from our siblings—even we need new kinds of families to supplement, if not to replace, the old ones. There is going to have to be a whole new grand-right-and-left promenade, as we sort ourselves into new constellations, new families, new clans.

These new families, to borrow the terminology of an African tribe, may consist either of friends of the road, ascribed by chance, or friends of the heart, achieved by choice.* Ascribed friends are those we happen to go to school with, work with, or live near. They know where we went last weekend and whether we still have a cold. Just being around gives them a provisional importance in our lives, and us in theirs. Maybe they still will matter to us when we or they move away; quite likely they won't. Six months or two years will probably erase us from each other's thoughts, unless by some chance they and we have become friends of the heart.

---

* The Bangwa of the Cameroons, described in Robert Brain's *Friends and Lovers*.

An achieved friend, a friend of the heart, is one who perceives me as one of the better versions of myself, who has troubled to map the oddities of my mind's geography, as I have of his. We have found the way past the blind alleys and the detours to the side roads that lead to the plazas where sometimes the music plays. We make good music, this friend and I, and we make good silences, too. Talk we can take or leave. As for politeness, we don't confuse it with generosity. My friend will tell me to get some new rims for my glasses at once, to stop yearning after someone who doesn't deserve me, but that even though I have wasted the last eighteen weeks of my life on a pointless and stupid endeavor, even considering my egregious imperfections, there still is hope. ("To be her friend," as someone said eulogizing the writer Jenny Moore, "was to be for a little while as good as you wish you were.")

My friend and I phone each other earlier and later than we would dare to bother others. Our talk starts out frivolous: Are brasses more pleasing than strings, long vowels than short ones, webbed feet than hooves, bridges than tunnels, tubs than showers? Two in the afternoon, we agree, is the dullest hour, forty the dreariest temperature, north by far the most inviting direction. At times we argue: Is far left more dangerous than far right? Does amity depend on enmity—for every Us does there have to be a Them? We travel together, too, when we can. In flush spells we go to see deserts and duomos; when cash and time are short a trip across town will do. Anywhere, just so we can gather, hone, and compare our reactions. Coming and going we absorb each other's histories: who brought us up, who taught us, where we were when the shots were fired, when the bombs fell, when the lights went out, what used to scare us and what still does.

To borrow Martin Buber's word, we have "happened" to each other. Our friendship may have begun with a thunderclap, the way romances do, with what Muktananda followers call *shaktipat*, or it may have grown so gradually as to catch us by surprise. Wishing to be friends, as Aristotle wrote, is quick work, but friendship is a slowly ripening fruit. An ancient proverb he quotes in his *Ethics* had it that you cannot know a man until you and he together have eaten a peck of salt. Now a peck, a quarter of a bushel, is quite a lot of salt—more salt, perhaps, than most pairs of people ever have occasion to share. We try, though. My friend and I break bread and pass salt together as often and at as many tables as we can. Between-times we see each other at our ugliest, forgive each other our falls from grace, make each other laugh aloud, and steer each other through enough seasons and weathers so that sooner or later it crosses our minds that one of us, God knows which or with what sorrow, must one day mourn the other. If I were sick enough to have good reason to want to die myself, he would let me do so in his house, as I would let him do in mine. When his mother dies, I will help him go through her things.

It would be splendid to live in a society that encouraged such friendships. Our does not. Ours is awash in what Robert Brain calls "emotional promiscuity . . . there are whole days when a busy person can come into no real contact with anyone else. Our culture has deprived us of any possible guidelines in making friends . . . Friendship must be taken as seriously as sex, aggression, and marriage. I have no qualms in elevating friendship into an imperative."

Neither have I. Nor have I qualms in repeating that if some of our friends are not in effect part of our family, then they ought to be, and soon. Friendships are sacred and miraculous, but they can be even more so if they lead to the equivalent of clans. If the important people in my life discern in my friend a fraction of the worth that I do, and if those who matter to him can understand his affinity for me, then we are on our way: the dim but promising outline of a new sort of family emerges. This sort of thing might happen oftener if we were to revive the old Latin custom of *compadrazgo*, co-godparenthood, a theme that would seem to deserve some new variations. *Compadrazgo*, as I understand it, is what binds you to me if we both have solemnly sworn to look after this newborn infant's spiritual, and maybe also material, welfare. So strong is this bond thought to be that it survives even when the baby in question does not. The bond links us as much to each other as it does to the family that chose us. At least one person is my friend largely because he and I orbit around two of the same fixed families, and not to honor any sworn oaths, either. Oaths aren't everything. Another friend of mine, who has fifteen godchildren, acquired four of them in an impromptu ceremony one secular afternoon on their parents' lawn—a far more affecting scene, she tells me, than any by a font in a church.

I know another woman, in Colorado, whose proudest moment was being "made a relative"—adopted, in effect—by the Sioux, in what she says was one of their "Seven Sacraments for This World and the Next." This ritual reached its peak when one Chief Eagle Feather took his knife to cut her left wrist, the one nearer her heart, and then to cut the wrist of the medicine man. As the tribal chant grew louder, the chief spat in both wounds, rubbed dirt and sage leaves into them, and bade the two to mix their blood together. Wrist-cutting and blood-mixing may seem a bit extreme, but I am taken all the same with such avenues to what anthropology texts refer to as "fictive" or "pseudo" kinship. If the real thing isn't handy, or isn't working, then maybe the ritual or the pseudo can fill the gaps. Few deny that such gaps are widening. How dull, as a Russell Baker column once said, to think of "a world where practically nobody has brothers or sisters, where there are very few relatives of any kind to come to dinner." Now and then Baker worries specifically about the disappearance of uncles, as does a bachelor friend of mine who practices law in Mexico. "Uncles," this bachelor once remarked, "are what we down here call a nonrenewable resource."

The thing to keep in mind is our need to devise new ways, or revive old ones, to equip ourselves with uncles and other kinfolk. Maybe that's what prompted whoever it was ordered the cake I saw in my neighborhood bakery, labeled "HAPPY BIRTHDAY SURROGATE." I like to think that this cake was decorated not for a judge, but for someone's surrogate mother or surrogate brother: loathsome jargon, but admirable sentiment. If you didn't conceive me or bring me up that doesn't mean you still cannot be—if we both decide you ought to be—a kind of parent to me. It is never too late, I like to hope, to augment our families in ways nature neglected to do. Susan Brown-miller, whose book *Against Our Will* earned her more money than she had expected and who has no close kin, wrote out a will leaving all she has to her friends who are, she explained, her family.

When some friends paid me the enormous compliment of naming me their child's legal guardian, should she be orphaned early, I agreed on one condition.

"You'll have to look after *me*," I said to the child in question, "if there's no one else around to, when and if I'm old and helpless. Is that a deal?"

"I guess so," she answered.

"It better be," I told her, "or I'll come back to haunt you, and I won't come back alone."

"Who will you bring?"

"Oh, maybe someone I've never even heard of right this minute," I said. Two friends who matter greatly to me as I write this were total strangers to me a year ago. Maybe they and I won't ever make much of a dent in any peck of salt, but I dare to trust that we might. Such trust, in fact, is much of the force that keeps me going. I have no use for the conventional wisdom that friendships may only commence in youth. As far as I am concerned, a new one might begin to-morrow morning, or ten years hence. So it is with our chosen clans, whose lifespans we can no more predict than we can our own.

The best chosen clans, like the best friendships and the best families, endure by accumulating a history solid enough to suggest a future. But clans that don't last have merit, too. We can lament their loss, but we shouldn't deride them. Better an ephemeral clan or tribe than none at all. A few of my life's most tribally joyous times, in fact, have been spent with people whom I have yet to see again. This saddens me, as it may them too, but dwelling overlong on such sadness does no good. A more fertile exercise is to think back on those times and try to figure out what made them, for all their brevity, so stirring. What can such times teach us about forming new and more lasting tribes in the future?

New tribes and clans can no more be willed into existence, of course, than any other good thing can. We keep trying, though. To try, with gritted teeth and girded loins, is after all American. That is what the two Helens and I were talking about the day we had lunch in a room way up in a high-rise motel near the Kansas City airport. We had lunch there at the end of a two-day conference on families. The two Helens both were social scientists, but I liked them even so, among other reasons because they both objected to that motel's coffee shop even more than I did. One of the Helens, from Virginia, disliked such fare so much that she had brought along homemade whole wheat bread, sesame butter and honey from her parents' farm in South Dakota, where she had visited before the conference. Her picnic was the best thing that had happened, to me at least, those whole two days.

"If you're voluntarily childless and alone," said the other Helen, who was from Pennsylvania by way of Puerto Rico, "it gets harder and harder with the passage of time. It's stressful. That's why you need support systems." I had been hearing quite a bit of talk about "support systems." The term is not among my favorites, but I can understand its currency. Whatever "support systems" may be, the need for them is clearly urgent, and not just in this country. Are there not thriving "megafamilies" of as many as three hundred people in Scandinavia? Have the Japanese not for years had an honored, enduring—if perhaps by our standards rather rigid—custom of adopting nonrelatives to fill gaps in their families? Should we not applaud and maybe imitate such ingenuity?

And consider our own Unitarians. From Santa Barbara to Boston they have been earnestly dividing their congregations into arbitrary "extended families" whose members all are bound to act like each other's relatives. Kurt Vonnegut, Jr., plays with a similar train of thought in his fictional *Slapstick*. In that book every newborn baby gets assigned a randomly chosen middle name, like Uranium or

Daffodil or Raspberry. These middle names are connected with hyphens to numbers between one and twenty, and any two people who have the same middle name are automatically related. This is all to the good, the author thinks, because "human beings need all the relatives they can get—as possible donors or receivers not of love but of common decency." He envisions these extended families as "one of the four greatest inventions by Americans," the others being *Robert's Rules of Order*, the Bill of Rights, and the principles of Alcoholics Anonymous.

This charming notion might even work, if it weren't so arbitrary. Already each of us is born into one family not of our choosing. If we're going to go around devising new ones, we might as well have the luxury of picking their members ourselves. Clever picking might result in new families whose benefits would surpass or at least equal those of the old. The new ones by definition cannot spawn us—as soon as they do that, they stop being new—but there is plenty they can do. I have seen them work wonders. As a member in reasonable standing of six or seven tribes in addition to the one I was born to, I have been trying to figure which earmarks are common to both kinds of families:

(1) Good families have a chief, or a heroine, or a founder— someone around whom others cluster, whose achievements as the Yiddish word has it, let them *kvell*, and whose example spurs them on to like feats. Some blood dynasties produce such figures regularly; others languish for as many as five generations between demigods, wondering with each new pregnancy whether this, at last, might be the messianic baby who will redeem us. Look, is there not something gubernatorial about her footstep, or musical about the way he bangs with his spoon on his cup? All clans, of all kinds, need such a figure now and then. Sometimes clans based on water rather than blood harbor several such personages at one time. The Bloomsbury Group in London six decades ago was not much hampered by its lack of a temporal history.

(2) Good families have a switchboard operator—someone like Lilia Economou or my own mother who cannot help but keep track of what all the others are up to, who plays Houston Mission Control to everyone else's Apollo. This role, like the foregoing one, is assumed rather than assigned. Someone always volunteers for it. That person often also has the instincts of an archivist, and feels driven to keep scrapbooks and photograph albums up to date, so that the clan can see proof of its own continuity.

(3) Good families are much to all their members, but everything

to none. Good families are fortresses with many windows and doors to the outer world. The blood clans I feel most drawn to were founded by parents who are nearly as devoted to whatever it is they do outside as they are to each other and their children. Their curiosity and passion are contagious. Everybody, where they live, is busy. Paint is spattered on eyeglasses. Mud lurks under fingernails. Person-to-person calls come in the middle of the night from Tokyo and Brussels. Catchers' mitts, ballet slippers, overdue library books and other signs of extrafamilial concerns are everywhere.

(4) Good families are hospitable. Knowing that hosts need guests as much as guests need hosts, they are generous with honorary memberships for friends, whom they urge to come early and often and to stay late. Such clans exude a vivid sense of surrounding rings of relatives, neighbors, teachers, students and godparents, any of whom at any time might break or slide into the inner circle. Inside that circle a wholesome, tacit emotional feudalism develops: you give me protection, I'll give you fealty. Such treaties begin with, but soon go far beyond, the jolly exchange of pie at Thanksgiving for cake on birthdays. It means you can ask me to supervise your children for the fortnight you will be in the hospital, and that however inconvenient this might be for me, I shall manage to. It means I can phone you on what for me is a dreary, wretched Sunday afternoon and for you is the eve of a deadline, knowing you will tell me to come right over, if only to watch you type. It means we need not dissemble. ("To yield to seeming," as Buber wrote, "is man's essential cowardice, to resist it is his essential courage . . . one must at times pay dearly for life lived from the being, but it is never too dear.")

(5) Good families deal squarely with direness. Pity the tribe that doesn't have, and cherish, at least one flamboyant eccentric. Pity too the one that supposes it can avoid for long the woes to which all flesh is heir. Lunacy, bankruptcy, suicide and other unthinkable fates sooner or later afflict the noblest of clans with an undertow of gloom. Family life is a set of givens, someone once told me, and it takes courage to see certain givens as blessings rather than as curses. Contradictions and inconsistencies are givens, too. So is the war against what the Oregon patriarch Kenneth Babbs calls malarkey. "There's always malarkey lurking, bubbles in the cesspool, fetid bubbles that pop and smell. But I don't put up with malarkey, between my step-kids and my natural ones or anywhere else in the family."

(6) Good families prize their rituals. Nothing welds a family more than these. Rituals are vital especially for clans without histories, because they evoke a past, imply a future, and hint at continuity. No

line in the Seder service at Passover reassures more than the last: "Next year in Jerusalem!" A clan becomes more of a clan each time it gathers to observe a fixed ritual (Christmas, birthdays, Thanksgiving, and so on), grieve at a funeral (anyone may come to most funerals; those who do declare their tribalness), and devises a new rite of its own. Equinox breakfasts and all-white dinners can be at least as welding as Memorial Day parades. Several of us in the old *Life* magazine years used to meet for lunch every Pearl Harbor Day, preferably to eat some politically neutral fare like smorgasbord, to "forgive" our only ancestrally Japanese colleague Irene Kubota Neves. For that and other reasons we became, and remain, a sort of family.

"Rituals," a California friend of mine said, "aren't just externals and holidays. They are the performances of our lives. They are a kind of shorthand. They can't be decreed. My mother used to try to decree them. She'd make such a goddamn fuss over what we talked about at dinner, aiming at Topics of Common Interest, topics that celebrated our cohesion as a family. These performances were always hollow, because the phenomenology of the moment got sacrificed for the *idea* of the moment. Real rituals are discovered in retrospect. They emerge around constitutive moments, moments that only happen once, around whose memory meanings cluster. You don't choose those moments. They choose themselves." A lucky clan includes a born mythologizer, like my blood sister, who has the gift of apprehending such a moment when she sees it, and who cannot help but invent new rituals everywhere she goes.

(7) Good families are affectionate. This of course is a matter of style. I know clans whose members greet each other with gingerly handshakes or, in what pass for kisses, with hurried brushes of side jawbones, as if the object were to touch not the lips but the ears. I don't see how such people manage. "The tribe that does not hug," as someone who has been part of many *ad hoc* families recently wrote to me, "is no tribe at all. More and more I realize that everybody, regardless of age, needs to be hugged and comforted in a brotherly or sisterly way now and then. Preferably now."

(8) Good families have a sense of place, which these days is not achieved easily. As Susanne Langer wrote in 1957, "Most people have no home that is a symbol of their childhood, not even a definite memory of one place to serve that purpose . . . all the old symbols are gone." Once I asked a roomful of supper guests who, if anyone, felt any strong pull to any certain spot on the face of the earth. Everyone was silent, except for a visitor from Bavaria. The rest of us seemed to know all too well what Walker Percy means in *The*

Moviegoer when he tells of the "genie-soul of the place which every place has or else is not a place [and which] wherever you go, you must meet and master or else be met and mastered." All that meeting and mastering saps plenty of strength. It also underscores our need for tribal bases of the sort which soaring real estate taxes and splintering families have made all but obsolete.

So what are we to do, those of us whose habit and pleasure and doom is our tendency, as a Georgia lady put it, to "fly off at every other whipstitch?" Think in terms of movable feasts, for a start. Live here, wherever here may be, as if we were going to belong here for the rest of our lives. Learn to hallow whatever ground we happen to stand on or land on. Like medieval knights who took their tapestries along on Crusades, like modern Afghanis with their yurts, we must pack such totems and icons as we can to make short-term quarters feel like home. Pillows, small rugs, watercolors can dispel much of the chilling anonymity of a sublet apartment or motel room. When we can, we should live in rooms with stoves or fireplaces or anyway candlelight. The ancient saying still is true: Extinguished hearth, extinguished family. Round tables help, too, and as a friend of mine once put it, so do "too many comfortable chairs, with surfaces to put feet on, arranged so as to encourage a maximum of eye contact." Such rooms inspire good talk, of which good clans can never have enough.

(9) Good families, not just the blood kind, find some way to connect with posterity. "To forge a link in the humble chain of being, encircling heirs to ancestors," as Michael Novak has written, "is to walk within a circle of magic as primitive as humans knew in caves." He is talking of course about babies, feeling them leap in wombs, giving them suck. Parenthood, however, is a state which some miss by chance and others by design, and a vocation to which not all are called. Some of us, like the novelist Richard P. Brickner, "look on as others name their children who in turn name their own lives, devising their own flags from their parents' cloth." What are we who lack children to do? Build houses? Plant trees? Write books or symphonies or laws? Perhaps, but even if we do these things, there still should be children on the sidelines, if not at the center, of our lives. It is a sadly impoverished tribe that does not allow access to, and make much of, some children. Not too much, of course: it has truly been said that never in history have so many educated people devoted so much attention to so few children. Attention, in excess, can turn to fawning, which isn't much better than neglect. Still, if we don't regularly see and talk to and laugh with people who can expect

to outlive us by twenty years or so, we had better get busy and find
some.

(10) Good families also honor their elders. The wider the age
range, the stronger the tribe. Jean-Paul Sartre and Margaret Mead, to
name two spectacularly confident former children, have both remarked on the central importance of grandparents in their own early
lives. Grandparents now are in much more abundant supply than
they were a generation or two ago when old age was more rare. If actual grandparents are not at hand, no family should have too hard a
time finding substitute ones to whom to give unfeigned homage. The
Soviet Union's enchantment with day care centers, I have heard,
stems at least in part from the state's eagerness to keep children away
from their presumably subversive grandparents. Let that be a lesson
to clans based on interest as well as to those based on genes.

Of course there are elders and elders. Most people in America, as
David T. Bazelon has written, haven't the slightest idea of what to
do with the extra thirty years they have been given to live. Few are as
briskly secure as Alice Roosevelt Longworth, who once when I visited her for tea showed a recent photograph and asked whether I
didn't think it made her look like "a malevolent Eurasian concubine
—an *aged* malevolent European concubine." I admitted that it did,
which was just what she wanted to hear. But those of us whose fathers weren't presidents may not grow old, if at all, with such style.

Sad stories abound. The mother of one friend of mine lay for
years, never far from a coma, in a nursing home. Only when her husband and children would sing her favorite old songs, like "Lord
Jeffrey Amherst," would a smile fleet across her face. But a man I
know of in New Jersey, who couldn't stand the state of Iowa or babies, changed his mind on both counts when his daughter, who lived
there, had one. Suddenly he'd take to inventing business trips to St.
Louis, by way of Cedar Rapids, phoning to say he would be at the
airport there at 11:31 P.M., and "BE SURE TO BRING JAKE!" I also was
heartened to talk to a woman in Albuquerque, whom I phoned during a short stopover there, not having seen her since a trip some
years before to the Soviet Union.

"Honey," she said when I asked how she was, "if I were any better
I'd blow up and *bust!* I can't *tell* you how *neat* it is to put some age
on! A lot of it, of course, has to do with going to the shrink, getting
uncorked, and of course it doesn't hurt to have money (no, we *don't*
have a ranch; it's only nine hundred acres so we call it a farm). But
every year, as far as age is concerned, I seem to get better, doing

more and more stuff I love to do. The only thing I've ever wanted and don't have is a good marriage. I keep marrying men like my mother; nothing I do ever pleases them. The only reason I'm still married now is it's too much trouble not to be. But my girls are growing up to be just *neat* humans, and the men they're sharing their lives with are, too. They pick nice guys, my girls. I wish I could say the same. But I'm a lot better off than many women my age. I go to parties where sixty-year-olds with blue bouffant hairdos are still telling the same jokes they told twenty-five or thirty years ago. Complacent? No, that's not it, exactly. What they are is sad—sad as the dickens. They don't seem to be *connected*."

Connectedness. That was the theme I kept looking for, traveling around the country, gathering enough family stories to fill several books. Few of the people I met felt as connected as they would have liked to. Bess, for example, was as eager for new connections at the age of 83 as a six-year-old is on his first day of school. When I signed Bess's guest book, there in her house on the Umpqua River in southern Oregon, she told me I was the first person she ever had met in all her 83 years who actually lived on Manhattan Island. Bess and her daughter Dorothy, who once stuffed stays into bathing suits, and Dorothy's janitor husband Ned, who used to work in a pie factory, lived in a five-bedroom, four-bathroom house with an enormous living room, a family room, a utility room, and one of the biggest eat-in kitchens I ever had seen. Bess's husband Tom and her sister Sally and her policeman nephew George had lived there too. These six Californians had saved and schemed for years, chipping in $10,000 each to build and occupy this dream house, but within three years after they moved in, Sally and Tom and George one by one all died.

I knew about this house because of Sandra, who is Bess's granddaughter, and Dorothy's and Ned's daughter. Sandra and I had met the year before. Sandra was, as she put it, "in the natural hazards prediction racket"—the foretelling of earthquakes, that sort of thing. She looked like a good bet for an earthquake herself; nothing, it seemed, could upset her. "If I seem sane," she had said, "it's because of my family. Everyone in the family I come from offers each other just all *kinds* of security. I am who I am, to a great degree, because of my great-grandparents. I'm a fanatic Democrat because of my mother's and grandmother's belief that without F.D.R. there'd have been no bread on the table." When she told me about her family's "geriatric commune," I said it sounded so ingenious I'd like to visit it someday. Do, she urged me. So a few months later, when by chance we were both in California, we arranged to drive north together.

Talk about hospitality. Talk about tidiness. No sooner did I step into that house than all my dirty clothes were tumbling around in Dorothy's Maytag, and Bess was bringing me a glass of fresh carrot juice, which she said was all she ever had herself until dinner, which was how she'd already lost three pounds. There was no problem you couldn't solve, Bess always said, if you kept your cool. A broom, Bess always said, was to sweep with, not to lean on. No, I'm wrong, it was Ned, Sandra's handsome father, who always said that. What Bess also always said was that as long as you had your feet on the ground, clean hands, a warm heart, and a belief in something beyond yourself, then you were doing all right.

Bess figured she had a lot of living left to do. At the age of 75, back when she lived at Leisure World, she learned for the first time to swim, and before long she was diving off the high board and had the lifeguard calling her his "Little Fish." She learned to paint china there too, so well that her hands forgot to shake. Lately she had got interested in square-dancing, only the trouble with that was you needed a partner. Would I like to see the square-dancing dresses she had made for herself, and the emerald green caftan she was making for Sandra for Christmas? Certainly I would.

For all of Sandra's 32 years her mother and grandmother had been making her dresses. Not that she ever had asked them to. By the time she was five they were reconciled to her wanting hunting knives and baseball bats instead of dolls. But in high school Sandra got to be Queen of her chapter of Job's Daughters, and what a costume they made for her then!

"I don't know *how* many times I lengthened that big long white robe, she grew so fast," Dorothy remembered. "When she got to be Queen it was right before Christmas, and sometimes it'd be two in the morning before we'd get to bed, staying up to get that robe ready for her Installation. She'd have settled for a lot less work than we went to—there wasn't any real reason for her to be done up to the gnat's eyebrow—but of course we're a family of perfectionists. Though that 'perfectionist' business has always baffled me; I just think of it as trying to do my very best. Maybe it's true, though. My brother up at Big Bear, he nearly cried over a mistake in the Formica, and he's such a perfectionist mechanic that the roads are just as smooth as velvet when he gets through with them. Anyway, when Sandra walked out there on that stage for her Installation, believe you me, it was worth all the work."

Horses and sheep were grazing on the hillsides that rose up from the Umpqua as we sat talking in the family room. Umpqua Umpqua Umpqua; the word bedazzled me; I wished it were my mantra. "Sheep have weak hearts," Dorothy was saying. "That's why we keep Fluffy penned up. Farmers shoot dogs that chase sheep." I also learned that Sandra had an older brother named Arthur, who as a small boy had been runner-up for a milk company's Beautiful Child contest; his photograph almost appeared on a calendar. A few years later he went to the Boy Scout Jamboree in Valley Forge, Pennsylvania. "It cost plenty, but the Kiwanis paid some, and it was too good of an opportunity to pass up. Every button, needless to say, was sewed on his uniform just right, because it was an international event. Arthur used to joke and say, 'If you guys don't treat me right I'm going to run away from home when I'm thirty-eight.' As it was, he didn't get married until he was thirty. His wife's name is Mi Sook; he met her when he was stationed in Korea. She already had three children and then they had two more together. Arthur gained forty-one pounds," Dorothy said, "and I offered him a dollar for every pound he lost, and he *has* begun to slim down."

Being so sudden a grandmother gave Dorothy a jolt; "I said to myself, My goodness, here's all this *family* I've never even seen! I ought to know how I should *feel* about those children! I kind of like the idea of giving kids a chance to get to know you. So what I did was I went to Korea. I'd got a kick out of the vacation trips we'd taken around the U.S.

"I flew to Korea, and Mi Sook and I had three weeks together getting to know each other on a one-to-one basis. I saw Seoul as no tourist ever would, and we watched soap operas together which *all* seemed to be about mother-in-law jokes, so Mi Sook and I would laugh. After that I made the decision to spend a week in Tokyo by myself. You know they have a twelve-story-high building there with *nothing* in it but silks? Of course with my tremendous interest in fabrics, I was in seventh heaven."

"You were in seventh heaven," said Sandra, "because Japan is a nation of Virgos." Virgo is said to engender the most meticulous and orderly people of all the signs of the Zodiac. This house on the Umpqua looked like a world Virgo headquarters, all right. But mostly it seemed sadly outsized. Without ever having met Sally or Tom or George, its deceased members, I missed them acutely. Dorothy and Ned and Bess talked of finding another family to move in and share all that space with them, but they weren't sure who, or even whether they really wanted to.

No house, I've heard it said, is ever the right size for long.

Maybe too much has been made of this business of everybody living under one roof. Clansmen don't seem to need or want all that propinquity: in 1977, 1.45 million single-family homes were built—more than ever before in history. I rather incline myself to a song my friend Dick Bausch once wrote to his parents and his brother, entitled "Wish We Could Live on the Same Street." The same street might be just right. The important thing is not to be too far apart. Much is to be said for—not to mention on—the telephone, whose intimacies for some of us are the single most sustaining blessing of technology. The sustenance frequent phone calls provide could, never be measured in message units. But a disembodied voice, however dear, won't quite do. Better to be able to walk in thirty minutes, or ride in ten, to at least one household so familial that your visits there need not be negotiated, where your future seems as implicit as your history.

But with how many people at a given time is such continuity possible? Pythagoras warned against "shaking hands with too many," but how many are too many? Have family circles an ideal diameter? Must one's friends be friendly with each other, as Aristotle counseled, "if they are at all to form as it were a happy family?" Is it too much to ask that the people I love should at least like each other enough to consider becoming a new family? What number of others, if there is such a thing, is most auspicious?

Two, of course, is the number with the most vigorous following. No kind of twosome goes unsung. Every child, Kenneth Keniston once said, needs to grow up with one person hooked on him. I would carry that further and say that every grownup needs the same thing. Freud and Tolstoy were wise to laud the magnificence of a life in which both work and love—one single, focused, reciprocated love, presumably—were flourishing. But it is the lot of many of us to live through long and arid spells when we are in love neither with a person nor with a project. Such spells are greatly cheered, as better times are too, by the presence of tribes and clans and families. The opposite of two, in other words, need not always be one: it might be some. But how many?

Five has always had its advocates. Five, social scientists claim, makes a group small enough for all to be heard, big enough to avoid deadlocks. Five, as Sir Thomas Browne observed in *The Garden of*

Cyrus, is among other things "the first rest and pause of numeration in the fingers." I know two fathers who both felt uneasy until their third children came along, giving them families of five. "Four people," one of these fathers told me, "just don't seem enough to make a family."

"Sixish is nice for living close and warm," a veteran New Haven communard said. "There's an expression in poker: The pot is right. The question is, Can you feel it? Do these people have something going? Is the whole more than the sum of its parts? It's hard to generalize, but seven and a half might be an ideal number. But of course if you're talking about decision-making, the perfect number is one."

"Minimum eighteen, maximum forty," said an Ann Arbor Unitarian, "though the optimum number for an extended family like ours, including children, is thirty-two."

"You have to keep in mind the Square Root Theory," said my friend Roger Vaughan. "Every time you add a new person to a group, you increase its complications exponentially. Two people, you see, mean four relationships; mine to me, yours to you, each of ours to the other. Add a third and the total relationships become nine. Add three more and the figure zooms to thirty-six."

"Nine people then, would mean eighty-one relationships?"

"That's right."

"Eighty-one's a lot."

"It sure is. What is it with you and nine, anyway?"

I tried to tell him. I don't mean nine people to be simultaneously in love with—what a state of affairs that would be—or necessarily to live with, though given space enough that might not be bad. What I mean is that nine seems a reasonable number of others with whom to seek weekly, if not daily, continuity, for whom to feel responsible, among whom to divide one's needs. It might be the most one can hope to connect with at any given period.

My search to confirm this hunch led me to the phenomenon of the "ten-group,"* ten being the historically average size of bands of hunters, soldiers, and athletes. Orthodox Jews may not officially pray until they have assembled a *minyan,* a group of ten. Residents of Boys' Town, Nebraska, live in groups of ten. Brigades of ten, Alexander Solzhenitsyn says in *Gulag Archipelago,* afford reliable protection and support. No doubt they do. But the decimal system seems to me both too obvious and too unwieldy. Nine, with its single digit and four different sets of components, has about it a compelling texture, a promising variety, a controlled tension.

* Antony Jay, *The Corporation Man.*

"Wouldn't you say that this train of thought of yours was, to put it kindly, a little more intuitive than rational?" a friend once asked.

"Of course I would."

"Where do you fit *yourself* into this hypothetical nine—if you have nine others doesn't it become a group of ten?"

"It would, if they all were connected with each other, but they're not. Besides, the nine others vary slightly from week to month, as people come and go." My friend shook his head. Still, one reason I feel in healthy spirits right now, on a Thursday noon, is that in the time since last Thursday noon I have not only had fruitful blocks of solitude but supped with, talked at length with, laughed with, and been hugged by nine of the people whom I think of as part of my family, even though not a one of them technically is. All these nine have at least a dim idea of what is on my mind, as I have of what is on theirs. Any of them, I think, would honor a four A.M. request from me for some gross inconvenience, as I would from them.

I have also had three heartening long-distance phone talks, with other such clansmen. Before long I'll be seeing them, too. Nine in the flesh, three on the phone. A surplus. An embarrassment of riches. Some of these people cherish each other, too, which makes me, as my mother might have put it, pretty darn lucky.

Some days my handwriting resembles my mother's, slanting hopefully and a bit extravagantly eastward. Other days it looks more like my father's: resolute, vertical, guardedly free of loops. Both my parents will remain in my nerves and muscles and mind until the day I die, and so will their other child, my sister, but they aren't the only ones. If I were to die tomorrow, the obituary would note that I was survived by my father and sister. True, but not true enough. Like most official lists of survivors, this one would be incomplete.

Several of the most affecting relationships I ever have known of, never mind been part of, have sprung not from genes or contracts but from serendipitous, uncanny bonds of choice. I don't think enough can be said for the fierce tenderness such bonds can generate. Maybe the best thing to say about them is nothing at all, or very little. Midwestern preachers used to hold that "a heavy rain doesn't seep into the ground but rolls off—when you preach to farmers, your sermon should be a drizzle instead of a downpour." So too with any cause that matters: shouting and lapel-grabbing and institutionalizing can do more harm than good. A quiet approach works better.

"I wish it would hurry up and get colder," I said one warm afternoon several Octobers ago to a black man with whom I was walking in a park.

"Don't worry," he told me, "like my grandmother used to say when I was a boy: hawk'll be here soon enough."

"What did she mean by 'hawk'?"

"Hawk meant winter, cold, trouble. And she was right; the hawk always came."

With regard to families, many would say that the hawk has long been hovering. "I'd rather put up with being lonely now than have to put up with being still more lonely in the future," *says a character in Natsume Soseki's novel* Kokoro. "We live in an age of freedom, independence and the self, and I imagine this loneliness is the price we have to pay for it." *Seven decades earlier, in* Either/Or, *Soren Kierkegaard had written that* "our age has lost all the substantial categories of family, state, and race. It must leave the individual entirely to himself, so that in a stricter sense he becomes his own creator."

If it is true that we must create ourselves, perhaps while we are about it we can also devise some new kinds of families, new connections to supplement the old ones. The second verse of a hymn by James Russell Lowell says that

> New occasions bring new duties;
> Time makes ancient goods uncouth.

Surely one outworn "good" is the maxim that blood relatives are the only ones who can or should greatly matter. Or look at it another

way: go back six generations and each one of us has sixty-four direct
ancestors. Go back twenty—only four or five centuries, not such a big
chunk of human history—and we each have more than a million.
Does it not stand to reason, since the world's population was then so
much smaller, that we all have a lot more cousins—though admit-
tedly distant ones—than we were brought up to suspect? And don't
these cousins deserve our attention?

One day, after lunch at a friend's apartment, I waited in his lobby
while he collected his mail. Out of the elevator came two nurses, one
on either side of a wizened, staring woman who couldn't have
weighed more than seventy pounds. It was all the woman could do
to make her way down the three steps to the sidewalk and the curb
where a car was waiting. The steps must have been to that woman
what a steep mountain trail would be to me; the nurses guided her
down them with infinite patience.

"Easy, darlin'," one nurse said to the woman.

"That's a good girl," said the other. The woman, my friend's doorman told us, was ninety. That morning she had fallen and hurt herself. On her forehead was something which, had it not been a bruise,
we might have thought beautiful: a marvel of mauve and lavender
and magenta. This woman, who was being taken to a nursing home,
had lived in my friend's apartment building forty years. Her relatives
all were dead, and her few surviving friends no longer chose to see
her.

"But how can that be?" I asked my friend. "We could never be
that alone, could we?"

"Don't be so sure," said my friend, who knows more of such matters than I do. "Even if we were to end up in the same nursing
home, if I was in markedly worse shape than you were, you might
not want to see me, either."

"But I can't imagine not wanting to see you."

"It happens," my friend said.

Maybe we can keep it from happening, maybe the hawk can be
kept at bay, if we give more thought to our tribes and our clans and
our several kinds of families. No aim seems to me more urgent, nor
any achievement more worthy of a psalm. So hosanna in excelsis,
and blest be the tie that binds. And please pass the salt.